Indian Theologies

Indian Theologies

In Search of Methods
and
Models for Theologizing

Edited by
Mathew Jayanth, SJ

Christian World Imprints™

&

Jnana-Deepa Vidyapeeth

First Published in 2017 by

Christian World Imprints™
Christian Publishing & Books from India
H-12 Bali Nagar, **New Delhi-110015**
info@christianworldimprints.com
www.ChristianWorldImprints.com
Phone: +91 11 25465925

&

Jnana-Deepa Vidyapeeth
Ramwadi, Nagar Road, **Pune 411014**
jdvoffice@jdv.edu.in
www.jdv.edu.in
Phone: +91 20 41036111

ISBN: 978-93-5148-048-8 (HB) ISBN: 978-93-5148-049-5 (PB)

Printed in India.

Contents

Contributors

Dr. Errol Aloysius D'Lima, a Jesuit of the Bombay Province, obtained a Doctorate in Theology from Graduate Theological Union, Berkeley in 1978 in the area of Sacramental Theology. He was on the teaching staff of Jnana-Deepa Vidyapeeth (Pontifical Athenaeum), Pune from 1978 to 2007, teaching courses in systematic theology. He contributes articles to theological journals and magazines; is a member of the Indian Theological Association (ITA) and was twice elected President (1996-2002). He is actively associated with activities connected with the Catholic Bishops Conference of India. He has jointly edited several books. At the request of the Inter-Ritual Committee of the Catholic Bishops' Conference of India, he has co-authored *Sacraments in General* (2005). He is general and sectional editor for *The Concise Encyclopedia of Christianity in India,* a venture of Jnana-Deepa Vidyapeeth.

Dr. Evelyn Monteiro, SCC obtained a Doctorate in Systematic Theology from Jesuit Faculty, Paris, France. Her area of specialization is ecclesiology. She teaches theology at Jnana-Deepa Vidyapeeth, Pune. She has published a book, edited a couple of books and published several articles. She has been elected as the Provincial of the Pune Province of the Sisters of the Cross of Chavanod.

Dr. George Thomas Kallunkal, a member of the Order of the Imitation of Christ, has a Doctorate from the Pontifical University of Teresianum in Rome on Spiritual Theology. He wrote his thesis on 'Towards a Realization of Christian Monastic Ideals in the Indian

Context, based on the Charism of our Congregation-Bethany Ashram'. He served for 12 years as Councilor General and 12 years as Superior General. He taught theology at Malankara Major Seminaries at Paurastya Vidyapeeth, Vadavathoor, BVP Pune, and at different Formation Centres in Kerala, and has been the Director of BVP, Pune. His area of specialization is Oriental Spirituality and Monasticism. He has also published many articles.

Dr. Joseph Lobo, a Jesuit belonging to the Karnataka Province of the Society of Jesus, holds a Doctorate in Systematic Theology in the area of Christology from the University of Innsbruck, Austria. He has published one book and several articles. He is Director of Jesuit Regional Theological Center, Bangalore and teaches several courses in theology.

Dr. Kurien Kunnumpuram, is a Jesuit belonging to the Kerala Province of the Society of Jesus. He holds a Doctorate in Theology from the University of Innsbruck, Austria. He has taught systematic theology at Jnana-Deepa Vidyapeeth, Pune for about forty years. He has published several books. He directs Retreats to Women Religious, conducts renewal program for them and has facilitated many provincial and general chapters.

Dr. Mathew Jayanth, SJ (Late), a Jesuit of the Calcutta Province, obtained a Doctorate in Theology and Anthropology from the Graduate Theological Union, Berkeley, and from the University of California, Berkeley. He wrote his dissertation on 'Eucharist and Social Ethics.' He taught several courses in the areas of systematic theology and theological methods at the under graduate and the Graduate levels at Jnana-Deepa Vidyapeeth (Pontifical Athenaeum), Pune. He has published several articles.

Dr. Rekha M. Chennattu, RA, is a member of the Religious of the Assumption, Province of India, and Professor of New Testament at Jnana-Deepa Vidyapeeth, Pontifical Institute of Philosophy and Religion, Pune, India. She has a Licentiate in Scripture from Pontifical Biblical Institute, Rome, and holds a Ph.D. in Biblical Studies from the Catholic University of America, Washington, D. C. She has presented papers at various international conferences and published more than 50 scholarly articles in journals and books in India and abroad. She is the author of the book, *Johannine Discipleship as a Covenant Relationship.* She was elected Provincial of the Indian Province of the Religious of the Assumption.

Dr. Selva Rathinam, is a Jesuit of the Karnataka Province and teaches biblical theology at Jnana-Deepa Vidyapeeth (Pontifical Athenaeum), Pune. He holds a Doctorate in Scriptural Studies from the Graduate Theological Union/Jesuit School of Theology, Berkeley. His areas of interest include Indian Biblical Spirituality, Zen meditation and Yogasanas. His area of research is the Old Testament, especially, the Hebrew Prophets. He endeavors to apply the postcolonial-subaltern (dalit) methodology to the Biblical texts. He has published several articles. He is at present the President of Jnana-Deepa Vidyapeeth.

Dr. Thomas Kuriacose, a Jesuit of the Delhi Province, obtained a Doctorate in Systematic Theology from Jesuit Faculty, Paris, France. He teaches theology at Jnana-Deepa Vidyapeeth, Pune. Besides teaching, he has been the Director of the Jesuit Secretariat for Dialogue in South Asia and the editor of *Jnanadeepa: Pune Journal of Religious Studies*. He has published several articles. His areas of special interest are ecclesiology, sacramental theology, interreligious dialogue and historical theology with special reference to India. He has also held the post of Dean of the Faculty of Theology of Jnana-Deepa Vidyapeeth.

Dr. V. Sebastian, is a Jesuit belonging to the Gujarat Province. He holds a Doctorate in Christianity and presently teaches systematic theology at Gujarat Vidya Deep, Vadodra (Gujarat). He had his theological training in Ahmedabad, and in Belgium. He has worked with tribal communities and has taken part in tribal rights movements. He has presented several papers at national seminars and written articles in the area of theology, culture, religion and socio-linguistics. His research areas and interests include nationalism, identity constructions, cultural studies and socio-linguistics.

Introduction

The Second Vatican Council generated great enthusiasm among the Indian theologians about initiating a new process of theologizing in India. Dr. Kurien Kunnumpuram, SJ and his colleagues took up the leadership and organized a seminar on theologizing in India. The book that came out of that Seminar, namely, *Theologizing in India*[1], can be considered as the first book to be published on Indian theological methods after Vatican II. That was about 35 years ago. Since then scholars in various fields of theology continued their search for ways of doing theology that are relevant to the Indian context. The search is going on and theologians from the Indian subcontinent are making valuable contributions to the process of theologizing in general. Now, the responsibility rests on the present day theologians to consolidate the previous efforts as well as to take the search for methods a step forward to make our theology more firmly rooted in the Indian soil.

The word 'method' calls for some clarifications. The term is ambiguous and it can be understood in different ways. Hence, it is necessary to ensure a certain degree of consensus on the meaning of the term. First, when taken in the ordinary sense, it can mean the steps followed or the technicalities involved in the process of theologizing. This understanding is applicable more to the fields of experimental sciences than to theology. In theology this aspect is

1 G. Gispert-Sauch M. Amaladoss and T. K. John, ed., *Theologizing in India* (Bangalore: Theological Publications in India, 1981).

subsumed under 'research methodology' and it is not our concern in this work.

The term 'mehod' can also mean the theoretical basis of theologizing. Here, the focus will be on how theologians use various philosophical, sociological, economic, or political theories for the purpose of theologizing. From this perspective, a theological method would mean the study of, for example, Augustine's use of Neo-Platonism, Aquinas' use of Aristotelian philosophy, Bultmann's use of Existentialism, Rahner's use of Neo-Thomism, Schillebeeckx' use of theories of interpretation, the use of Marxist social analysis by the Latin American Liberation theologians, the use of deconstructionism of Derrida as a critical tool by some of the Feminist Theologians, and the use of the *Vedanta* philosophy by some of the Indian theologians.

Such studies provide very useful information regarding the diversity of methods in the history of theologizing. And yet, it is not in this sense that we intend to use the term 'method' here. Our understanding will go into the very fundamentals of theologizing, into the very process of understanding the faith claims that we make. Accordingly, the initial, and yet crucial, question that would engage us is: To what extent one's faith and value commitments, political allegiance, self-perception, one's socio-cultural context and worldview influence both the process and the content of one's theology? This will generate an insight into one of the vexing problems concerning Indian theologizing, namely, the specific nature of the existing Indian theologies and the rationale behind it.

Only after identifying the specific nature the Indian theologies assume and the reasons for it, we would be in a position to ask more fundamental questions that impinge on our quest for relevant Indian theological methods. These questions, in turn, empower us to look deeply into the inner recesses of our life as theologians.

The questions are fundamental precisely because they concern our very existence as Indian theologians: our identity and our task as theologians, our purpose and goal of theologizing, our physical and mental location as theologians, the consequences and the process of our theologizing. In fact, these questions take us into the heart of theological methods. Hence, we shall briefly analyze various aspects of our existence as theologians.

1. **Identity:** Here the question is: Who is an Indian theologian? In India no one can claim to be a theologian solely on the basis of one's vast knowledge and information on theological subjects. Theology in India is qualified as *brahmavidya* which presupposes certain initial familiarity with *Brahman*/ the Divine. The primary prerequisite for an Indian theologian is a personal experience of God, especially in the person of Jesus. Thus, we ask: Are we persons with a deep experience of God in our lives and conscious of the God-experiences of our people?
2. **Task**: Here the question is: What does a theologian do when one enters in the process of theologizing? One could faithfully repeat the dogmas of the Church and their traditional interpretations while remaining totally oblivious of the ability of such formulations to communicate the truths of the faith in the changed context. But an Indian theologian has the formidable task of interpreting ever-new the Christian faith affirmations in such a way as to bring out their significance for living our faith in our context. Thus we ask: Are we persons who try to make the faith a living reality in our own lives and the lives of the people?
3. **Purpose/Goal:** Here the question is: Why do we theologize in the first place? It is possible that one might theologize to promote one's own vested interests and ideologies; to display one's intellectual acumen and, thereby, advance one's sense of self-worth. However, an Indian theologian has to be concerned about building human communities of love, peace, harmony, equality and solidarity. A theologian's reflections not only seek to give expression to this concern but also embody it in one's commitment to building the nation and the Church according to this vision. Hence we ask: Has an Indian theologian a clear

perception of the goal or aim of one's theologizing in India?

4. **Location**: Here the question is: Where is an Indian theologian located physically and mentally? It is possible that a theologian located physically in the Indian context could find oneself alienated from the Indian ethos. This happens when one allows one's worldview to be shaped by the concerns, values, and priorities of a consumerist, hedonist society and culture as they exist elsewhere in the world today and is fast becoming a fashion in India as well. Hence we ask: Is the worldview of an Indian theologian rooted in and shaped by the socio-cultural, politico-economic, religious and moral ethos of our nation?
5. **Consequences**: Here the question is: What are the consequences of an Indian theologian's theologizing? There was a time when no one bothered to ask this question and unwittingly supported the vested interests of certain dominant groups at the expense of the weaker sections of society. Theology, instead of empowering people, subdued and subjugated the will of the poorer sections to resist oppression, domination and exploitation. Therefore we ask: Does the theologizing of an Indian theologian empower people to challenge the dehumanizing forces and to live a meaningful life?
6. **Process:** Here the question is: How does an Indian theologian conceive the hermeneutic task of theologizing? In the past and even today there were and are theologians who conceived the process of theologizing as 'theological archaeology' and focused on finding out the exact wordings of dogmatic statements and scriptural texts oblivious of the hermeneutical challenges involved. Moreover, being unaware of the operation of one's own pre-understanding or prejudices in every process of understanding, theologians tended to project their own assumptions as objective truth. However, finding the exact wordings and meaning of the text is only one part of the theologian's task. The other part consists in bringing the text (dogma

> or scripture) alive and making it powerful to address the existential situation of the people. This process has to take into account the influence of the unexamined assumptions operating largely at the subconscious level. Thus we ask: Does an Indian theologian seek to bridge the gap between the past of the text and the present of the people in order to make the text meaningful and relevant to our people without reducing the text into an ideological weapon?

Making a theologian aware of these concerns and questions is the main function of a theological method. In other words, when we have specified and accepted the **identity** of an Indian theologian, become aware of the **task** a theologian is called upon to perform in the Indian context, attained certain clarity about the **goal or purpose** of theologizing, become conscious of the **location** of an Indian theologian and the **consequences** of one's theologizing for the people of India, and, attained certain competence in the **process** of theologizing in India, we can say with confidence that we are well into Indian theological methods.

This book, which is the fruit of a seminar on Indian Theological Methods held at Jnana-Deepa Vidyapeeth in 2010, is designed to facilitate reflections on Indian ways of theologizing by generating a keen awareness of the identity, task, goal and location of an Indian theologian, as well as the consequences and process of theologizing. Accordingly, the book consists of ten chapters. The first two chapters by Dr. Kurien Kunnumpuram and Dr. Errol D'Lima present the scenario of theological methods in general. The following four chapters by Dr. Sebastian Vazhapilly, Dr. Selva Rathinam, Dr. Joseph Lobo, and Dr. Thomas Kuriacose and put us in touch with the Indian theological scenario. The seventh paper by Dr. Evelyn Monteiro makes us aware of the crucial contribution that the women's perspective can make to Indian theological methods. The paper by Dr. George Thomas Kallunkal highlights the importance of the Oriental theological reflections for developing an Indian theological method. Dr. Rekha Chennattu's paper offers certain hermeneutical keys for developing an Indian reading of the Bible. The final paper on Methods and Models of Education: Re-visioning the Teaching and Learning Process by Dr. Mathew Jayanth was not a part of the seminar; however, it is included here with a view of advancing reflections on efficient communication of theology in the Indian context.

The first chapter of the book, "Theological Method in Vatican II" by Dr. Kurien Kunnumpuram, SJ, highlights the contribution of the Second Vatican Council to the search for Indian theological methods. He argues that the Council was not concerned about developing new theological methods. However, its approach to the Church, Revelation, the Modern World, the Church's Missionary Activity and other issues opens up avenues for new ways of theological thinking. Kunnumpuram analyzes a few important texts to show that the Council adopts a dialectical approach to the word and the world which, in turn, points to the need to go beyond the traditional ways of doing theology. He goes to illustrate with the help of selected texts the changed attitude of the Church to the modern world. This change, as he shows, is characterized by a movement from the traditional ambiguous and hostile attitude to a more positive and accepting attitude.

In order to discuss the Church's approach to the world, Kunnumpuram focuses on the phrase "the signs of the time" – a phrase that was close to the heart of Pope John XXIII. This theologically loaded phrase is, in fact, a theological principle. Theologically it emphasizes the need to discern the on-going revelation of God in the longings and aspirations of the people in the contemporary times as well as in the happenings in the history of the world. In other words, theology must begin with God's action in people's lives and in world history. As a methodological principle it challenges us, first, to recognize what God is communicating at present; then, to respond to it and, finally, to reflect upon God's on-going revelation and the existential response accorded by humans.

Thus, the theological principle enshrined in the phrase "signs of the time" transforms the world into the locus of God's action and this change prompts a new understanding of God's revelation. Kunnumpuram highlights in his article that the Council no longer considers revelation narrowly as the divine communication of a set of supernatural truths. Rather, it is seen as God's saving presence in history. It is this revelation, as implied in "the signs of the time" that needs a faith interpretation so that seeing God's presence and action in one's own life and in the world people may be led to deeper faith. This presence, according to him, is the continuing revelation that comes to us as grace seeking a response of faith. In other words, in the Council's understanding, revelation is grace and grace is revelation and it is encoded in "the signs of the time" that the contemporary world offers. This approach to the world and this understanding of revelation bridge the gap between revelation/grace and the secular world. The world is looked at as a reality infused with divine presence/grace requiring a faith response.

In the final section of his article, Kunnumpuram discusses the impact of Vatican II on the Indian methods of theologizing. Giving particular emphasis on Christology, he shows that the new methods of theologizing in India emerge from the lead given by the Second Vatican Council and he expects that the Indian Church will take forward this lead even more vigorously into the future.

Developing Indian theological methods can never be an isolated endeavor. It is a task that calls for diachronic and synchronic dialogue. Diachronically or vertically the effort of Indian theologians is related to the history of theological method, both in the East and the West, spanning over two thousand years. Synchronically or horizontally it is related to the contemporary efforts in developing theological methods that are going on in India and the rest of the Christian world. This bidirectional dialogue in critical openness to learn from others and with courage to respond to the specific demands arising from the context of the life experiences of our people is a non-negotiable element in our theological venture.

We have numerous partners for our diachronic conversation. The dialogue with the Western Church could, probably, begin with Origen, the father of systematic theology and move forward to Augustine, Thomas Aquinas and Scholasticism, Neo-Scholasticism which will take us to the contemporary conversation partners in Orthodox, Liberal, Neo-Orthodox schools with differing approaches such as Transcendental approach, method of Correlation of various kinds, liberation models of numerous varieties, and the emerging dialogical models. Similarly, the Eastern Churches offer many great dialogue partners in St. Ephraim, who initiated a poetic mode of theologizing consonance with the Eastern flair for symbols and metaphors and many others. This would open up a rich array of possibilities for finding resources for developing Indian theological methods.

While acknowledging the relevance and benefits of such dialogues and, at the same time, knowing the impossibility of such an undertaking in a short paper, Dr. Errol D'Lima, SJ, in his essay, "Theological Method in the Indian Contest", proposes to review three models of theologizing that emerged in the 19th century and attempts to retrieve important elements for developing models of theologizing in India. He discusses the Orthodox model, the Liberal Model and the Neo-Orthodox Model with the help of the grid/pattern of Context, Agents, and Outcome as developed by David Tracy in his *Blessed Rage for Order*. His analysis of these models highlights some of the important and general methodological principles that are involved in every process of theologizing.

The first principle that D'Lima chooses to emphasize is that theologizing is an activity of a believing community. Theologizing happens when a community of faith begins to interpret its faith in response to the questions that emerge from the context. This interpretation, in the light of the Scripture and the Tradition, seeks to transform the life of the community. Thus, theologizing has to do with the interpretation of the faith of the community in response to the questions in the light of the sources of faith with a view to effect transformation. The perception of the context and its significance for theologizing can differ, as will be clear from the discussion below.

According to D'Lima, the Orthodox model understands the context as something static, having little significance for theological activity. For, this model looks at theological activity itself as noetic, focused on the articulation of reveled truths, an activity that can be carried on without reference to the questions arising from the context. The Liberal model, on the other hand, following the spirit of Enlightenment, links theological activity with the context of scientific enquiry and gives importance to reason and its ability to discover truth. In the process, the Christian faith is sidelined and the content of faith becomes another object of enquiry. Thus, while the Orthodox model ignored the context, the Liberal model ignored faith. Following a middle path, the Neo-Orthodox model acknowledged the importance of the secular world and the need to address the issues facing the modern world from a faith perspective. In this way, D'Lima shows that the context has a decisive influence on the nature of theologizing.

The second principle that emerges from the grid is the agents which D'Lima explains as the elements that influence theologizing. In the Orthodox model the self-understanding of the Church as the sole possessor of truth and, hence, its perceived responsibility to establish that truth throughout the world were the agents that influenced theologizing. In the Liberal model the use of critical method, development of sciences, study of history and the development of hermeneutics were the elements that exerted influence on the Liberal way of theologizing. In the Neo-Orthodox model the secular world with its socio-political changes and the emerging pluralism acted as agents. Thus, the context of theologizing determines the nature of theological activity through various agents or elements that characterize the context.

The third aspect in the grid is the outcome of theologizing. It refers to the result of doing theology in terms of answers, solutions, or responses to the questions/issues emerging from the context. In the Orthodox model, the outcome was the creation of a universal Church marked by uniformity that neglected the relevance of the local Churches. The outcome of the Liberal model was the decrease of faith in the revealed religions and, as a reaction, the Catholic Church withdrew into its shell, thereby, stifling the possibility of pioneering studies in various fields of theology in dialogue with the world. The outcome of the Neo-Orthodox model was the bridging of the gap between the secular and the sacred, respect for other religions and the development of a spirit of dialogue. This shows that the results of theologizing defer one from the other depending on the context and the agents.

On the basis of his analysis of the three models of theologizing, D'Lima points out some of the lessons for developing theological methods in India. First, with regard to the Context of theologizing, methods of Indian theologizing must begin with an analysis and understanding of the context that offers categories to articulate the experience of faith. Second, regarding the Agents of theologizing, there is a need to initiate and facilitate a dialogue between the Indian context and the Christian Tradition. Third, concerning the Outcome of theologizing, the Christian faith should enable the believer to recognize God's action in the world of pluralism and to collaborate actively in bringing about a just and humane society based on the values of God's Reign in this world. At the same time, the theologizing intended for the context of India must also be seen as orthodox by the universal Church.

When we attempt for a vertical dialogue in the Indian context, suddenly we realize that we do not have a long history of specifically Indian ways of theologizing. This is because up until the Second Vatican Council theology in India followed a process of dependent theologizing. The Western/Roman model of theologizing was taken as the valid and universal model. As D'Lima has pointed out, it was the result of an Orthodox model of theologizing enforced in the Catholic Church. The accepted principle seemed to be that one theology for one Church universal without realizing that that one theology was a local theology developed in the West. History shows that it was not easy to challenge this mindset.

However, a few theologians who realized the multi-religious, multi-lingual and pluralist context of India felt the need for developing an authentic Indian Church, a contextualized interpretation of the person of Jesus Christ, theologizing in Indian categories of thought and using Hindu scriptures as resources for theologizing. Apart from the earlier attempts at Indianization by the Jesuit missionaries like Robert De Nobili, John de Britto and others, in more recent times, say from the mid-19th century, there are theologians who took up the challenge of doing theology in Indian ways. Brahmabandab Upadhyaya, a Brahmin convert to Catholicism from Bengal, advocated the use of Vedanta philosophy for articulating Christian faith in the Indian context, just as the Fathers of the Church used Greek philosophy. With great desire to make Christianity truly Indian, he also advocated the formation of an Indian church. Understandably, Brahmabandab is the only one from the Catholic side who followed this way of thinking for which he had to pay dearly. From the Protestant side there are eminent personalities like A.J. Appasamy, Parani Andi, Vengal Chakkarai, Chenchaiah, Sadhu Sundar Singh, Pandita Ramabai and others who tried to make a breakthrough in Indian ways of theologizing. Following in their footsteps, immediately before and after the Second Vatican Council, theologians like Amalorpavadas, J.B. Chettimattam and a few others sought to advance the process of theologizing in India.

The critique of their approach was that they tried to develop an Indian model of theologizing in dialogue with the classical religious texts and philosophical systems of Hinduism. In the process they identified Indian culture with Brahminical culture ignoring and neglecting the presence of numerous other cultures. In the paper, "Cultural Constructions of Indian Christian Theology: Exploring its Presuppositions and Implications", Dr. V Sebastian, SJ, makes a critical study of the theological endeavors of these pioneers from the perspective of their assumptions and their consequences. He argues that what is taken as Indian 'culture' is the hegemonic discourse of a particular group, namely, of the classical/Sanskritic Hinduism. Though it has been made normative through colonial administration and other complex mechanisms, the presence of other discourses belies its normative claims. He begins with an analysis of the central hermeneutic principle of the role of presuppositions in knowing and underscores that presuppositions entail acceptance of their logical implications. From the perspective of this theoretical principle he examines the Western classical theology and points out its three major presuppositions, namely, the immutable nature of truth, the permanency and universality of human nature, and one culture – the high culture identified with the Greco-Roman culture – as normative form for all cultures. According to Sebastian, the Indian theologians challenged these assumptions of the West in their attempt to promote an Indian Christian theology.

However, the Indian theologians, observes Sebastian, fell into the same trap that they were trying to avoid. They uncritically accepted the cultural constructions of the colonial administrators and the British Orientalists about India. The colonial-Orientalist nexus, based on the sacred texts, spearheaded a view of Indian culture as monolithic. It identified India with the classical tradition and the Indian classical tradition with the Hindu socio-cultural and religious ethos and gave birth to the notion of a pan-national culture and equated it with the Hindu culture. Sebastian points out that this fallacy of the Hindu culture as normative for the whole of India has become an operating principle for many Indian nationalists in the past and for the present day Right Wing political parties. The Indian theologians adhered to this normative view of the Indian culture and, as a consequence, the Indian theologizing became a mirror image of the Western Classical theology.

In developing Indian theological methods, it is important, cautions Sebastian, to transcend such normative view of Indian culture and accompanying cultural stereotypes by acknowledging and accepting the fact that Indian culture is constituted by numerous cultural traditions, both great and little, each having a legitimate claim on being an integral part of the Indian tradition. This being the case, there cannot be a single Indian theology; there can only be Indian theologies and, accordingly, there ought to be a plurality of Indian theological methods.

The study of the presuppositions, limitations and the consequences of an approach to theologizing based on a dominant, hegemonic view of the Indian culture raises the questions: what are the options left for us to develop genuine theological methods for India? Can we have an overarching perspective that can accommodate the plurality of cultures that constitute the culture of India? Dr. Selva Rathinam, SJ, in his paper, "Postcolonial Biblical Interpretation for India," suggests that postcolonialism as an interpretative theory offers a theoretical framework for relevant ways of theologizing in India.

Postcolonialism, understood not chronologically as coming after colonialism but as a discourse that focusing on the cultural effects of colonialism, seeks to bring to the forefront the marginalized, subjugated, neglected and ignored voices. The problem with the hegemonic discourse, as we have noted earlier, is that it excludes large sections of the people and their experiences. As Sebastian has argued and as Selva Rathinam reiterates, the Indian theologizing was done from the perspective of the hegemonic view of culture constructed and propagated by the colonizers and the Orientalists which was readily accepted by the pioneers who endeavored to find Indian ways of theologizing. A move away from this mode, according to Selva Rathinam, is the goal of postcolonialism.

As the title of his paper indicates, Selva Rathinam's focus is specifically on postcolonial biblical interpretation. However, his argument in the paper has methodological import for theologizing in general. Thus, in order to substantiate his argument, he, after a brief discussion on the development of postcolonialism, analyses the biblical interpretation as practiced in colonial India. He points out that while the Orientalist mode sought to enhance biblical interpretation by borrowing hermeneutic tools from Sanskritic traditions, the Anglicist mode adopted the Western historical critical method to make Christian faith historical and objective as well as to demote other faiths to a-historical and mythical levels. The Nativistic mode, on the other hand, looked to the vernacular traditions for guiding biblical interpretation. This mode has to face the problem of isolationism that results in the ghettoization of theology. These modes of biblical interpretations/theologizing in the pre-Independent, colonial India failed to address the real issue of exclusion.

To suggest appropriate methods of biblical interpretation for India, Selva Rathinam borrows the concepts of *otherness* as developed by Edward Said, *deconstruction* as interpreted by Gayatri Spivak and *hybridity* as coined, elaborated and popularized by Homi Bhabha. The concept of *otherness* helps to unmask the ideology of domination that underlies the colonial discourse. The concept of *deconstruction*, as a subaltern strategy, exposes the incompatibilities between the explicit and implicit meanings in the colonial discourse. And, finally, the concept of *hybridity* seeks to destabilize the status quo by asserting the cultural alterity.

The incorporation of these concepts into the interpretative theory of postcolonialism, according to Selva Rathinam, enables one to identify the subjugated and submerged protest or oppositional voices and to bring them into the sphere of public discourse. In the process there takes place the subversion of the traditional, ascribed meaning of the hegemonic discourse in favor of subaltern voices. In this way, postcolonialism challenges the customary way of paying attention to the hegemonic, the professional and the negotiated codes of a discourse at the exclusion of the protest or oppositional code and directs attention to the protest voices in the discourse. Thus, postcolonialism becomes a subaltern strategy to replace the hegemonic discourse.

One of the primary functions of a theological method in India is to develop appropriate strategies to expose, subvert and transcend the ideologies underlying the dominant discourse. At present Indian theologies, to a greater or lesser degree, are unwittingly co-opted into the hegemonic discourse. This happens mainly because we lack effective strategies to understand and resist the machinations of the dominant culture to subdue and subjugate the protest voices of large sections of people. Selva Rathinam holds that postcolonialism, as a critical theory and a strategy, is capable of providing the necessary strategic methodological principles not only for biblical interpretation in India, but also for developing theological methods suitable for Indian ways of theologizing.

The papers of Sebastian and Selva Rathinam have examined some of the presuppositions of the Indian theologies developed in the past through the process of a vertical dialogue. They have highlighted the falsity and the dangerous consequences of doing theology from the perspective of a solely hegemonic cultural world view to the exclusion of others. While Sebastian emphasizes the need for an awareness of the dangerous presuppositions as a necessary prerequisite for theologizing in India, Selva Rathinam proposes the critical theory of postcolonialism as a method to overcome the limitations entailed in the traditional ways of doing theology in India. However, the constructive process of developing truly Indian methods of theologizing requires a horizontal dialogue over and above the vertical one.

This is exactly what Dr. Joseph Lobo, SJ, is attempting in his paper, "Towards an Interreligious Dialogical Theologizing in India: Its Presuppositions, Preconditions and Implications." A horizontal dialogue calls for an awareness of the context and its specific characteristics, a clear perception of the goal of theologizing, an understanding of the nature of the agents of theologizing, a vision of the main features of the methods of doing theology and an awareness of the challenges involved. Lobo focuses on these elements of a horizontal dialogue and proposes an interreligious dialogical process of theologizing in the Indian context.

As regards the context, Lobo situates people's existence marked by glaring disparities and contradictions along the economic, political, and socio-cultural and religious axes and identifies the goal of theologizing in this context as integral liberation of the people. In order to achieve this goal, he argues that those who share the Indian situatedness and seek to respond to the context in a liberative manner need to come together as 'theologizing communities' which he calls 'multi-religious theologizing communities' (MTCs). In this way he affirms that the theological activity is done by a community. However, this community is neither exclusive nor inclusive, but a pluralistic or interreligious community. Thus, Lobo proposes a wider concept of a theologizing community.

The main methodological features of theologizing, according to Lobo, are, first, the lived experiences of the people of their situatedness, of the divine, and, of the drive toward harmony and unity. Second, dialogue with religious traditions in their entirety, and, third, sharing the personal experiences of one's own religious tradition within the theologizing community and sharing the fruits of theologizing with those who are not directly involved in the process.

What are the requirements and challenges of an interreligious dialogical ways of theologizing? Lobo specifies five spheres that demand special attention. First, the socio-cultural and religious sphere calls for genuine respect, appreciation and acceptance of the plurality of cultures and religions, as well as solidarity in the situatedness of the people. Second, in the theological sphere, the purpose of theologizing needs to be understood in terms of mediation between the socio-cultural, economic and political institutions, on the one hand, and religious experiences, on the other. Hence, it needs to be cross-cultural and cross-traditional. Third, in the sphere of hermeneutics, the context of theologizing is marked by different historical and existential realities, and, hence, a faith based interpretation calls for a cross-cultural and cross-traditional retrieval of religious traditions. Fourth, the praxical sphere demands that the theologizing process ends up in liberating praxis. And, fifth, in the ecclesial sphere, since the theologizing community is a wider concept, there is a need for expanding the notion of 'ecclesia'.

The pioneers who initiated doing theology in the Indian context endeavored to enter into a conversation with the dominant Hindu religious and philosophical texts and systems. The drawbacks of such attempts have been adequately perceived by theologians doing theology in India today. The need for a wider horizontal dialogue – a dialogue that invites wider participation of diverse cultures, different religions, various caste groups, varied economic classes, as well as different sexes – is keenly felt as integral to the theologizing process in India. According to Lobo, the ground condition for such a dialogue is the existence of pluralistic communities where the horizontal dialogue can become an experiential reality. Only from such communities can genuine Indian theologies emerge. Lobo's proposal for an interreligious dialogical theology based on shared situatedness, shared experiences of the Divine across religious traditions and shared praxis presupposes the formation of inclusive, pluralistic communities that could transcend the boundaries of religious traditions and generate genuine Indian theologies from within its shared common life.

One obvious lacuna in the Indian theologizing process, as emphasized by the previous three authors, is the conspicuous absence of the common people as partners in conversation. In their dialogue the Indian theologians, by and large, preferred the middle class, sophisticated intellectuals as partners. Entering into dialogue with the Indian intelligentsia is not bad in itself. But the real problem is the exclusion of the common people – the poor, the disenfranchised, and the subaltern. Indian theological methods that do not take into account the stories, songs, myths, oral traditions, artistic expressions, and forms of worship that are the carriers of the life history of the ordinary people, cannot be considered as promoting effective ways of theologizing in India.

Dr. Thomas Kuriacose, SJ, in his paper, "Implications of Peoples' History for a Theological Method in India", addresses the methodological issue of incorporating the common people's history into the process of theologizing in India. In his paper, he briefly highlights the theological significance of history and shows that history is sacramental or revelatory in that it is in history that God's presence and actions take place. Precisely because of this, history becomes the *locus* of people's encounter with God. Hence, history is not merely an objective, disinterested narration of past events; it is the power that enlightens the present and leads the present toward the future of God.

From this perspective, Kuriacose discusses the importance of People's History. It is the location of ordinary people's encounter with God – an encounter in which they perceive God's invitation to strive toward the future that God sets for them. It is the drama of their life with God – a drama that involves God's reaching out to the people in myriad forms with the offer of life and freedom and the people's positive response or lack of it to this offer. From a faith perspective, people's history is their history with God which needs to be interpreted in order to discern and explicate God's self communication in the midst of their history. This is the task that the Indian theologians are called to perform.

However, by focusing exclusively on the history of 'great people' and 'important events' to the exclusion of a majority of our people, Indian theology has forfeited its right to speak to, for and of the common people. In the process it has lost its power to respond to the needs and aspirations of the ordinary people. For, it has listened only to the dominant voices and is responding to them. Hence, there is no compelling reason for the ordinary people to listen to it. Secondly, by closing itself off from God's self communication in and through various people's movements, Indian theology has lost important resources for theologizing. Relevant theologies in India can emerge only in the process of discerning God's presence and actions in the aspirations and struggles of people for freedom, equality, respect, dignity, justice and ecological well-being as well as in the process of articulating, clarifying and explaining in a prophetic and transformative way the meaning and significance of the specific manner of God's presence and actions in people's history. In this regard, Indian theologies and theologians have not fared well!

It is here, reiterates Kuriacose, that one should locate the sinfulness of Indian theologies and theologians. They have been deaf to the cries and blind to the needs of the poor and the marginalized.

This realization ought to lead Indian theologians to conversion so that they may recognize the people's history as a constitutive element of Indian theological method and theology may regain its prophetic and transformative function. For this, Indian theologies have to take a different route – a route different from the models developed in the West as well as from that formulated by Indian theology from the perspective of and dialogue with the hegemonic culture. Taking a different route would entail examining the stories, songs, oral traditions, myths and art forms of the ordinary people as well as an openness to and willingness to participate in various people's movements with a view of discerning God's voice in them. In short, the Indian people's history must become a dialogue partner for theology to become truly Indian.

Is it necessary for theology to enter into dialogue with women as a separate group? Are not women, as a subjugated, oppressed, silenced and discriminated group, included in people's history and, hence, theology's dialogue with people's history encompasses women's history as well? Theoretically, it is not necessary to consider women as a separate group and their history can be considered as a part of the people's history. However, just as history became the history of 'great men and their deeds' to the exclusion of the subaltern, so also people's history can become the history of men in subaltern groups to the exclusion of women. This possibility is clearly seen in the hegemonic discourse which seldom includes the voice of women from the dominant cultural groups. Granted that women's voices are taken up in the hegemonic discourses as well as in the subaltern discourses, the questions still remain: Should not women speak for themselves instead of depending on men to speak *for* them? Should not theology enter into direct dialogue with women?

In her paper, "A Feminist Theological Method for India: Dance of Emancipation, Empowerment, and Enabling," Dr. Evelyn Monteiro, SCC, seeks to underscore the significance of theology's dialogue with Indian women of all sections and to propose a theological method for such a dialogue. She begins with clarifying some important concepts such as 'femininity' and 'feminism', and 'feminist' and 'feminist theology', and, in the process, traces the trajectory of the emergence and development of feminism and feminist theology from a global perspective. Coming to the Indian scenario, she points out that though Indian secular feminism has made great advance in terms of developing theories and methods, Indian feminist theology is only gradually emerging as a distinct voice with characteristic methods of its own. In her paper she attempts to delineate the outlines of an Indian feminist theological method.

The primary task of feminist theology in India, according to Monteiro, is to articulate and interpret the faith experiences of Indian women. She is aware that this poses insurmountable difficulties because the experiences, including the faith-experiences, of women in India change according to their location. There are urban and rural women, educated and uneducated women, high caste, low caste and outcaste women, high class, middle class and low class women, married and unmarried women, and, women belong to diverse religious traditions, cultures, and linguistic groups. These differing locations determine, influence and differentiate women's experiences and, hence, women can never be considered as a homogeneous category in India. It implies that there needs to be different feminist theologies and, accordingly, different feminist theological methods.

These differences, however, do not rule out the fact that there are factors shared by all feminist theologies. The centrality of gender in determining the nature of social relationships, the experiences and viewpoints that emerge from such scripted relationality, the privileged perspectives from the underside of history gained through these same experiences, the experiential knowledge of the false ideologies perpetuated by male-dominated societies and the awareness of the need for deconstructing the oppressive and dehumanizing systems with a view of reconstructing and transforming them into life affirming systems, and, finally, the centrality of body as the locus of experience and knowledge as well as the source of one's identity and the realm of one's integrity – these elements, however differently they may be understood and approached, are integral to feminist theology everywhere.

At the same time, there are certain factors that call for special attention from Indian feminist theology. They include, as already pointed out, the fact of the diversity of experiences of Indian women, the fact of their belonging to different religious traditions, the fact that women constitute the poorest of the poor in the Indian society and that they are the victims of violence and death, and finally, the fact that the socio-cultural structures affect women differently. These specific factors that affect women's existence in India require a feminist critical pedagogy and praxis to raise women's consciousness in order to dismantle the dehumanizing systems constructed by the male-dominated Indian society.

Accordingly, taking inspiration from Elizabeth Schüssler-Fiorenza, Monteiro outlines in broad strokes an Indian feminist theological method. Since the Indian feminist theology is a theology from the perspective of women in struggle, its method must begin with the stories of women's multiple experiences. These stories and their interpretation must focus on raising the consciousness of women regarding their actual situation, the reasons for its existence and the causes that perpetuate it. With the help of this feminist consciousness, women engage in the acts of questioning and deconstructing with a view of generating a changed and new consciousness that is capable of empowering them to dream new dreams, to act decisively and to network with other women in struggle. Thus empowered, women will be enabled to fashion new visions and new goals and to march toward their actualization in future. This, in gist, is the essence of the 'dance of emancipation, empowerment and enabling.'

Fashioning Indian feminist theologies and Indian feminist theological methods are women's project. But it is not envisaged as a project solely for and by women. For, the purpose of Indian feminist theologies, as Monteiro specifies, is to help construct a new way of being a participatory Church of equal discipleship and build a new society of integral human relationships. Hence, it is an invitation extended to all, women and men, to be human and recognize God's image in one another. It is "a project where emancipated, empowered and enabled women work in partnership and mutuality of relationship with men for the transformation of society and for building a just and life-giving human and cosmic order for all".

It is clear from the previous papers that to develop genuinely Indian theological methods there is a need for vertical and horizontal dialogue. While the vertical dialogue establishes a link with the history of the development of Indian theology, the horizontal dialogue seeks to initiate a connection with the oppressed, subjugated, silenced and excluded groups of people by paying attention to the voices of the subalterns, people's history and entering into dialogue with women. There is yet another dimension to the horizontal dialogue which emerges from the ecclesial context of India. The Catholic Church in India is made up of the Latin Church and two Oriental Churches, namely, the Syro-Malabar and the Syro-Malankara Churches. There are also other Christian denominations that are part of the Indian ecclesial context. This situation makes it necessary to enter into dialogue among the three Catholic Churches and between the Catholic Churches and the Churches of other denominations in order to find ways of theologizing in India. Sharing the spiritual, liturgical, and theological riches of these Churches through a process of open dialogue can make great contributions to the task of developing Indian theological methods.

In this context, the paper of Dr. George Kallunkal, OIC, assumes great importance. In his paper, "Relevance of Oriental Theological Method for the Development of an Inculturated Indian Theological Method", Kallunkal focuses on the question of inculturation and its relation to the method of Indian theologizing. He argues that the Indian theological methods do not emerge from a vacuum. It must originate from the life of the people. In order this to happen, the Christian faith must become an integral part of that life. In other words, faith must become incarnate in the cultures of India. The development of authentic Indian theological methods can emerge only from within the context of an incarnated/ inculturated faith.

Accordingly, Kallunkal examines the resources of Oriental traditions as well as of the Indian cultural and spiritual ethos with a view of establishing connections between them that could pave the way for developing theological methods for inculturated Indian theologies. First, he points out the distinguishing characteristics of Oriental theology. They include rootedness in scripture, liturgy-centeredness, and Narratological approach to theology. Secondly, he identifies the spirit that permeates Oriental theology from the perspective of its mystical, spiritual, and contemplative character as well as in its apophatic approach, ascetical practices and monastic way of life. These characteristics and the spirit that pervades Oriental theology resonate with the general Indian disposition in approaching the transcendent and the spiritual atmosphere of India. This correspondence needs to be explored further in order to advance the search for Indian ways of theologizing.

The exploration will have to take into account how stories, music and symbols, rather than rational and metaphysical categories, are employed in communicating the experience of the divine in the Indian context as well as in the Christian scriptures. Both, the Oriental Christians and the people of India, share the awareness that God/ the Divine is a Mystery and this awareness provides a common platform for articulating the Christian experience of God as Mystery in the idioms emerging from the Indian spiritual atmosphere. They are well expressed in the narrative stories, musical styles and symbolic mediation. Moreover, the ascetical practices undertaken in the context of a monastic lifestyle can also furnish a credible mode of witnessing to the process of theologizing in India. There is also a need for emphasizing the liturgical dimension of theology in India not only by inculturating the liturgy but also by the transformation of life that results from liturgy leading toward commitment to the social and ecological issues facing the nation.

Thus, in the context of the co-existence of three Catholic Churches and many Protestant denominations in a pluralistic cultural and religious context, calls for theological methods that cut across the boundaries of individual Churches and denominations and that resonate with the religious atmosphere and cultural ethos of India. According to Kallunkal, inculturation, understood as a presupposition, as a process and as an outcome of theologizing in India, can be a powerful source for developing relevant Indian theological methods.

The centrality of dialogue and its various dimensions for developing Indian theological methods have been established beyond doubt. A crucial aspect of this dialogue, that remains to be seen, is interreligious dialogue. The Indian religious scenario is marked by the coexistence of many religious traditions. In the context, Christian life, practice and, even, the thought processes need to take an interreligious character. Christian existence in isolation might have been considered as an ideal in the past. However, today the principle of incarnation questions the rationale of such an approach to Christian life in India. Hence, it is important that the Indian ways of theologizing must promote a Christian existence that is essentially dialogical. In other words, theological methods in India have to advance an interreligious existence for all, especially for Christians.

Integral to the interreligious dialogue is the manner in which the scriptures are interpreted. The Indian religious traditions have developed specifically Indian ways of interpreting their scriptures from within the overarching Indian worldview and respecting the characteristic sensibilities of the Indian religious ethos. Accordingly, they have also developed methods of interpretation that allow scriptural texts to resonate with the visions and goals of life. They have shown how to bring scriptures close to the life of the people and to make them serve the purpose of life.

By and large, Indian biblical scholars, in their overconfidence in the suitability of the Western modes of interpreting scriptures, ignored the resources and methods for interpretation readily available in India. Frustrated with the sterility and irrelevance of the methods of interpretation inherited from the West, Dr. George Soares-Prabhu, perhaps the first well-known Indian scripture scholar, spearheaded a process of Indian ways of reading the Bible. His untimely death in an accident marked a big setback to this endeavor. Hardly anyone, ever since, has come forward to take the baton from him and to lead the process ahead.

It is against this background that the paper, "Reading the Bible in the Indian/Asian Context," by Dr. Rekha Chennattu, RA., becomes significant. Her paper was not presented at the seminar; and, yet, it is included in this collection because it has methodological import from the perspective of developing an Indian reading of the Bible. In the paper, she briefly analyzes the past attempts at developing an Indian Biblical hermeneutics and highlights the three strands of these attempts. They are the use of Indian traditional methods for interpreting the Christian scriptures, the use of *dhvani* method and the interpretation based on Indian realities and concerns. The last of these takes two distinct perspectives, namely, the socio-political perspective and the Indian feminist perspective.

The purpose of Chennattu is to identify certain hermeneutical keys for developing an Indian reading of the Bible. For this, she, first, analyses the Hindu worldview and shows that the striking feature of the Hindu worldview is its emphasis on the immanence of the transcendent Divine. Second, she analyses the goal of the interpretation of the scriptures in India and underscores that liberation and transformation, rather than attainment of intellectual clarity and understanding, are the expected outcome of the process of scriptural interpretation. In the Indian context, the biblical interpretation ought to aim at these goals as its first priority. From this perspective, Chennattu proposes two hermeneutic keys for an Indian reading of the Bible. First, rootedness in and fidelity to the text is fundamental to the interpretation of the scripture which calls for the use of all modern exegetical and hermeneutical tools. Second, the interpretation should emphasize sensitivity to and relevance for the Indian context. This will demand the application of the specifically Indian principles of interpretation as shown in the three main strands of Indian biblical hermeneutics.

The final chapter, "Methods and Models of Education: Reflections on Re-visioning the Teaching and Learning Process" by Dr. Mathew Jayanth, SJ, deals with the question of communicating theology. This paper was not among those presented at the seminar and it does not directly deal with the process of theologizing as such. However, teaching theology itself involves a theologizing process and, hence, the choice of methods of teaching and learning should be such that they promote appropriate ways of theologizing in the Indian context. The goal of the paper is to provide various models of education that can be differently combined to realize the purpose of philosophical and theological education. Jayanth discusses four basic models of education and the models that derive from them. He analyzes the contemporary system of theological and philosophical education in India in the light of the strengths and weakness of each of these models and offers suggestions for the renewal of teaching and learning philosophy and theology.

His basic argument is that teaching-learning activity is largely determined by theories of education. Hence, the success of any attempt at the renewal or reform of the philosophical and theological education is predicated upon a keener perception of the models and theories of education. There are certain models of education that are incompatible with the goals of philosophical and theological education; and still they are unwittingly employed in the teaching and learning process in the institutions of philosophy and theology. This happens mainly due to lack of familiarity with alternative models of education that compels teachers to adhere to the familiar traditional models. His discussion of various models and theories of education opens up possibilities for re-visioning the philosophical and theological education as well as for exploring effective methods of teaching and learning.

Indian theological methods are not matters of technique. They concern the awareness of who an Indian theologian is, the what, why and how of the theological activity of a theologian and the consequences of one's theological undertakings for the Indian churches and the nation. The essays in this book deal with various dimensions of theologizing in the Indian context. The book does not claim to offer a finished product. Rather it initiates reflections on Indian theological methods and makes a plea for ongoing critical reflection on the process of theologizing in India that could shape and advance genuinely Indian theological ways of doing theology in the years to come.

Chapter 1

Theological Method in Vatican II

Kurien Kunnumpuram, SJ

As far as I can make out, the Second Vatican Council did not develop a new theological method. But its approach to the Church and the world in the Pastoral Constitution on the Church in the Modern World led to the emergence of a new method of theologizing. And scattered through the Council's documents are several passages that lend support to this new method.[0]

This paper begins with a brief description of the new method of theologizing which emerged from the work of Vatican II. It goes on to show that the emergence of this new method was made possible by a two-fold change: The Council adopted a new attitude to the world and developed a new understanding of revelation. It then briefly highlights the impact this new method has had on theologizing in India. By way of conclusion the paper points out some of the things we can learn from the Council's approach to theologizing for doing theology in India today.

I. A New Method of Theologizing

1. While discussing the ecclesiology of the Pastoral Constitution, Avery Dulles remarks:

> The theological method accompanying this type of ecclesiology differs from the more authoritarian types of theology that have become familiar to us in past centuries. This method may be called "secular-dialogic": secular, because the Church takes the world as a properly theological locus, and seeks to discern the signs of the times; dialogic, because it seeks to operate on the frontier between the contemporary world and the Christian tradition (including the Bible), rather than simply apply the latter as a measure of the former.[1]

This new theological method consists in the dialectics of the world and the Word. It seeks to interpret the Christian faith in the light of the events and experiences of today as well as to understand the events and experiences of today in the light of the Christian faith.

2. There are several passages in the documents of Vatican II which explicitly or implicitly lend support to this method. While speaking of the help which the Church receives from the modern world, the Pastoral Constitution states:

> With the help of the Holy Spirit, it is the task of the whole people of God, particularly of its pastors and theologians, to listen to and distinguish the many voices of our times and to interpret them in the light of the divine Word, in order that the revealed truth may be more deeply penetrated, better understood, and more suitably presented. (*GS* 44)

There are three things in this text which need to be noted.

(i) The phrase "many voices" is a translation of the Latin "*Varias loquelas*", which has a very rich meaning. Commenting on this passage Yves Congar points out:

> That the Council understands by language something other and more than a mere means of expression – and that in itself is no small thing! – is evident from the fact that all the faithful, and especially pastors and theologians, are invited to study and listen to the numerous languages of our time. It is therefore a matter of all the modes of expression of the immeasurable researches and discoveries of the human mind throughout time and space.[2]

(ii) The dialectical interaction between the many voices of our times and the Word leads to a faith understanding of the events and experiences of today as well as a deeper grasp of divine revelation.

(iii) It is the whole people of God, and not merely the theologians, that theologize. All of them seek a faith understanding of life and reality.

3. In the Introduction to the Pastoral Constitution the Council asserts:

> At all times the Church carries the responsibility of reading the signs of the times and of interpreting them in the light of the Gospel, if it is to carry out its task. In language intelligible to every generation, she should be able to answer the ever recurring questions which men ask about the meaning of this present life and of the life to come, and how one is related to the other. We must be aware of and understand the aspirations, the yearnings, and the often dramatic features of the world in which we live (*GS* 4).

In this passage, the stress is laid on interpreting the signs of the times, the events and experiences of today, in the light of the gospel. The passage points out that it is necessary for the Church and its theologians to have a deep understanding of the modern world.

4. While discussing the relationship between the gospel and culture the Pastoral Constitution remarks:

> Living in various circumstances during the course of time, the Church, too, has used in her preaching the discoveries

> of different cultures to spread and explain the message of Christ to all nations, to probe it and more deeply understand it, and to give it better expression in liturgical celebrations and in the life of the diversified community of the faithful (*GS* 58).

There is a two-way relationship between the gospel and culture. On the one hand, culture helps the Church to probe the message of Christ and understand it more deeply. On the other hand, the Church can use different cultures to spread the faith, to explain it and celebrate it in its liturgy and, thus, enrich the life of the faithful in a variety of ways.

This topic is dealt with at greater length in the Decree on the Missionary Activity of the Church (See *AG* 22). The Council explains how the young churches which come into existence as a result of the Church's missionary activity take to themselves, in imitation of the plan of Incarnation, the riches of the nations (See *AG* 22). Here Vatican II is describing the process of inculturation. In this context it declares:

> If this goal is to be achieved, theological investigation must necessarily be stirred up in each major socio-cultural area, as it is called. In this way, under the light of the tradition of the universal Church, a fresh scrutiny will be brought to bear on the deeds and words which God has made known, which have been consigned to sacred Scripture, and which have been unfolded by the Church Fathers and the teaching authority of the Church. Thus it will be more clearly seen in what ways faith can seek for understanding in the philosophy and wisdom of these peoples. A better view will be gained of how their customs, outlook on life, and social order can be reconciled with the manner of living taught by divine revelation. As a result, avenues will be opened for a more profound adaptation in the whole area of Christian life (*AG* 22)

If the incarnation of the Christian faith in the cultures of peoples is to be effectively carried out, then the Church has to engage in a serious theological investigation. In the cultural context of the peoples the Church has to engage in a new reflection on God's revelation recorded in sacred Scripture and unfolded in the work of the Fathers of the Church and the teaching of the magisterium. Such a reflection will show how faith can gain a new understanding in the philosophy and wisdom of these peoples. Further, the Christian faith can shed light on the customs, outlook on life and the social order of these peoples and show to what extent they are compatible with the manner of life taught by divine revelation. Thus, gradually avenues will be opened for a thorough inculturation of the whole of Christian life.

These two passages, which we have discussed in this section, too lend support to the new method of theologising which emerged from the work of Vatican II.

5. Further, while dealing with culture and Christian formation the Pastoral Constitution points out the need for an interdisciplinary approach to theology and theological formation:

> Those involved in theological studies in seminaries and universities should be eager to cooperate with men versed in other fields of learning by pooling their resources and their points of view. Theological research, while it deepens the knowledge of revealed truth, should not lose contact with its own times, so that experts in various fields may be led to a deeper knowledge of the faith (*GS* 62).

If theologizing requires an interaction between the experience of the people today and the Christian faith, then one must realize that various disciplines can throw light on human life and human experience.

Besides, advances in the various fields of human knowledge raise many questions that are of vital significance for human life, and theology must deal with them (See *GS* 62). The natural sciences, for instance, often challenge the obsolete world-view implicit in the Church's dogmatic formulations, and invite us to interpret these in terms of the new, emerging world-view. The human and the social sciences give us valuable insights into human nature and the functioning of society, which can be of great help to theologians. Historical studies reveal to us the gradual development of institutions, doctrines and rites, thus liberating us from what Michael Novak has called "the non-historical orthodoxy".

In their own way literature and art too are important for theology. They seek to give expression to human nature, human experiences and human problems. They try to throw light on humans' suffering and joy, their needs and their potentialities, and to outline a happier destiny in store for them. "Hence they can elevate human life, which they express under many forms according to various times and places" (*GS* 62).

Vatican II gratefully acknowledges the contributions these disciples make: "Thanks to the experience of past ages, the progress of the sciences and the treasures hidden in the various forms of human culture, the nature of man himself is more clearly revealed and new roads to truth are opened. These benefits profit the Church too" (*GS* 44).

These disciplines enlarge and enrich human experience and can play an important role in the process of theologizing.

As has been stated above, the emergence of this new method of theologizing was made possible by a new attitude to the world which the Council adopted and a new understanding of revelation which it developed.

II. A New Attitude to the World

1. Right from the beginning the Church's attitude to the world was ambiguous.[3] On the one hand, it looked upon the world as an object of God's love, since God created it and continued to care for it. On the other hand, it regarded the world as hostile to God, since it had closed itself against God in its sinful self-sufficiency. Both John and Paul, among the New Testament writers, gave expression to this ambiguity. During the centuries of Roman persecution the Church adopted a very negative attitude to the world. It thought of itself as a community of believers surrounded by a wicked world. Baptism was the moment of decision when

a person renounced the spirit of the world and embraced the spirit of Christ. The Didache has preserved a text which shows that the Eucharistic celebration concluded with the words: "Let grace come, let this world pass away".[4]

The Church of the Middle Ages was somewhat ambivalent in its approach to the world. It fostered a spirituality based on contempt for the world. As Alfons Auer has pointed out:

> The basic attitude of the Middle Ages was one-sidedly that of flight from the world. The monastic, ascetical ideal prevailed also in the world; medieval Christianity was predominantly shaped by monks. Its ideal of life had a fascinating effect also upon laymen; one thought one could serve God best and most uncompromisingly when one bade farewell to the world.[5]

There was, on the other hand, an effort made to subjugate the world to the Church or even to absorb it. To quote Auer once again:

> In the greatness of the Middle Ages its very limitations become all the more apparent. No other age was able to achieve to the same degree a blending of the terrestrial and heavenly kingdoms into a single universal order in which the temporal realms were directly ordered to the spiritual reality of the Church, and even – in order to maintain this order – directly or at least indirectly subjugated to ecclesiastical regulation. This unitary order necessarily resulted in a situation in which temporal matters were not adequately considered with respect to their inherent value nor sufficiently seen as fashioned according to their own laws. In the long run, the sacred order of the Middle Ages amounted to the same thing as Monophysitism.[6]

In a way the modern phenomenon of secularization is a reaction to this tendency on the part of the Church to absorb the world and not to respect it in its otherness. Gradually human beings, human society and its institutions, the arts and the sciences, work and professions began to assert their autonomy with respect to the Church and to affirm their intrinsic value. However, the Church reacted to this process quite negatively. As Avery Dulles observes,

> The papal encyclicals from Gregory XVI (1831-46) to Pius XII (1939-59) continually deplore modern errors. *The Syllabus of Errors*, published by Pius IX in 1864, comes to a climax with Error No. 80: "The Roman pontiff can and should reconcile himself with, and adjust to, progress, liberalism, and recent civilization." In 1907 the Church condemned Modernism, a movement that had begun as an effort by Catholics to bring the Church abreast of the times. Much later, just as World War II was breaking out, Pius XII issued his first encyclical, *Darkness over the Earth* (*Summi Pontificatus*, Oct. 20, 1939), reflecting remnants of this antimodernist mentality.[7]

2. Pope John XXIII had quite a different attitude. In his Apostolic Constitution convoking Vatican II he emphatically declared: "Distrustful souls see only darkness burdening the face of the earth. We, instead, like to reaffirm all our confidence in our Saviour, who has not left the world he redeemed".[8] And in his opening address to the first session of the Council he made it clear that he was not one of those who "in these modern times... can see nothing but prevarication and ruin".[9] Pope John's positive attitude to the modern world has had a great impact on *Gaudium et Spes*. That is probably why it has turned out to be one of the most inspiring documents of the Council.

Right at the beginning the Pastoral Constitution explains how it understands the modern world:

> Therefore, the Council focuses its attention on the world of men, the whole human family along with the sum of those realities in the midst of which that family lives. It gazes upon the world which is the theatre of man's history, and carries the marks of his energies, his tragedies, and his triumphs;

> that world which the Christian sees as created and sustained by its Maker's love, fallen indeed into the bondage of sin, yet emancipated now by Christ (*GS* 2).

The document regards the difficulties and imbalances brought about by the rapid changes which are taking place in the world as a 'crisis of growth' (*GS* 4).

The Council has a positive attitude to the process of secularization. In unmistakable terms it declares:

> If by the autonomy of earthly affairs we mean that created things and societies themselves enjoy their own laws and values which must be gradually deciphered, put to use, and regulated by men, then it is entirely right to demand that autonomy. Such is not merely required by modern man, but harmonizes also with the will of the Creator. For by the very circumstance of their having been created, all things are endowed with their stability, truth, goodness, proper laws, and order. Man must respect these as he isolates them by the appropriate methods of the individual sciences or arts (*GS* 36).

Such a view leads to the recognition of the freedom and legitimacy of the arts and the sciences. As *Guadium et Spes* puts it,

> The Church is not against the use by human arts and sciences of their own principles and methods in their respective fields; therefore it acknowledges this lawful freedom and affirms the legitimate autonomy of culture and especially of the sciences (*GS* 59).

3. What is perhaps most significant in the Pastoral Constitution is that it conceives the role of the Church in the modern world as that of a servant. Inspired by no earthly ambition, the Church wishes only to carry forward the work of Christ who came not to be served but to serve (*GS* 3). Hence, "Christians cannot yearn for anything more ardently than to serve the men of the modern world ever more generously and effectively" (*GS* 93).

The document spells out concretely the kind of service that the Church can render to human persons, human communities and human activity in the world:

> Pursuing the saving purpose which is proper to her, the Church not only communicates divine life to men, but in some way casts the reflected light of that life over the entire earth. This she does most of all by her healing and elevating impact on the dignity of the person, by the way in which she strengthens the seams of human society and imbues the everyday activity of men with a deeper meaning and importance. Thus, through her individual members and her whole community, the Church believes she can contribute greatly toward making the family of man and its history more human (*GS* 40).

This new attitude to the world calls for a new way of dealing with it. The Council speaks of 'dialogue' which is a sign of the Church's love for and solidarity with the world (See *GS* 3). And the Church is interested in dialoguing with all kinds of people in the modern world. After having spoken of dialogue within the Church and with non-Catholic Christians and their communities, the Council says:

> Our thoughts also go out to all who acknowledge God and who preserve precious religious and human elements in their traditions; it is our hope that frank dialogue will spur us all on to receive the impulses of the Spirit with fidelity and act upon them with alacrity. For our part, our eagerness for such dialogue, conducted with appropriate discretion and leading to truth by way of love alone, excludes nobody; we would like to include those who respect outstanding human values without realizing who the author of those values is, as well as those who oppose the Church and persecute it in various ways (*GS* 92).

III. A New Understanding of Revelation

1. Before Vatican II revelation was understood as God's communication of supernatural truths. But this is not the way the Council looks at revelation. As Richard P. McBrien points out:

> The council no longer tried to define revelation as "the sum total of truths disclosed by God for our salvation and preserved in doctrinal form by his one true Church." Revelation is given in and through history, and especially in the central Christ-event.[10]

In other words divine revelation is God's saving intervention in human history. As the Constitution on Divine Revelation observes:

> This plan of revelation is realized by deeds and words having an inner unity: the deeds wrought by God in the history of salvation manifest and confirm the teaching and realities signified by the words, while the words proclaim the deeds and clarify the mystery contained in them (*DV* 2)

God acts in history, and interprets God's actions. God speaks to us and confirms God's words through deeds.

In a true sense one can say that divine revelation is available to us only in human experience and as human experience. If God's revelation takes place through God's words and deeds, we can receive it only by observing God's deeds and by listening to God's words. Speaking of God's self-revelation to Israel, Vatican II states: "To this people which He had acquired for Himself, He so manifested Himself through words and deeds as the one true and living God that Israel came to know by experience the ways of God with men…" (*DV*. 14).

Further, while dealing with the transmission of divine revelation the Council observes: The apostles "handed on what they had received from the lips of Christ, from living with him, and from what he did, or what they had learned through the prompting of the

Holy Spirit" (*DV* 7). Commenting on this passage, Joseph Ratzinger (now Pope Benedict XVI) remarks:

> The point is certainly not to play off the theology of salvation history against word theology, but in place of a narrowly doctrinal conception of revelation, as had been expressed in the Tridentine word theology, to open up a comprehensive view of the real character of revelation, which – precisely because it is concerned with the whole man – is founded not only on the word that Christ preached, but in the whole of the living experience of his person, thus embracing what is said and what is unsaid, what the apostles in their turn are not able to express fully in words, but which is found in the whole reality of the Christian existence of which they speak, far transcending the framework of what has been explicitly formulated in words.[11]

2. There is reason to believe that Vatican II understood revelation as the experience of God's grace. This is clear from the way it understands faith. For the Council, faith is one's total self-surrender to God and the acceptance of God's revelation (See *DV* 5). But faith can also be understood as an experience of God's grace and our response to it. The Council, while describing the genesis of faith, mentions two elements: (1) the interior help of the Holy Spirit which moves the heart and opens the eyes of the mind to assent to God's revelation; (2) the grace of God which precedes and accompanies the act of faith (See *DV* 5). Here grace refers to the experience of God as grace. I am inclined to believe that Vatican II looks upon faith as our response to the experience of grace. In *Lumen Gentium*, there is a statement which reads:

> Those also can attain to everlasting salvation who through no fault of their own do not know the gospel of Christ or His Church, yet sincerely seek God and, moved by grace, strive by their deeds to do His will as it is known to them through the dictates of conscience (*LG* 16).

During the voting on the text in 1964 an amendment (*modus*) was suggested: "The necessity of faith is also to be affirmed." The Theological Commission rejected the suggested amendment with the explanation: "Faith is contained in the expression 'under the influence of grace'." This is quite significant. For, the Council is here dealing with those who are ignorant of the Gospel of Christ and his Church. Hence, the faith in question is not the Christian faith. These are people who sincerely seek God and, moved by grace, strive to do his will. Now according to the explanation given by the Commission, the grace of God at work in them also includes saving faith. In other words, God through his grace calls them and their response to this call of God is faith. In fact the Council has explicitly stated that "God in ways known to Himself can lead those inculpably ignorant of the gospel to that faith without which it is impossible to please Him" (*AG* 7).

If, according to the Council, faith is one's response to the experience of God's grace, then the experience of grace is revelation.

Vatican II seems to think that revelation is available to all people since God liberally bestows His grace on them all. The Council is convinced that we can find revelation in the experience of ordinary men and women today. "All believers of whatever religion have heard God's revealing voice in the discourse of creatures" (*GS* 36). And the Church has to learn to hear the voice of God not only in Scripture and tradition, but also in the events of secular history. Hence it has the duty to "scrutinize the signs of the times and interpret them in the light of the Gospel" (*GS* 4). That is why the Church "labours to decipher authentic signs of God's presence and purpose in the happenings, needs and desires" of the people of our age (*GS* 11).

IV. The Impact on Indian Theology

1. It is undeniable that Vatican II has had a great impact on theology in India. It has led to a new way of looking at theologizing. In a perceptive paper on doing theology in India, Samual Rayan wrote:

> The theology we do in India is Indian, local and contextual. It takes our Christian faith and our concrete historical

> situation seriously. The situation has many dimensions: social, cultural, intellectual, political, economic, aesthetic, cosmic and religious. We know that these act on us, shaping our perceptions and sensibilities, affecting our responses and decisions. They cannot but be an ingredient of our theological reflection and of its articulation. Theology is understood as reflection on our faith-experience in the light or shade of life lived in its actual context, with its problems, struggles, tears, and hopes; or, conversely, it is a reflection on life in the light of faith. We bring the two – life and faith – to face each other and to dialogue, questioning and critiquing each other, exploring each other's depths and enriching each other, challenging each other.[12]

Rayan is here describing in his own way the understanding of theologizing that emerged from the work of Vatican II. Particularly noteworthy is the sentence: "Theology is understood as reflection on our faith-experience in the light or shade of life lived in its actual context, with its problems, struggles, tears, and hopes; or conversely, it is a reflection on life in the light of faith."

2. With regard to the content of theology in India two trends are noticeable. The first one is an attempt to reinterpret the traditional themes of theology in the context of the Indian situation today. Thus serious efforts have been made by the Indian Theologians to articulate an Indian Christology.

Michael Amaladoss has sought to discover the significance of Jesus for us in the multi-religious context of India by exploring images like Jesus the sage, the *guru*, the *satyagrahi,* the *avatar*, the servant and so on.[13] Sebastian Kappen has attempted to articulate an understanding of Jesus in the secular context of the country.[14] There have been many other attempts made to elaborate an Indian Christology.[15]

The way Amaladoss interprets the many religions of India is by making a distinction between the Eternal Word and the Incarnate Word. In a recent article he wrote:

Jesus as the Word of God is enlightening every human being coming into the world (cf. Jn 1:9), while as the Word Incarnate he is interacting only with those who are relating to him in faith. Whatever Jesus does, the Word of God does in him. But the power and the extent of the Word of God is not limited to the humanity of Jesus. I would like to point out that once again we are not making an effort to explain what Jesus is in himself, playing with the Greek concepts of 'person' and 'nature'. We are trying to understand how Jesus is relating to humans. We are trying to protect his universal outreach to all humans, while seeking to preserve his special relationship to the Christians who know and confess their faith in him. The relationships are not the same though they may be equally effective, because the divine dimension is present in both cases. Once again, we are not promoting abstract theologizing, but reflecting on the significance of Jesus in a multi-religious context."[16]

3. Yet another trend in Christian theology is to articulate an Indian Christian response to some of the burning issues and problems of our country. Thus, in its annual meeting in 1997 the Indian Theological Association (ITA) discussed the question of ecological crisis and formulated a statement: "Ecological Crisis: An Indian Christian Response".[17]

The Association also discussed another serious issue: The Challenge of *Hindutva*. This was the main theme of the annual meeting of ITA in 2000. It has issued a well formulated statement on *Hindutva*.[18]

A careful study of all these writings reveals the fact that the Indian theological enterprise has been greatly influenced by the method of theologizing that emerged from the work of Vatican II.

Conclusion

Before I conclude this paper I would like to briefly point out some of the things we can learn from the Council's approach to theologizing:

1. Living and relevant theology is born of a dialectical interaction between the world and the Word. It involves two steps: (1) An attempt to interpret the Christian faith in the light of the events and the experiences of today; (2) An effort to understand the events and the experiences of today in the light of the Christian faith.
2. We need to adopt a positive attitude to the modern world and observe carefully all the developments that are taking place there. This world is the object of God's love.
3. God is present and active in the world today. To read "the signs of the times" means to discern the presence and purpose of God in the events, needs and desires of people today (See *GS* 11).
4. We need to adopt an interdisciplinary approach to theologizing. Various disciplines can throw light on human persons, human societies and developments in the world today.

It is my fond hope that all of us will make serious efforts to make theologizing in India a vibrant enterprise.

Endnotes

1. Unfortunately the English translation of the documents of Vatican II does not use inclusive language. It speaks of 'man' when it means the "human person' and 'mankind' when it means 'humankind'. This is also true of some of the theologians cited in the paper.
2. A. Dulles, *Models of the Church* (Garden City: Doubleday and Company Inc., 1974), 85-86.
3. Y. Congar, "Commentary on Part I, Chapter 4 of the Pastoral Constitution," in H. Vorgrimler, *Commentary on the Documents of Vatican II*, Vol. 5 (London: Burns and Oates Ltd., 1969), 219-220.
4. See J. Neuner, "The Role and Responsibility of Lay People in the Struggle for a New Society" in *The Indian Church in the Struggle for a New Society*, ed. D. S. Amalorpavadass (Bangalore: NBCLC, 1981), 447-456.
5. Didache 10, 6.
6. A. Auer, "The Changing Character of the Christian Understanding of the World" in *The Christian and the World*, compiled by Canisianum (Innsbruck, 1965), 6.
7. *Ibid.*, 8-9.
8. A. Dulles, *Models of the Church*, 84.
9. As reported in W. M. Abbot, ed., *The Documents of Vatican II* (London: Geoffrey Chapman, 1966), 100.

10. As reported in W. M. Abbot, *The Documents of Vatican II*, 712.
11. R. P. McBrien, *Church, the Continuing Quest* (London: Newman Press, 1970), 25.
12. J. Ratzingar, "Commentary on Chapter II of *Dei Verbum*", in H. Vorgimler, *Commentary on the Documents of Vatican II*, vol. 3 (London: Burns and Oates Ltd., 1966), 182.
13. S. Rayan, "Doing Theology," in *Theologizing in Context: Statements of Indian Theological Association*, ed. J. Parappally (Bangalore: Dharmaram Publications, 2002), 11.
14. See M. Amaladoss, *The Asian Jesus* (Chennai, IDCR, 2007).
15. See S. Kappen, *Jesus and Freedom* (New York: Orbis, 1977).
16. See J. Parappally, *Emerging Trends in Indian Christology* (Bangalore: IIS Publications, 1995).
17. M. Amaladoss, "Towards an Indian Theology," in *Theological Explorations*, ed. J. Kavunkal (Delhi: ISPCK, 2008), 29.
18. This statement of ITA is found in *Theologizing in Context*, ed. J. Parappally, 252-264. The papers presented at this meeting of ITA have been published. See J. Mattam and J. Kavunkal, ed., *Ecological Concerns: An Indian Christian Response* (Bangalore: NBCLC, 1998).
19. This statement of ITA is found in *Theologizing in Content*, ed. J. Parappally, 290-309. The papers presented at this meeting of ITA have been published. See J. Mattam and P. Arockiadoss, ed., *Hindutva: An Indian Christian Response* (Bangalore: Dharmaram Publications, 2002).

Chapter 2

Theological Method in the Indian Context

Errol Aloysius D'Lima

Introduction

Method is usually associated with the steps taken to realize a goal that is seen to be attainable, desirable and productive. The steps are envisaged in a logical succession. In doing Christian theology, one can conceive of a series of steps followed in different areas connected with theology. To theologize is to account for the faith experience of a Christian community, and while keeping in mind the community's concerns and intentions, seeks to enhance and transform human existence. It attempts to clarify concepts expressing a faith experience, to respond to life's challenges in the light of the Christian Tradition as a whole, to articulate the hermeneutical questions that a context throws up, and, more importantly, to live out an action-based programme that echoes the words and deeds of Jesus Christ himself. The steps followed by the theologian in theologizing must enable him/her to make an appropriate response to the questions asked. What steps would be helpful when theologizing in India?

One way of attempting to study theological method is to review all the possible patterns of theologizing used in the history of the Church. The scope of such a study is daunting. Another way is to review more recent attempts at theologizing, e.g., those that date from the 19th century to the present time. We opt for the second way since it was with the 18th century Enlightenment that the Axial Age Religions were first closely scrutinized.[1]

The different attempts at theologizing will be in terms of a grid/ pattern that (a) includes a certain **context** in which theologizing occurs, (b) pays attention to the **agents** involved in theologizing and (c) notes the **outcome** of such theologizing in the ongoing history of the Church and world. In India, this mode would help to identify or recognize significant aspects of the point of departure, understand better the task of the theologizing subject, and arrive at a fruitful goal. In fine, it would assist in sketching out a method of theologizing in today's India.

In keeping with this procedure, the approach found in David Tracy's book *Blessed Rage for Order, The New Pluralism in Theology* has been adopted in part.[2] However, the presentation is tailored to fit the intent of my paper. Hence there will be modifications and additions which may not necessarily reflect Tracy's work. At the start, the three terms (context, agents and outcome) are considered. Secondly, three efforts to theologize are examined. In conclusion, an attempt will be made to sketch a mode for theologizing in India today.

Part I: A Pattern for Theologizing

A pattern for theologizing is a structure that is meant to facilitate the process of theologizing. Members of a community recognize its help in their common approach to problems, questions and challenges and in finding solutions, answers and responses to these. Assessing an attempt at theologizing by referring it to the gird/pattern could make one aware of the success or failure of methods used in theologizing. Further, such assessment could suggest how theologizing can be done in today's India.

(a) Context

Theologizing must be seen taking place in a believing community. It must benefit both the individual persons as well as the community as a whole. The point of departure for theologizing can be an issue that religion is asked to resolve, or a faith practice that requires theological validation, or a prophetic stance that obliges establishment religion to engage in introspection. In all of these a question is asked that calls for an answer through the theologizing process. Theologizing usually uses scriptural texts, magisterial statements, Christian faith traditions and human experience for its purpose. In times past, the context was mostly seen as linked with concepts, doctrinal claims and philosophical systems. In such a context, the main concern was an orthodox formulation of faith and dogmatic claims, e.g. the historical Jesus and the Christ of faith.

After the Enlightenment and the emergence of the humanistic and social sciences the context had to do with questions and issues arising from human experience that was perceived as pluralist. The postmodernist world has questioned the assumptions made about worldviews, human destiny and the transcendent. Theologizing in such a context will surely be challenging.

(b) Agents

The agents are those elements that constitute or influence the theologizing subject. They could be an individual, a school of thought, groups of persons bound together by an ideology, various organs of authority that preside over or represent human communities, and events that bring about a crisis situation in a community. The persons, entities and aspects that affect and effect the process of theologizing can be seen as agents. The human agent keeps in mind that the faith perspective with which he/she begins to theologize must be preserved and given pride of place in the outcome of theologizing.

(c) Outcome

The result of a theologizing process can be varied. Not all the results that ensue are intended by the theologizing subject. The end product of a process of theologizing is meant to be a solution, an answer or a response to an issue raised in a particular context. While such an answer is meant to deepen the faith experience of the community, it must also effect transformation in a community of persons so that the way of life lived by the community manifests virtues like love, forgiveness, compassion, integrity, caring and, in general, respect for the rights and dignity of others. Such transformation must be seen at the individual and social levels.

In the course of this paper, we shall examine models of theologizing from the perspective of context, agents and outcome.

Part II: A Study of Three Models of Theologizing

(1) The Orthodox Model

The Orthodox model is seen as emerging from those in charge of the Church. Their intention is to make sure that the traditional faith of the Church – especially as reflected in the *depositum fidei* – is preserved intact whenever the gospel message is proclaimed in new situations. Such a model tends to favour a conservative approach to questions raised in and by the community and stresses continuity between doctrinal stances of today and those of the past. The Church in the 19th century was concerned about the truths of the faith and saw dogmas as articulations that adequately expressed revealed truth. It made little space for a reinterpretation of dogmatic truths in new situations. Further, the experience of theologizing was seen primarily as a noetic activity that was universally valid.

(a) The Context

The teaching church tends to favour such a model since it provides continuing stability to the institutional church. It uses "proof texts" to support positions held by the establishment, e.g. the mode of exercising authority in the Church, the role of the hierarchy and that of the laity, etc. The claims of a system – e.g. scholasticism – become reference points of great importance for elaborating a Christian systematic theology. In fact, scholastic theology had become the staple in seminary studies till Vatican Council II. (This was especially so with the Catholic Church; not so with the Protestants.)

Issues that arose in different places and at different times were articulated and solved in terms of a unitary system, e.g. Thomism from the 13th century or the synthesis of Joseph Kleutgen (1811-83) in the 19th century. Scholastic philosophy – with its claim of being a *philosophia perennis* – provided a suitable system in terms of which Christian theology could be elaborated. With the active encouragement of popes, especially Leo XIII (1878-1903), it provided an umbrella under which theological issues were discussed and resolved well into the middle of the 20th century.

Naturally, the establishment theologians viewed with suspicion the Enlightenment age that raised questions about positive religion and the divine authority it relied on.[3] Until that time, however, the authority of the Magisterium was enhanced as it handed down its decisions – *Roma locuta est, causa finita est* – about questions concerning orthodox theology.

(b) The Agents

The official church's stance in the 19th century was limited by its self-understanding.[4] The Church believed that it possessed the only truth that mattered and it had the mandate from Christ to proclaim it throughout the world. Little or no space was allowed to inculturate the Christian message. The gospel text, the magisterial pronouncements and the missionary thrust preserved a European flavour and the tasks of interpretation and dialogue did not feature in the theologizing subject's mindset.[5]

Such theologizing suited a centralized administration in the Church and added to its universal importance. It also suited the colonialists who continued holding on to their colonies with the excuse that they were furthering the mission of Christ in bringing Christianity to the world beyond Europe. The political and ecclesiastical establishments combined well in governing the people in the colonies since the mission theology and the colonizers' practice of Christianity were transplanted in the colonies with little regard for native susceptibilities. Little, if any, space was given to the colonized people to develop indigenous religions with their own theologies and spiritualities.[6] Latin continued being the uncontested *lingua franca* of the Church authorities which gave them an undue advantage over the vast majority of believers who were not Latin-literate!

(c) The Outcome

Theology that was mostly drawn from manuals and text books ensured that throughout the world the same mindset prevailed as regards the belief and practices of Christianity. This gave the universal Church a feeling of unity and made for a well-knit government but neglected the building of the local churches with their particular cultures and languages. The definition of papal infallibility in Vatican I strengthened the feeling that the Church could seldom, if ever, be mistaken in its pronouncements and decisions. "Creeping infallibility" made its presence felt more and more.[7] The *idem semper* of the conservative group in Vatican II sums up well the consequence of following the orthodox model of theologizing. How could *aggiornamento* take place if Church doctrine was to be merely restated, not reinterpreted?

(2) The Liberal Model

(a) The Context

The Liberal model of theologizing arose from the spirit of the European Enlightenment in the 18th century. The classical definition of the Enlightenment is as follows:

> Enlightenment is man's exodus from his self-incurred tutelage. Tutelage is the inability to use one's understanding without the guidance of another person. This tutelage is self-incurred if its cause lies not in any weakness of the understanding, but in indecision and lack of courage to use the mind without the guidance of another. 'Dare to know (*sapere aude*)! Have the courage to use your own understanding; this is the motto of the Enlightenment.[8]

Often seen as anti-religion, the Enlightenment – via the Kantian critique – gave rise to the scientific method, the development of the sciences, the study of history, the development of hermeneutics and a critique of all authority, especially religious authority. Protestant liberal theology stressed an anti-dogmatic approach. The History of Religions School laid stress on the comparative study of religion in understanding Christianity.[9] This was also the age when the question of the Jesus of history and the Christ of faith was discussed.[10] Catholic liberalism remained within the limits of religious orthodoxy but looked for a scientific approach in matters of faith. The Modernist controversy, however, affected both the Catholic as well as the Protestant side.[11]

> From the new philosophies, the new natural sciences, and especially from the new historical disciplines, Christian theologians in every church tradition found major and minor theological claims severely challenged. Yet it is not the cognitive challenge alone which occasioned the deepest crisis for the liberal and modernist Christian theologians. Rather, the liberal theologian's ethical and existential commitment to that secular faith constitutive of the critical drive present in all modern science is at the heart of the liberal enterprise.[12]

(b) The Agents

The liberal model had much to do with (German) scholarship. One recalls the Tubingen School founded by Ferdinand Christian Baur (1792-1860) as well as the attempts of various theologians to study primitive Christianity, e.g. David Friedrich Strauss (1808-74) and his 'mythical' Life of Christ (1835). This model inspired theologians to use critical methods in the study of the scriptures, dogma and Church history. They often ended up by paying little attention to Christian faith itself. The Catholic faculty of theology (1817) emphasized the need of retaining the faith commitment in theologizing . The Catholic Church was wary of these critical methods and reacted by condemning Modernism and various theories that seemed to be overly rationalistic. However, Leo XIII did set up the biblical commission to study the scriptures in the Catholic Church and to answer questions concerning biblical matters. But it was only with the encyclical *Divino Afflante Spiritu* (1943) of Pius XII that biblical criticism in the Catholic Church received its *magna carta*! In general, the siege mentality that had its origin in the Reformation and continued in the Catholic Church until Vatican II was all too apparent in theologizing.

(c) The Outcome

The fear of what a rational and critical approach could do to the faith of the Church was seen in Vatican Council I which was announced by Pope Pius IX two days before *Quanta Cura* (1864) – to which the Syllabus of Errors was attached – was published. The attack against Modernism by Pope Pius X saw not only the emergence of the oath against Modernism (*Sacrorum Antistitum*, 1910) but the stagnation of pioneering studies concerning the bible, church doctrine and systematic theology.[13]

In general, the findings of historical criticism that liberal theologizing approved of seemed to effect a lessening of faith in revealed religion. Scientific method was seen to dispense with Christian belief and the teaching authority of the Church. However, the contribution of historical criticism and the scientific method would benefit the Church during the period of neo-Orthodox theologizing.

(3) The Neo-Orthodox Model

The quest of the historical Jesus ended in failure.[14] Karl Barth (1886-1968) sensed the 'bankruptcy' of liberal theology when he saw his former professors confirm the Kaiser's idea that the acquisition of colonies by Germany could be seen as extending the kingdom of God. Dialectical theology was seen as the answer since the analysis of history could not, by itself, yield a Jesus of faith![15] In fact, while seeing Christian faith in Jesus Christ as non-negotiable, the neo-Orthodox theologians sensed the importance of situating such faith in the context of culture, contemporary world-views and evolution. In a word, the scientific disciplines that were found in the world of the secular were not seen as antagonistic to the world of the sacred, of faith and Christian piety.

(a) The Context

The need for continuing research in the fields of scripture, systematic theology, liturgy and moral theology was felt keenly in the Catholic Church at the end of 19th century. Modernism accentuated that need. The Liturgical Movement received fresh impetus from the congress held in 1909 in Malines. Systematic theology was in search of a more sustaining foundation than scholastic Thomism. Could this foundation be constituted by the bible and patristics?

In addition, the political and social changes taking place in the world obliged the Catholic Church to consider seriously questions concerning salvation outside the Church. The Church's relationship to newly independent nations in the post-colonial era had to be rethought and new questions were raised about the compatibility of faith with the concrete tenor of life in an age of science and technology. The people of many of the newly independent nations which emerged after the end of World War II were of faith persuasions other than Christian. How was the Church going to relate to them in the scenario of pluralism?

(b) The Agents

The emergence of the *Nouvelle Theologie* in the 1940's suggested new ways of studying scripture and understanding dogma. The theologies implicit in the church's understanding of scripture and liturgy were underlined in the encyclicals written by the popes from the time of World War II and later.[16] Besides, the efforts of theologians and the announcement of Vatican Council II by Pope John XXIII, three months after he was elected pope, echoed the basic insights of the neo-Orthodox method in the areas of scripture, ecclesiology, liturgy, human rights, and the world of the secular and priestly training. Those who look to Vatican II for a theology that would displace traditional (e.g. scholastic) theology would be disappointed. However, the holding of Vatican II validated the emerging new self-understanding of the Church, recognized the positive worth of the secular, and began a process of renewal in the way theology was envisaged and realized.

(c) The Outcome

The world of the secular and that of the sacred were not seen as opposed to each other. Respect for other religions and a spirit of dialogue came to the fore and the self-understanding of the Church began to be seen in terms of the world at large. It was in this spirit that *Gaudium et Spes* was composed, salvation history was recognized in the concrete happenings in the world, and the importance of hermeneutical approaches in theologizing conceded. The *aggiornamento* of Pope John XXIII had begun.

Concluding Remarks of Part II

1. Theologizing is not a method of justifying God's actions in the history of the world. It is rather an attempt to critique and transform the human situation in the light of God's revelation – natural or supernatural, categorical or transcendental, cosmic or personal. This comes out very strongly in the neo-Orthodox model both among the Protestants as well as the Catholics. The aspect of the mystery of God is a *sine qua non* in the process of theologizing. Hence, the classical definition deriving from Anselm (c. 1033-1109), i.e., *fides quaerens intellectum* (faith seeking understanding) should lead to the accounting of human experience in the light of faith:

> Like St. Augustine, Anselm saw in faith the precondition of the right use of reason *(*'credo ut intelligam'); but it yet remains our duty, so far as we can, to exercise our minds in apprehending revealed truth. The whole of his theology is a working out of this programme.[17]

In his theology, Anselm used intellectual reasoning rather than scriptural or patristic sources to find meaningfulness in Christian faith. But faith in the mystery of God remained the point of departure in theologizing.

By contrast, the Liberal model was so caught up with the tools of historical criticism that it even subjected God's revelation to the forum of reason and ended up by neglecting faith in God as the starting point for theologizing. It is for this reason that Karl Barth reacted so strongly against the liberal model and responded with his famous commentary on Romans (1918) and later on in the Barmen Declaration (1934) at the first synod of the Confessing Church.

2. Theologizing is not merely an inductive or deductive process. It is carried out by a community of faith that reflects on its experience in the light of the Christian Tradition. When the Catholic Church holds that the guarantee of the Christian Tradition is articulated in the teaching of the Magisterium it is relying on the neo-Orthodox model of theologizing. Yet, this model has its shortcoming. It is more concerned with the past than with the present or the future. In fact unless the Church encourages a dialogue between the beliefs it holds and the newness of a situation that has come about, its theology will be dysfunctional in that the answers given will not be a response to the questions asked.

The process of theologizing cannot be the mere intellectual effort of an individual theologian if it is to enhance human existence. It must be situated in a faith community that raises questions and searches for answers. Those answers will be the product of the professional theologian who is firmly inserted in a faith community. The answers will rely on the scriptures, the Catholic Tradition, human experience and spiritual discernment. The neo-orthodox model strives to do this.

3. Theologizing must take account of the a-priories it begins with. The 19th century believed that it could put together a significant historical picture of Jesus Christ. It was Albert Schweitzer's *The Quest of the Historical Jesus* (Ger. 1906, Eng. 1910) that showed up the futility of such an undertaking:

> The Quest of the historical Jesus was a failure. It had to be a failure both historically and theologically. Historically, because it is neither the aim of our Gospels nor within their scope to provide material for a biography of Jesus. They are not meant to give a 'Life of Jesus', but to proclaim his words and actions as God's revelation and salvation....

> Theologically, the critical study of the life of Jesus had to fail, because it attempted to ground faith in scientific history, by making an historical reconstruction, the so-called 'historical Jesus', the immediate object of faith. This was once again to ask the impossible of scientific history, that it lay a foundation for present truth and thus for present faith[18]

4. Vatican II can be seen as a gift and task, a gift made possible by the Spirit present in the Church and a task that challenges theologians to bring about the realization of the vision of Vatican II in the world.[19] However, no single theology is sufficient for all time since salvation history continues in a world that is evolving and so Vatican II must be seen as a point of arrival (the gift) and of departure (the task). That is what we must address ourselves to in the following part.

Part III: Theologizing in Today's India

The *aggiornamento* begun in Vatican II continues in the decades following the Council. On the one hand the reform of the liturgy was mandated in the light of certain principles set down in *Sacrosanctum Concilium* (nos. 7ff): concerning the signs used, their meaningfulness and the full and active participation by the laity. The 1983 Code of Canon Law reflects some of the changed conditions (responsibilities to be undertaken) in which members of the Church live their lives as Christians, e.g. the setting up of pastoral councils, finance committees, etc. In *Gaudium et Spes*, the Church is actively engaged in the world of the secular and has taken a pro-active stand in matters of dialogue with other faiths.

On the other hand, while the International Theological Commission was established as an advisory board to the Congregation for the Doctrine of Faith (CDF), the person who heads the commission is also the prefect of the CDF. The danger of the Orthodox model alone prevailing in the commission cannot be discounted! During the pontificate of John Paul II, a series of documents warning against pioneering ventures – especially in the field of religious pluralism – seemed to inhibit authentic dialogue with other religions. Many see in the present official decisions concerning the Lefebvre group, the permission to celebrate the Latin Mass and the liturgical norms that have been set down by Rome as a throwback to the pre-Vatican II days. Collegiality is still not too apparent in the Roman style of functioning.

Yet, bold initiatives have been taken and the result has been the flourishing of local and regional churches, contextual theologies and new apostolic ventures.

(a) Contextualized Theology

Contextualizing theology is one of the most fruitful tasks that different theologizing subjects are engaged in.[20] Thomism suited the age of the *summas* and a church administration that held on to an essentialist philosophy for the world. Theology conceived contextually underlined the important principle that the text could be understood meaningfully when the theologizing subject took into account the difference that came from the various contexts in which theologizing was done. Thomism with its structured system was assumed to be meaningful and relevant in all contexts. Such theology gave no quarter to specific differences arising from varied contexts and as soon as this limitation was recognized, new theologies emerged with their own particular methods.

Feminism asked searching questions to a theology that was unaware of its ill-founded patriarchal presumptions. In the interpretation of the scriptures, in the assessment of people's needs, in decision-making in the Church, those presumptions were unearthed and scrutinized. The prevailing theology could not pretend to be gender-neutral.[21] Black theology, Tribal theology and Dalit theology began with very specific contextual understandings of Christian theology.[22] Among these contemporary efforts, those of the Liberation theologians in the late 1960's first drew attention to contexts. Since then theologizing method that began with a faith perspective took serious notice of the social, economic and political contexts. Doing theology in a context has come to stay.

Among the Protestants, a theological system that was fashioned around the analogy of being was anathema. But the systems that were sketched by Paul Tillich (1886-1965) – the theological method of correlation, by Rudolf Bultmann (1884-1976) – the human existential state and the faith event, and Emil Brunner (1889-1966) with his understanding of natural theology, indicated that the mystery of God could be safeguarded even as the specifically human situation could be redeemed. On the Catholic side, the transcendental method worked out by Karl Rahner (1904-1984) with the help of Marechal's (1878-1944) dynamism of the intellect tried to achieve the same objective. In our own days, *Minjung* theology in South Korea, African theology, Water-buffalo theology (Kosuke Koyama) and Federation of Asian Bishops' (FABC) theology have attained respectability.

For India, theological method should begin with an analysis and understanding of the context that offers categories through which the experience of faith is made understandable. The New Testament communities did exactly this to record the experience of the Christ event. Many of the Fathers of the Church did the same when they had to account for the Christian God experience for their communities of believers. Theologizing will then be a constant going to and fro of the theologizing subject between the question uncovered in the context and the answer that is discerned in Christian Tradition as a whole. Finally, theologizing is a task that is carried out not merely for a particular community alone but also for the universal Church. The theologizing intended for the context of India must also be seen as orthodox by the universal Church. It is the Magisterium in the Church that exercises its function so that what Jesus Christ proclaimed in his day is authentically interpreted in our times.

(b) The Hermeneutical Context of Theology

The theology present in Vatican II offers an opportunity to understand the hermeneutical approaches of those engaging in theologizing. To those who formed the first committees to prepare the council, the aim was to set down the main guidelines within which decisions, or rather endorsements, would be forthcoming from the council fathers. To those who actually took part in the proceedings, these guidelines were seen as restrictive and new committees were set up. The intentions of each of the two groups were different in respect to what the council was supposed to do. The difference came about because one group came from a background which assumed that the Church's self-understanding was static for all time; the other saw change in the world as an invitation to the Church to live out the vision of Jesus Christ in a new key.

The event that was Vatican II could be seen as a "text". The "behind" of the text was the accumulated tradition of the Church. The first group paid attention to the "behind" of the text and decided that *aggiornamento* meant a reaffirmation of the past, especially in doctrines. The second group, while aware of the "behind" of the text, decided that the "front" of the text had still to be discussed and formulated in the council. In the events that transpired during the council, it would seem that the Spirit was with the second group.

Theologizing in India cannot afford to be concerned only with the "behind" of the text because then it will have little to say to the India of today with its pluralism and poverty, its rising eminence and its glaring disparities. The "front" of the text challenges the theologizing subject to initiate and facilitate the dialogue between the Indian context and the Christian Tradition. What will be the self-understanding of the Church in the context of religious pluralism? Would the Christian community not need to reinterpret its creed, cult and symbol system so that their meaningfulness is grasped by those of other faiths?

(c) Theology of Dialogue

Dialogue begins with an understanding of unity underlying diversity and the presumption that the God whom the Christian worships in faith has also left God's footprints in religions other than Christianity. It is the same God who calls all persons into unity. The Christian paradigm of faith should enable the believer to recognize God's action in the world of pluralism and to collaborate actively in bringing about a just and humane society based on the values of God's Reign in this world. Dialogue is a means of achieving both.

Dialogue advocates an enriching of the partners who engage in it. There is one plan of salvation and the method of theologizing should take note not only of the Catholic community, but also of the

Christian community as well as of the community of humankind. Dialogue must be an occasion for understanding and feeling with the other. To achieve this, historical consciousness is necessary so that one does not indulge in (pious) platitudes or the denial of the dark periods of the Church in its history.

The message of dialogue will be propagated more credibly if the Church authorities engage in dialogue more frequently with those within the Church, especially with the local Church and the theologians who are investigated for alleged heterodoxy. True dialogue does not mute the prophetic element of the gospel message nor does it ignore the 'option for the poor'.

Resume

The purpose of this paper was to indicate what could be learnt from past models of theologizing. To this end, three models were examined and lessons were drawn. In part three, under three headings, suggestions have been made for elucidating a method of theologizing in India with reference to the three models.

Endnotes

1. John Bowker, ed., *The Oxford Dictionary of World Religions* (Oxford/New York: Oxford University Press, 1997), 116.
   "**Axial age**. Period around the 6th cent. BCE, when religions were instrumental in effecting great changes in history and civilization. The term was used by Karl Jaspers to draw attention to the rise to prominence of great religious leaders and innovations which established the basis of the great civilizations until the disturbance of those patterns by the European enlightenment and expansion of trade and empire. He drew attention to Zoroaster, the Upanishads, the Buddha, Mahavira, Confucius, the emergence of Taoism."
2. David Tracy, *Blessed Rage for Order: The New Pluralism in Theology* (New York: The Seabury Press, 1975). My presentation will reflect more specifically the matter found in pp 22-63.
3. The Enlightenment showed up the inadequacy of a discipline that is self-authenticating. The stage was set for theology to become interdisciplinary in its method as well as for the Church to become accountable to different constituencies including that of science, e.g. evolution, etc. The rise of capitalism and the emergence of an industrialized society rested on the premise that progress was it own justification and that accountability to all groups of human beings – the working class – was not necessary.

4. The document Syllabus of Errors with its 80 theses that were condemned was attached to the encyclical *Quanta Cura* (Dec. 8, 1964). It was meant to be an attack on the errors of its time, but it also showed a Church that was ill at ease with the changing world around it. It is unfortunate that the Church did not engage in introspection. In fact the Ultramontane forces viewed the Syllabus as justifying their position.
5. One recalls the controversy surrounding the Chinese and Malabar Rites controversy after the death of Matteo Ricci (1552-1610). It was only in 1939 that Pope Pius XII ruled in favour of Ricci's attitude to the traditional honours given to Confucius and the cult of ancestors.
6. The effort of Brahmabandhab Upadyaya (1861-1907) is a case in point.
7. The term "creeping infallibility" implies that even without the formal exercise of infallible teaching, members of the Church are led to believe that they are bound to follow whatever the Church teaches without questioning.
8. Quotation from Claude Welch's *Protestant Thought in the Nineteenth Century,* Vol. I, 1799-1870 (New Haven and London: Yale University Press, 1972; reprint, 1974), 32. The quotation itself is from I. Kant's *Immanuel Kants Werke*, 11 Vols. (Berlin 1912-18), 4:169.
9. Adolf Harnack (1851-1930) and his thesis of the hellenization of Christianity is well known. A good treatment of this problem is found in Heinz Zahrnt, *The Historical Jesus,* trans. from the German by J. S. Bowden (London: Collins, St. James Place, (1960).
10. Refer Martin Kahler's (1835-1912) *The So-called Jesus of History and the Historic Biblical Christ,* ed., C. E. Braaten (Philadelphia: Fortress Press, (1892), 1964).
11. F. L. Cross and E. A. Livingstone: *The Oxford Dictionary of the Christian Church,* 3rd ed. (Oxford University Press, reprinted with corrections, 1997), 1098: "**Modernism**. A movement within the RC Church which aimed at bringing the tradition of Catholic belief into closer relation with the modern outlook in philosophy and other sciences and social ideas. It arose spontaneously and independently in several different countries in the later years of the 19th century...It reached the height of its influence in the first years of the 20th century. It was formally condemned by Pius X in 1907."
12. David Tracy, *Blessed Rage for Order,* 25.
13. The oath against Modernism was rescinded in 1967 by the Congregation of the Doctrine of the Faith.
14. Albert Schweitzer (1875-1965) *The Quest of the Historical Jesus: A Critical Study of Its Progress frm Reimarus to Wrede* (London: Adam & Charles Black, (Ger. 1906), (Eng. 1910), 1948).
15. On the Protestant side, some neo-orthodox theologians are Karl Barth, Emil Brunner (1889-1966), Rudolf Bultmann (1884-1976), Paul Tillich (1886-1965), Reinhold Niebuhr (1892-1971) and Helmut Richard Niebuhr (1894-1962). On the Catholic side, the following may be considered neo-orthodox theologians: Karl Rahner (1904-1984), Edward Schillebeeckx

(1914-2009), Henri de Lubac (1896-1991), Georges-Yves Congar (1904-95), Marie-Dominic Chenu (1895-1990) and others.

16. *Divino Afflante Spiritu* (1943) and *Mediator Dei* (1947).
17. *The Oxford Dictionary of the Catholic Church*, 74.
18. Heinz Zahrnt, *The Historical Jesus*, 47.
19. Refer Jacob Kavunkal, Errol D'Lima and Evelyn Monteiro, ed., *Vatican II: a Gift and a Task.* International Colloquium to Mark the 40th Anniversary of Vatican Council II (Mumbai: St. Paul's, 2006).
20. Refer Jacob Kavunkal, Errol D'Lima and Mathew Jayanth, ed., C*hurch in the Service of Asia's Peoples* (Pune: Jnana-Deepa Vidyapeeth, 2003).
21. Lynda L. Coon, Katherine J. Haldane, and Elisabeth W. Sommer, ed., *That Gentle Strength: Historical Perspectives on Women in Christianity* (Virginia: University of Virginia, 1990). Anne E. Patrick, *Liberating Conscience: Feminist Explorations in Catholic Moral theology* (New York: Continuum, 1997).
22. James H. Cone and Gayraud S. Wilmore, ed., *Black Theology: A Documentary History,* Volume One: 1966-1979 (Published in 1993) and Volume Two: 1980-1992 (Published in 1993) (11th reprint, New York: Maryknoll Orbis Books, 2008).

    M. Amaladoss, "Theologizing in a Tribal Context: Some Methodological Observations," *Sevartham* (1984) 3-10.

    Hugo Gorringe, *Untouchable Citizens: Dalit Movements and Democratisation in Tamil Nadu*, Cultural Subordination and the Dalit Challenge, Vol. 4, ed., Simon R. Charsley and G. K. Karanth (New Delhi: Sage Publications, 2005).

Chapter 3

Cultural Constructions of Indian Christian Theology

Exploring its Presuppositions and Implications

V. Sebastian, SJ

A school text book, *Gujarati Seventh Book* (1938) prepared by the Vernacular Text Books Revision Committee, has the following information for students in a chapter entitled "Aryans and Non-Aryans":

> Aryans were fair skinned and well-built. They worshipped fire, sun and wind as their gods, and recited mantras about them... Heroic men among them established kingdoms and established their dynasties .... The non-Aryans were dark skinned, flat-nosed and practiced superstitious religion and were cruel by nature. Aryans called them *Dasyus* or slaves. In the beginning, non-Aryans harassed the Aryans but eventually, the non-Aryans had either to flee to the forests

> or had to become the servants of Aryans... Among those non-Aryans who came from outside, there were two main groups – Dravidians and Kolars. Kolars were uncivilized and the Dravidians were a little more civilized. When the Aryans went to South India, they saw the settled Dravidians there... Eventually the Dravidians adopted some of the civilized ways of the Aryans. Some among the non-Aryans have improved by coming into contact with Aryans and by mixing with the Rajputs... The gods of the Aryans are fair and manifest love towards human beings. But the gods of non-Aryans are malevolent and evoke fear and trepidation. Non-Aryans worship ghosts, devils, and offer sacrifices to them... It should not be forgotten that in spite of these differences, non-Aryans are also human beings. There are some good qualities in them.[1]

From mid-nineteenth century onwards, children of impressionable age in British India were regularly fed with such myths and identity constructions through school text books. Drawing mainly from the classical Hindu texts and Aryan Race Theory, these myths were by and large the creations of Orientalists like Colebrook and Max Muller, imperial historians such as Hunter and Wheeler and colonial administrators such as Hastings and H. H Risley. This is not just about the Aryan and the non-Aryan. It belongs to a much larger and powerful discursive horizon which began to take shape in the beginning of the nineteenth century colonial India. These stereotypes, derived mainly from what is known as the 'textualized' approaches, have a lasting influence in interpreting India and its past. This particular form of interpretation about Indian and its past has found currency not only in the academic circles but also in the right wing political discourses, which tend to put a high premium on the Indian 'golden' past.

I would like to propose in this paper that one specific form of theology in India which draws its framework and categories from the Hindu classical traditions share the colonial-Orientalist-nationalist-right wing cultural presuppositions. There had been various attempts to make Christianity intelligible in India. Much of these attempts, especially of those of the nineteenth and twentieth centuries resulted in the formation of what had come to be known as Indian Christian theology. Most of these attempts within the framework of Indian Christian theology originated from one central idea, namely, Christian theology is dressed in Western clothing and that such a situation needs to be changed, if the message of Jesus Christ is to have relevance in India. In spite of variations in the way the pioneers tried to articulate an 'Indianized' theology, most of these pioneering attempts drew their categories from what is known as the 'classical traditions' of India. The central concern in these efforts remains constant: theology in India needs to be articulated through 'Indian' categories. In this paper I would like to assess the reasonableness of these attempts – mainly focusing on its cultural presuppositions.

This paper suggests the following theses: (1) Indian Christian theologians wanted to do away with Western theology, its cultural assumptions, and it ways of thinking. But ironically, the cultural presuppositions of Indian Christian theologians are the mirror image of the cultural assumptions of Western Christian theology. Therefore, the criticism which Indian Christian theologians reserved for Western theology is equally applicable to Indian Christian theologians. (2) Indian Christian theology, which was built on the basis of classical Indian philosophical categories, participates in the colonial-Orientalist readings of the Indian past. Such reading and interpretation of India privilege one particular interpretation/worldview to the exclusion of other interpretations/worldview. This interpretation of what constitutes Indian past and Indian 'culture' is based mainly on what is known as the 'textual' approach to Indian realities. More importantly, this approach which has found currency in the secular academic circles and in the right wing political discourses tends to reinforce structures which privilege those who are powerful in society. (3) If the above two perspectives are true, then, we need to have a closer scrutiny of the presuppositions of Indian Christian theology. If Indian Christian theology which is built on the basis of classical Indian categories entails a normative view of culture, the alternative to this hegemonic model would be an empirical approach to culture exemplified in social sciences such as sociology and anthropology.

Presuppositions are intrinsic in any human knowing because we cannot take a single step toward knowing without making *some* presupposition. Presupposition is a fundamental frame of reference that helps perceive reality. Presuppositions form a horizon, and background in our inquiry thus becoming a tacit dimension in our knowing. Presuppositions refer us to the basic structure of one's experience with the world, and this structure makes articulation of that experience possible. In other words, they are a pre-articulated, unthematic structure of beliefs which directs consciousness to perceive, organize and understand the objects and events it encounters.[2] As Polanyi has pointed out, our articulated scientific believes are based on unarticulated foundations. These unarticulated foundations, in any area of knowledge, whether in science or outside of it, are presuppositions. According to Polanyi, presuppositions are intrinsic to our interpretative framework as "we may be said to dwell in them as we do in our own body."[3]

It is important to note that our presuppositions entail certain logical implications. Nygren explains: "If I have affirmed a proposition, I cannot *logically* at the same time deny something which that proposition implies; I *must* affirm all its logical presuppositions."[4] In other words, by asserting the proposition, I have already affirmed some presuppositions and these (presuppositions) are 'implicit in my own assertion.' The major difficulty in understanding presupposition is this: presuppositions are not themselves subject to proof.[5] Presupposition is by necessity relational and therefore it cannot exist in itself. According to Nygren, presuppositional analysis has to do with the relation between our propositions; and what the analysis seeks to do is to show that the propositions necessarily include certain presuppositions and to indicate what these presuppositions are.[6] Any discourse would involve the use of propositions and there is an intrinsic link between propositions and presuppositions.[7] This paper proposes to make explicit some of the cultural assumptions which are implicit in Indian Christian theology. From the view point of method, we need to ask whether the presuppositions which we bring along in the construction of theology are reasonable or not.

A word about the method of this paper: This paper does not deal directly with the 'content' of Indian Christian theology. I take it for granted that we are familiar with the theological orientation under consideration. I am more interested here in the dynamics and historical factors pertaining to cultural constructions and presuppositions. This paper has four sections. The first section focuses briefly on the cultural presuppositions of Western classical theology. The second section looks at the cultural presuppositions of Indian Christian theology. The third section focuses on the colonial-Orientalist interpretations of what constituted Indian past. The fourth section looks at the problems and limitations involved in the normative view of culture.

1. Method and Presuppositions of Classical Theology

Let me begin with one simple historical data, which most of us know very well. Till around 1960s, in the Roman Catholic Church, the liturgy and the Eucharist were in Latin. Before 1960s, the Roman Catholic Church all over the world administered sacraments, sang hymns, and conducted official business almost exclusively in Latin language. The Eucharistic celebration was in Latin, irrespective of the fact that people understood it or not. Seminarians were taught philosophy and theology in Latin and they conducted examinations in Latin. In short, Latin was the official language of the Roman Catholic Church. This situation began to change with the Second Vatican Council (1962-65). There are reasons why the Catholic Church functioned in this way. There is a specific understanding about human beings, truth and culture behind such a way of functioning. Scholars have called this old way of approaching reality as 'Classical' approach in philosophy and in theology. So, the question is: how did they operate in old theological system? What are their assumptions and presuppositions? What are the implications of classical or old theology?

In spite of variations and differences between various schools of theology, they shared some common assumptions about truth, human nature and culture. Most of these assumptions have their basis in Greek philosophy. For example, St. Augustine and Thomas Aquinas, two influential theologians of Christianity, built their theology on Greek philosophical categories. We shall note three important assumptions of old theology: (1) about truth (2) about human nature and (3) about culture.

One of the important classicist assumptions was about the nature of truth. Classicist theology believed in immutable nature of truth. The classicist theologians believed that truth do not change; it possesses a permanent nature. It is true that times change and that circumstances change cases. But within the classicist frame, "all that change is accidental. The same eternal principles are equally valid and equally applicable despite the flux of accidental difference."[8] The classicist "knows that circumstances alter cases but he/she is far more deeply convinced that circumstances are somehow accidental and that, beyond them, there is some substance or kernel or root that fits in with classicist assumptions of stability, fixity, immutability. Things have their specific natures; these natures, at least in principle, are to be known adequately through the properties they possess and the laws they obey. Over and above the specific nature there is only individuation by matter, so that knowledge of one instance of a species is knowledge of any instance.[9]

The second important assumption was about human beings and about human nature. The classicist believed in the permanency and universality of human nature. In other words, they thought that human beings everywhere in the world have one common nature.[10] There are differences between human beings but these differences do not really affect the human nature which is universal. In classical understanding, human nature is inherent or intrinsic to human beings. They believed that once you know aspects of human nature, then it would be the case in all other cases. Once you know one instance, then you know all other cases. Human nature was studied in metaphysical psychology with a long and subtle catalogue of virtues and vices, and the great things humans could accomplish with the grace of God. However, such study was not part of some ongoing process; everything essential had been said long ago; the only urgent task was to find the telling mode of expression and illustration that would communicate to the uneducated of today the wisdom of the great people of the past. As the study of humans was static, so, too, human was conceived in static fashion.[11]

Another important assumption of classical theology was about culture. Of course, the Greeks and Romans did not use the term culture at all. As we know, the concept of culture is a modern construct. The Greeks spoke about cultivating the mind through the principles of *paideia* and *areté*. And this cultivation and human perfection, which represented the noblest and highest human achievements, was meant mainly for the aristocracy.[12] These Greek ideals had considerable impact on human perfection conceived by Western philosophy and theology. Classicist philosophers and theologians assumed that only one cultural form (way of life) represented the highest form of culture. And this culture was the best and all other cultures were inferior or defective.[13] And this one culture was the 'norm' to judge other cultures and ways of life. And the best and the highest form of culture in this thinking was the Greco-Roman model. This idea of culture is known as the "high-culture." This high-culture for them is the embodiment of all that is beautiful, best and refined. The classics of Greece and Rome were seen as the highest achievements of humanity. Opposed to this idea of high-culture, the Greeks developed the notion of 'barbarian.' For the Greek, the barbarian was the uncultured and unrefined. Ancient India had a similar idea, namely, the *Mleccha*.[14] Classical theology held for many centuries what might be called a normative notion of culture. The classicist notion of culture was normative: at least *de jure* there was but one culture that was both universal and permanent; to its norms and ideals might aspire the uncultured, the barbarians or the natives.[15] Perhaps one of the well known portrayals of culture as the pursuit of refinement, perfection of human beings, and as the quest for noble and higher aspirations, was propounded by Mathew Arnold (1822-1888) in his book *Culture and Anarchy* (1869). For Arnold, the creators and custodians of these noble ideals are the elite of a given society.[16] Arnoldian concept of culture as 'high culture' gained currency in the nineteenth century.

The nineteenth century thinkers like Arnold as well as classical anthropologists interpreted the human being and human nature typologically. They sought to construct an image of the human being as a model and as an archetype. And in that process they essentialized the human being and human nature. Classical anthropology sought to uncover the human being by focusing on 'commonalities' in culture. In such approach, the actual differences among individuals and groups are rendered secondary.[17] The trouble with grand formulations about human beings and human nature consists in the fact that they miss out countless variations and immense diversity. The efforts to fit immense diversities into a prefixed frame irons out real differences. Geertz writes: "If we want to discover what man amounts to, we can only find it in what men are: and what men are, above all other things, is various."[18] As Geertz pointed out, "we become individual under the guidance of cultural patterns, historically created systems of meaning in terms of which we give form, order, point, and direction to our lives. And the cultural patterns involved are not general but specific."[19] In classicist understanding, culture was conceived normatively rather than empirically. The modern understanding of culture is not 'normative' but empirical. Modern cultural anthropology tries to understand each culture in its own terms.

2. Cultural Presuppositions of Indian Christian Theology

Historically, the search for an Indian Christian theology is intrinsically linked to the self-understanding of Western theology which saw itself as normative and universally valid. From the viewpoint of history of theology the emergence of an Indian Christian theology has much to do with the attempts to make Christianity intelligible and meaningful in India. It has been pointed out time and again by theologians and thinkers that Hellenized Christian tenets, doctrines, dogmas and categories are extrinsic to Indian mindsets. Christianity in general and Roman Catholicism in particular have been described, besides being esoteric, as alien to the cultural ethos of the people of India. Theologians and thinkers have pointed out that if Christianity is to have relevance, it needs to be presented in a way that is intelligible to the people of India. I guess most of us are familiar with such formulations articulated by various theologians in India.

Within this context, some Christian thinkers attempted to reorient Christianity in Indian soil in order to make it intelligible. Indeed, their task had been pioneering in this direction. They did make attempts to synthesise Christianity with classical Hindu Philosophical categories and Indian spiritual heritage. Christian thinkers like Brahmabandhav Upadhyaya, members of the Calcutta School, among others, were convinced that classical Hindu philosophical categories were the conditions for the possibility of making Christian message meaningful in Indian soil. There is an impressive collection of theological literature using this classical Hindu cultural and religio-philosophic orientation produced by both Indians and non-Indians who belong to Catholic and Protestant traditions.[20] This specific orientation has been termed as *Indian Christian Theology* by a considerable number of theologians.[21] The quest for making the Christian message meaningful in India is still in the process of evolution. However, the theological tradition that began from De Nobili of making Christianity intelligible through the mediation of classical Hindu cultural and religio-philosophic symbols, categories and thought patterns still has an appeal in many parts of India.

If there is a commonality shared by Indian Christian theology, in spite of divergences in the approach, then, it is the appropriation of the so called classical Indian traditions. These classical traditions refer to what is commonly perceived as the mainstream religious, philosophical, spiritual, mystical and aesthetic orientations in India; they are part and parcel of the so called classical culture. For instance, in the common parlance, Indian classical music and classical dances are differentiated from Indian folk dances and music. In Indian Christian theology the mainstream classical traditions are identified as "Indian." In fact there is a triple identification involved in Indian Christian theology: (1) "Indian" is identified as belonging to the classical tradition (2) Conversely, classical tradition is identified as "Indian" (3) The "Indian" tradition is identified with Hindu socio-cultural and religious ethos.

This triple identification is quite common in Indian Christian theology and in most cases, this identification is something taken for granted by Indian Christian theologians. Such identification forms one of the chief presuppositions of a considerable number of theologians in India. It is not merely the nomenclature involved in an Indian Christian theology that is problematic, but more so the cultural presuppositions encoded within it. One of the main presuppositions behind the so called Indian Christian theology is that there is just one Indian culture which is represented by the so called classical cultural ethos of India. But from the perspective of an anthropologically informed theology such a presupposition would seem highly questionable.

The implicit notion of culture contained in an Indian Christian Theology seems to be the mirror image of Western classical theology. To put it differently, Indian Christian theology works within the same cultural framework with which Western Classical theology functioned. Several Indian Christian theologians criticized theology in India being too western. Paradoxically, Indian Christian theologians themselves seem to be harboring the same cultural presuppositions of Western classical theology. It would seem that the criticism which Indian Christian theologians have reserved for Western Christian theology may be equally applicable to the so called Indian Christian theology based on a normative understanding of culture. Both Classical Western theology as well as Indian Christian theology seems to be operating within the classicist cultural framework.

The very nomenclature "Indian Christian Theology" in the singular is indicative of the *normative* cultural presupposition. Such singular approach correlates Indian Christian theology with "Indian" culture, which is the *culture*. The implicit correlation is between Indian Christian theology = Indian culture = High culture = *the* culture. The use of terms such as "Indian culture", "Indian theology" and "Indian Christology" in the singular is quite common in the writings of considerable number of theologians. For instance, L. Klostermeir sees the aim of an "Indian Christology" as being able to express in Hindu terms Christ as the living relationship of everybody with the ultimate.[22] Such singularity of 'Indian Christology' cuts deeper than mere nomenclature. If there is a development of a 'Tribal Christology' and a 'Dalit Christology' then, how are we to make sense of an "Indian Christology" in the *singular* that uses classical categories? As K. Tanner points out,

> Unlike the anthropological notion, high culture is not a term highlighting differences among those who display it.

> General process of refinement and the basic nature of results need not vary over time and space. Differences among the cultured are at most quantitative, matters of degree: one can be more or less cultured. The word culture when used in a high culture or evaluative sense is therefore found in the singular rather than in the plural: there is *a* high culture to be shared in varying degrees by cultured persons, ***but no high cultures.***[23]

The first difficulty involved in Indian theology in the *singular* is cultural one. Those theologians who speak of an Indian theology presuppose that there is something like an Indian culture.[24] Most of these theologians take it for granted that the so called classical culture of India reflects 'Indian' culture. In other words, they take the Sanskritic or classical culture as the norm. Normative understanding of culture takes one culture, usually the dominant culture to judge and evaluate other cultures. Indian Christian theology which draws its inspiration from classical Hindu categories depends, either directly or indirectly on the colonial constructions of Indian past. Indeed, Hindu categories existed for many centuries, but the privileging of the classical Hindu system took place during the colonial period. And this popularization of Hindu texts did have an impact on Christian thinkers such as Brahmabandhab Upadyaya, a friend of Vivekananda.

3. Orientalists' Textual Approach and its Implications

It would be interesting to note that in spite of India's considerably long history, systematic understanding about it had been relatively recent one. In this context Romila Thapar's observation is pertinent: "A major contradiction in our understanding of the entire Indian past is that this understanding derives largely from the interpretations of Indian history made in the last two hundred years."[25] British Orientalists and colonial administrators played an important role in the systematic retrieval, interpretation and construction of Indian history. Early British Orientalists, under the leadership of Warren Hastings, sought to know India so as to govern it effectively and in that process they engaged in a systematic investigation into Indian past. Indeed, they had the help and support of the Indian elites (pundits) who provided the manuscripts, helped in the translation process and in the interpretation of Indian past. The colonial-Orientalist interpretation of Indian past was basically a hermeneutic process based on the Indic texts. In their quest to understand India and its past Orientalists such as Wilkins, Duncan, Halhead, Jones and Colebrooke focused on Hindu Sacred texts.

The Orientalists seems to have been convinced that these texts were indeed accurate guides to the culture and society of the Hindus.[26] The perception of Indian society which was derived from the study of texts with the cooperation of *pundits* and *sastris* had important consequences. The subsequent scholarly attention was focused almost exclusively on the textualised Hinduism or Sanskritic Hinduism. Towards the end of the nineteenth century Müller's translations in a way encouraged what has been called a 'textual' approach to Hinduism. The textualized approach to Indian realities had far reaching consequence.

In the first place, what came to be known as Indian 'classical texts' underwent significant transformations during colonial period, especially with the Orientalist interventions. Muller considers the published Vedas as a 'book.' Circulated mostly through strict oral tradition,[27] the very idea of printing the Vedas went against time-honored epistemic boundaries and the notion of *adhikara* about *Sruti*, the highest form of Sacred Scriptures. Until it was published, the Vedas were never thought of as 'books.' Now during colonialism most of these ancient texts came to be considered as 'classical' texts and books. But the very concept and taxonomy of the 'classical' was something of a novelty and the term itself was used very rarely till the nineteenth century in Europe. In its long development the concept of the classical in the West carried always the ideological connotations of privileged access to cultural and epistemic domains. Interestingly there is no word in Sanskrit or in any other Indian languages which is equivalent or parallel for words 'classical' 'classic' or classicism.

Secondly, the colonial-Orientalist perspectives led to the interpretation of the Vedic past as the 'golden age.' The fascination of the Orientalists such as Jones, Colebrooke and Max Müller with the discovery of a Hindu age of splendor made them draw parallels with

Greek classical period. Colebrooke propounded a new synthesized image of the Indo-Aryan period as a 'golden age.' Colebrooke as well as Max Müller dramatically contrasted Vedic period with the beliefs and practices of contemporary Hindu society. This image of the Hindu 'golden' age would be taken up enthusiastically by Indian nationalists towards the end of the nineteenth century in their effort to create a pan-national identity.

Thirdly, as Romila Thapar points out, given their textual approach, "Orientalism encouraged a Brahmanical view of early Indian society and anthropologists, who more often work on the ground as it were, have tended to see Indian society and religion from the perspective of Brahmanical texts."[28] Such view led to a consistent view that the Brahmins were the dominant group in society. This was the function of the view which came from the texts themselves – a view which sees the Brahmin as the center of the social order, which prescribes differential punishments for crimes based on one's varna status, which prohibits other varnas than Brahmins from learning certain texts, and which generally exalts the sacredness of the Brahman.[29]

Fourthly, the textual approach to Indian society had a huge impact on the social structures. We cannot go into minute details of this impact. I would like to mention two important administrative measures which changed the very character of Hindu social structures in the nineteenth century. The first was the introduction of the personal law and the second was the introduction of the decennial census. The Orientalists codified *dharmashastra* texts with a view of creating a stable and consistent Hindu personal law, thereby fossilizing dynamic traditions and jeopardizing regional variations. This they did by applying the concept of 'legal precedence' which was totally alien to Hinduism.[30] Similarly, decennial census which began in 1871 used the taxonomies derived from brahmanical texts. For example, census commissioner H. H Risley used the principle of 'social precedence' to categorize the Hindu society. It was an effort to get a 'clear' picture of Indian society, but the ground realities were far more complex. Soon the census officials ran into serious trouble because the demarcation lines between 'caste' and 'tribe' were very nebulous. The category 'brahmin' appeared more or less distinct;

but as they went down the hierarchical ladder, who belonged where became a matter of bitter dispute.[31]

Fifthly, one of the major stereotypes created by administrator-Orientalist scholarship is the projection of Hinduism as a monolithic 'religion.'[32] "While most Indians encountered the Veda through the oral medium, Müller's publication of the Veda created a reified product, decontextualized from its audience, and popularized the idea that the study of Hinduism meant the study of a body of texts."[33] The 'textual' approach in understanding and interpreting India and its past, the dominant method adopted by the Orientalist scholars, created a particular view about India, was deeply embedded in Indian classical traditions. As Gauri Viswanathan points out, although "Sanskritic Hinduism was far from representative of the worship of diverse peoples, it was made to define a whole range of heterogeneous practices that were then lumped together to constitute a single religious tradition termed "Hinduism."[34]

The Colonial-Orientalist interpretations about India and Indian past have left long lasting consequences. Impressionable youngsters in the schools and colleges have been regularly fed with stereotypes in the nineteenth and twentieth centuries. The interpretation about India and its past for past two hundred years or so has taken a particular direction and orientation – both in the academic and political discourses.

4. Hegemonic Cultural Constructions

Indeed, such interpretations have not gone unchallenged. Several historians and thinkers such as D. D Kosambi, Romila Thapar, Sumit Sarkar, and Amartya Sen have challenged the assumptions of such hegemonic interpretations. As I mentioned before, Indian nationalists at the tail end of the nineteenth century took up many of the stereotypes created by the colonial-Orientalist nexus. According to Romila Thapar, "nationalist historians made little attempt to change the basic paradigm put forward by European Orientalist scholarship, a paradigm conditioned certainly by paucity of evidence but equally by European intellectual preconceptions within a colonial framework."[35] Hindu leaders like Vivekananda took up the concept of the Hindu 'golden' age and popularized the notion that India is essentially a 'religious' and 'spiritual' nation. This is what Vivekananda consistently said in many of his lectures: "To the other nations of the world, religion is one among the many occupations of life… But here, in India, religion is the one and the *only* occupation of life."[36] According to Vivekananda, "the Indian mind is first religious, *then* anything else."[37] Vivekananda was not the only one to project such images about India. Such portrayal 'spiritual India' can be seen in the writings of Aurobindo Ghosh also. Someone familiar with colonial history would immediately recognize the fact that the Orientalists such as Max Müller had played a big role in the creation of such myths. This notion of 'spiritual India' is the staple diet in the contemporary Right Wing political discourses. Often such interpretations are fed into school text books and popular discourses. We need to ask further: Does such interpretation stand on reasonable grounds? According to Romila Thapar, a well known historian, 'Indians in the pre-eighteenth century never claimed that they were more spiritual than other peoples, or that the Indian way of life was concerned solely with things spiritual. The ideal of the earlier texts that the best life on earth is a balance between *dharma, artha, and kama*, shows a healthy unconcern for any obsession with either the spiritual or the material.'[38]

The essentialized view which equates Indian identity with Hindu identity can be seen at various levels – the right-wing political discourses, common parlance, and writings about Indian 'culture,' academic circles and in theology. Nirad Chaudhuri's writings reflect such essentialized view: "They [the Hindus] are the masters and rulers… They are also the only source of energy for the country considered as a human machine; and it is their desires and aspirations which are keeping it running. No other element counts." He writes further: "… At least, I have no hesitation in saying that if the history of India has taken a certain course in the last fifty years, or for that matter in the last thousand, that is due, above all, to the Hindu character. It has been the most decisive determining influence on the historical process. I feel equally certain that it will remain so and shape the form of everything that is being undertaken for and in the country."[39] Obliterating India's cultural diversity has been the main agenda of the right wing political ideologies. There is a systematic attempt by political parties belonging to this ideological persuasion to project the Hindu culture as the culture of India. They are unable or unwilling to recognize the pluralistic cultural traditions of the Indian subcontinent. A recent article by the former RSS chief K. S. Sudarshan in the *Third Millennium* posits India's fundamental unity in the Hindu cultural ethos.[40] As past two decades of Indian political landscape reveal, the unwillingness to affirm the cultural and religious plurality of India often have led to violent confrontations between communities. What is a serious concern is the systematic infiltration of such narrow and distorted perceptions into India's bureaucratic, judicial, and administrative infrastructure. Even more worrying is the 'Hindutva' judgments by the judiciary during the NDA rule which equated *Hindutva* with 'Indianness' and Indian culture as Hindu culture.[41]

The distorted interpretation of India and its past is not limited to the domain of politics alone. Several scholars have pointed out the manner in which contemporary academic discourse about Indian culture, religion, and Indian past are deeply embedded in colonial constructions. According to sociologist Sujata Patel, much of the Indological, sociological and anthropological discourses in India are embedded either directly or indirectly in colonial categories.[42] It is not uncommon to see the projection of Aryan model of societal structure, with its hierarchies and inequalities, in the scholarly circles as the core of Indian tradition.[43] There are some prominent social scientists who are critics of Indian secularism seeking a return to traditional religious ethos of India. For most of these social scientists, Indian religion means primarily Hindu tradition.[44] Not only social sciences but much of philosophy and theology taught in India participate, either directly or indirectly, in the Orientalist and nationalist stereotypes. What has been projected as 'Indian Christian Theology,' reflects the same presuppositions of colonial constructions of religion and of Hinduism.

A normative interpretation of culture usually either excludes or sidelines India's cultural diversity. Historically speaking, India is the product of a large number of cultural influences. For example, the contribution of Buddhism, in terms of philosophy, morality, higher education, art, and architecture, can hardly be ignored when the cultural past of India is discussed. Buddhism had been a significant catalyst in the cross cultural encounter between ancient India and several Asian countries.[45] Christianity which has been present in India at least for a thousand and six hundred years has contributed significantly in a number of areas such as science, astronomy, linguistics, literature, cartography, medicine, printing, and educational institutions. The contribution of Islam, at least from the tenth century, had a considerable influence in terms of art, architecture, science, music, literature, and administrative institutions.[46] There is a sizable Adivasi population who had been present in India even before Hinduism came into existence. Jainism and Sikhism also have contributed to the cultural heritage of India. There had been cultural, scientific, mercantile exchanges between India and other civilizations such as Greek, Persian, Arab, and Chinese. There had been also Jewish and Parsee communities for several centuries in India. The characterization of India as 'Hindu civilization,' according to Amartya Sen, tends to 'add some highly deceptive credibility to the extraordinary distortion of history and manipulation of the present realities.'[47]

Conclusion

The specific theological orientation under consideration – known as Indian Christian Theology – entails a normative understanding of culture. In other words, it sets up a dominant form of culture as the norm in its hermeneutical enterprise. The most crucial limitation with the notion of an 'Indian theology' would be its inability to address specific, diverse and particular cultural experiences. It could be argued that by Indian Christian theology we mean only a theology which has its origins and roots in India. The obvious question would be then: Where does it have its origins and roots within the time-space categories? If the phrase Indian Christian theology is to have concreteness, then it has to account for the time-space dimensions of it. The so called 'Indian' Christian theology (read as Sanskritic) has its specific historical, spatial, and temporal origins. To universalize from the particular (Sanskritic) cultural and philosophical categories and to project it as 'Indian' would involve ethnocentric assumptions. Such normative approach presupposes that other cultures do not possess the ability and categories to make sense of the Christian message. Such normative approaches of Indian Christian theology which use classical Hindu categories are mirror images of Western cultural presuppositions.

What can take other cultures seriously is an empirical understanding of cultures. Culture is relative in the sense that it is the meaning system which had been created by a given group of people. It reflects and draws from the meaning systems of a particular people. It is a meaning system intelligible to those who partake in it. Communities are the achievement of common meaning and there are levels and degrees of this achievement. There is no 'common' meaning and there is no one Indian 'culture.' What is usually projected as Indian 'culture' is the hegemonic discourse of a particular group – classical/Sanskritic Hinduism. Their experiences cannot be made normative for the whole of India. However, it had been made normative through colonial administration through complex mechanisms. When we speak about theological method, these dynamics and mechanisms need to be kept in mind.

Endnotes

1. Department of Public Instruction, *Gujarati Sathmi Chopdi* [Gujarati Seventh Book], Prepared by the Vernacular Text Books Revision Committee, 8th ed. (Bombay: The British India Press, 1938), 156-159.
2. T. Peters, "The Nature and Role of Presupposition: An Inquiry into Contemporary
Hermeneutics," in *International Philosophic Quarterly,* 14, No. 2 (June, 1974): 210.
3. M. Polanyi, *Personal Knowledge: Towards a Post-Critical Philosophy* (New York: Harper & Row, 1958), 60.
4. A. Nygren, *Meaning and Method* (London: Epworth Press, 1972), 206.
5. Ibid., 221.
6. Ibid., 222.
7. A proposition is "that which is proposed or stated; the content of a declarative sentence, capable of truth and falsity." S. Blackburn, *The Oxford Dictionary of Philosophy* (Oxford: Oxford University Press, 1994), 307

8. B. Lonergan, "The Future of Thomism," in *A Second Collection: Papers by Bernard J. F. Lonergan, SJ*, ed., William Ryan, SJ and Bernard Tyrrel, SJ (London Darton, Longman & Todd, 1977), 47.
9. B. Lonergan, *Method in Theology* (Minnesota: The Seabury Press, 1979), 48.
10. Bhikhu Parekh, *Rethinking Multiculturalism: Cultural Diversity and Political Theory* (New York: Palgrave, 2000), 16-23.
11. B. Lonergan, *Method in Theology*, 48.
12. Both *paideia* and *arête* represent Greek educational ideals, which aimed at the perfection of young men. See, Werner Jaeger, *Paideia: The Ideals of Greek Culture, Vol. I, Archaic Greece, the Mind of Athens*, trans. Gilbert Highet, Second edition (New York: Oxford University Press, 1973).
13. B. Parekh, *Rethinking Multiculturalism*, 16.
14. Romila Thàpar, "The Image of the Barbarian in Early India," in *Cultural Pasts: Essays in Early Indian History*, idem (Delhi: Oxford University Press, 2007), 235-270.
15. B. Lonergan., *Method in Theology*, xi.
16. Mathew Arnold, *Culture and Anarchy*, ed. Dover Wilson (First published in 1869. Reprint: Cambridge: Cambridge University press, 1981).
17. Clifford Geertz, "The Impact of the Concept of Culture on the Concept of Man," in *Man in adaptation: The Cultural Present*, Vol. 2, ed. Yehudi A. Cohen (New York: Aldine de Gruyter, 1974),19-32, here, 30.
18. Ibid., 31.
19. Ibid.
20. See for example, A. J. Appaswamy, *Christianity as Bhakti Marga: A Study of the Johannine Doctrine of Love* (Madras: The Christian Literature Society, 1928); R. Boyd, *An Introduction to Indian Christian Theology* (Madras: The Christian Literature Society (1969), 1975); idem, *Khristadvaida: A Theology for India* (Madras: The Christian Literature Society, 1977); J. Chethimattam, "Vedanta and Christian Experience," *Indian Theological Studies* 1 (1962): 222-30; 277-89; M. Dhavamony, "Indian Christian Theological Method," *Studia Missionalia* 45 (1996): 57-94; idem, "Indian Christian Theology." *Studia Missionalia* 45 (1996): 95-117; idem, "Indian Perspectives in the New Paradigms of Theology," in *Paradigm Change in Theology*, ed. Hans Kung and David Tracy (Edinburgh: T. & T. Clark LTD, 1989), 424-36; K. Klostermaier, "Indian Christian Theology," *Clergy Review* LIV, no. 3 (1969): 175-98; idem, *Indian Theology in Dialogue* (Madras: The Christian Literature Society, 1986); J. Mattam, *Land of the Trinity* (Bangalore: TPI, 1975); idem, "Interpreting Christ to India Today: The Calcutta School," *Indian Journal of Theology*, 23 (1974): 206-218; idem, "Modern Catholic Attempts at Presenting Christ to India," *Indian Journal of Theology*, 23 (1974): 191-205; A. Mookenthottam, *Towards a Theology in the Indian Context* (Bangalore: Asian Trading Corporation, 1980); R. Panikkar, *The Unknown Christ of Hinduism* (London: Darton, Longman and Todd, 1964); Sr. Vandana, "Indian Theologizing -the Role of Experience,"

in *Theologizing in India*, ed. G. Gispert-Sauch M. Amaladoss. T. K. John (Bangalore: Theological Publications in India, 1981), 81-115; J. Vattanky, "Theological Implications of Nyaya System," *Vidyajyoti* (1983): 334-41; idem, Current Nyaya Studies and Contemporary Indian Theology." *Vidyajyoti* (1990): 507-16.

21. See especially, R. H. S. Boyd, "The Philosophical Context of Indian Christian Theology with Special Reference to P. Chenchiah," in *Indian Voices in Today's Theological Debate*, ed. Horst Burkle and Wolfgang M. W. Roth (Lucknow: Lucknow Publishing House, 1972), 47-69; K. Klostermair, "Indian Christian Theology," in *Indian Theology in Dialogue* (Madras: The Christian Literature Society, 1986), 65-88; M. Dhavamony, "Indian Christian Theological Method," *Studia Missionalia* 45 (1996): 57-94; idem, "Indian Christian Theology." *Studia Missionalia* 45 (1996): 95-117.
22. Quoted by R. H. S. Boyd, *An Introduction to Indian Christian Theology*, 303.
23. K. Tanner, *Theories of Culture: A New Agenda for Theology* (Minneapolis: Fortress press, 1997), 5. Emphasis added.
24. See, R. Panikkar, "Indian Theology: A Theological Mutation,' Theologizing in India, 25; M. Dhavamony, "Indian Christian Theological Method," *Studia Missionalia*, 45 (1996), 59.
25. Romila Thapar, *The Past and Prejudice* (New Delhi: National Book Trust, 1979), 3.
26. Bernard Cohn, "Notes on the History of the Study of Indian Society and Culture," in *Structure and Change in Indian Society*, ed. Milton Singer and Bernard Cohn (Jaipur: Rawat Publications, 1996), 6-7.
27. William Albert Graham, *Beyond the Written Word: Oral Aspects of Scripture in the History of Religion* (Cambridge: Cambridge University Press, [1987]1993), 71-74.
28. Romila Thapar, "Communalism and Historical Legacy: Some Facets," in *Communalism in India: History, Politics and Culture*, ed. K. N. Panikkar (New Delhi: Manohar, 1991), 21.
29. Bernard Cohn, "Notes on the History, 7.
30. See, D. Derrett, *Hindu Law Past and Present: Being An Account Of The Controversy Which Preceded The Enactment Of The Hindu Code, The Text Of The Code As Enacted, And Some Comments Thereon* (Calcutta: A. Mukherjee & Co., Private Ltd., 1957); M. Galanter, *Law and Society in Modern India* (Delhi: Oxford University Press, 1989); Richard W. Lariviere, "Justice and *Panditas*: Some Ironies in Contemporary Readings of the Hindu Legal Past," *The Journal of Asian Studies*, 48, no. 4 (November 1989), 757-769; Bernard Cohn, "Law and the Colonial State in India," in *Colonialism and its Forms of Knowledge: The British in India* (Delhi: Oxford University Press, 1997), 57-75; Rosane Rocher, "British Orientalism in the Eighteenth Century: The Dialectics of Knowledge and Government," in *Orientalism and the Postcolonial Predicament: Perspectives*

on South Asia, ed., C. Breckenridge and Peter van der Veer (Delhi: Oxford University Press, 1994), 215-49.

31. See, Bernard Cohn, "The Census, Social Structure and Objectification in South Asia," in *An Anthropologist among the Historians and Other Essays*. idem (Delhi: Oxford University Press, 1987) 224-254; Arjun Appadurai, "Number in Colonial Imagination," in *Orientalism and the Postcolonial Predicament: Perspectives on South Asia*, ed. Carol Breckenridge and Peter van der Veer (Delhi: Oxford University Press, 1994), 314-339; Nicholas B. Dirks, *Castes of Mind: Colonialism and the Making of Modern* India (New Jersey: Princeton University Press, 2001. Reprint, Delhi: Permanent Black, 2003).
32. See, S. N. Balagangadhara, *The Heathen in His Blindness: Asia, the West, and the Dynamic of Religion* (Leiden: E. J. Brill, 1994 and New Delhi: Manohar, 2005); Ronald Inden, *Imagining India* (Cambridge: Balckwell Publishers, 1994); Richard King, *Orientalism and Religion: Postcolonial Theory, India and 'The Mystic East* (New Delhi: Oxford University Press, 1999); Romila Thapar, "Syndicated Hinduism," in *Hinduism Reconsidered*, ed. Günther-Dietz Sontheimer and Hermann Kulke (New Delhi: Manohar Publishers, 2001), 54-81; Gauri Viswanathan, "Colonialism and the Construction of Hinduism," in *The Blackwell Companion to Hinduism*, ed. Gavin Flood (Oxford: Blackwell, 2003), 23-44; Richard King, "Orientalism and the Modern Myth of Hinduism," in *Numen*, 46, no. 2, 1999): 146-185; Heinrich von Stietencron, "Hinduism: On the Proper Use of a Deceptive Term," in *Hinduism Reconsidered*, 32-53; Robert Eric Frykenberg, "The Emergence of Modern 'Hinduism' as a Concept and as an Institution: A Reappraisal with Special Reference to South India," in *Hinduism Reconsidered*, 82-107; Brian K. Pennington, *Was Hinduism Invented? Britons, Indians, and the Colonial Construction of Religion* (Oxford: Oxford University Press, 2005); Geoffrey A. Oddie, *Imagined Hinduism: British Protestant Missionary Constructions of Hinduism 1793-1900* (New Delhi: Sage, 2006); David N. Lorenzen, *Who Invented Hinduism? Essays on Religion in History* (New Delhi: Yoda Press, 2006).
33. Kwok Pui-lan, "Introduction: Gender, Colonialism, and the Study of Religion," in *Postcolonialism, Feminism and Religious Discourse*, ed. Laura E. Donaldson and Kwok Pui-lan (New York: Routledge, 2002), 19.
34. Gauri Viswanathan, "Colonialism and the Construction of Hinduism," 25.
35. Romila Thapar, "Nation Building, Development Process and Communication: Towards a Renaissance: Some Historical Perspectives Drawing on Early Times," in *In Search of India's Renaissance*, Vol. II, (Chandigarh; Centre for Research in rural and Industrial Development, 1992), 23.
36. Italics added. Vivekananda, "India's Message to the World," in *My India, Arise* (Calcutta: Ramakrishna Math and Ramakrishna Mission, 1993), 2-3.
37. Italics added. Vivekananda, "The Future of India," in *My India, Arise*, 74-75.
38. Romila Thapar, *The Past and Prejudice*, 7.

39. Nirad Chaudhuri, *The Continent of Circe* (London: Catto and Windus, 1965), 86.
40. According to Sudarshan, "the Church is engaged in creating dissention in the Hindu society by projecting the diversity as basic differences and strike at the inherent unifying factor of *Hindutva* or Hinduness." K. S. Sudarshan, "Our Hindu Nation and Indian Christian Identity," *Third Millennium* X (January-March, 2007): 88.
41. Anil Nauriya, "The Hindutva Judgments: A Warning Signal," *Economic and Political Weekly*, 31, No. 1 (6 January, 1996): 10-13; Brenda Cossman and Ratna Kapur, "Secularism: Bench-Marked by Hindu Right," *Economic and Political Weekly*, 31, No. 38 (21 September 1996): 2613-2630.
42. Sujata Patel, "Sociological Study of Religion: Colonial Modernity and 19th Century Majoritarianism," *Economic and Political Weekly* XLII, No. 13 (March 31, 2007): 1089-1094.
43. See for example, Louis Dumont, *Homo Hierarchicus: Caste System and its Implications, R*evised English Edition. (Chicago and London: The University of Chicago Press, 1970); T. N. Madan, "Secularism in its Place," in *Secularism and its Critics*, ed. Rajeev Bhargava (New Delhi: Oxford University Press, [1998] 2006), 297-320.
44. T. N. Madan and Ashis Nandy are prominent among these social scientists. See, Joseph Tharamangalam, "Indian Social Scientists and Critique of Secularism," *Economic and Political Weekly* XXX, No. 9 (March 4, 1995): 457-461.
45. De La Vallée Poussin, "Buddhism," in *The Legacy of India*, ed., G. T. Garratt (Oxford: Clarendon Press, 1937), 162-184.
46. Abdul Qadir, "The Cultural Influence of Islam," in *The Legacy of India*, ed., G. T. Garratt, 287-304.
47. Amartya Sen, *Identity and Violence: The Illusion of Destiny* (London: Allen Lane-Penguin Books, 2006), 48.

Chapter 4

Cultural Postcolonial Biblical Interpretation for India

Selva Rathinam, SJ

At the first sight, the above title sounds naïve. Historically, India is a postcolonial nation which has celebrated even the golden jubilee of its liberation from the British colonizers in 1997. Consequently postcolonialism must be the ideology appropriate to interpret the Bible in India. This term 'postcolonial' refers to the "reading and writing practices grounded in some form of colonial experience occurring outside Europe but as a consequence of European expansion into and exploitation of 'the other' worlds."[1] In countries which have been victims of imperialism, postcolonialism is the need of the hour to achieve an identity "uncontaminated by universalist or Eurocentric concepts and images."[2]

In this paper[3] I would like to point out some aspects of its theoretical positions as I understand them. After exploring the historical development of postcolonialism in general and of biblical interpretation in India in particular, we shall focus on three concepts contributed by three key figures to the postcolonial strategy and finally we shall conclude with some concrete marks of the postcolonial reading of the Bible.

A. What is Postcolonialism?

1. Colonialism

According to the *Oxford English Dictionary*, the word colonialism comes from the Roman 'colonia' meaning 'farm' or 'settlement.' It referred to Romans who settled in other lands but still retained their citizenship. Unfortunately, the above meaning refers only to the colonizers and avoids any implication of an encounter between peoples, or of conquest and domination.[4] Although the process of colonialism was different in different parts of the world it invariably resulted in the most complex and traumatic relationships between the original inhabitants and the newcomers.

The process of 'forming a community' in the new land necessarily meant *unforming* or re-forming the communities that existed there already, and involved a wide range of practices including trade, plunder, negotiation, warfare, genocide, enslavement and rebellions. Such practices produced and were produced through a variety of writings – public and private records, letters, trade documents, government papers, fiction and scientific literature. These practices and writings are an important part of all that the contemporary studies of colonialism and postcolonialism try to make sense of. So colonialism can be defined as the conquest and control of other people's land and goods.[5]

Colonialism in this sense has been a recurrent and widespread feature of human history. Modern European colonialism cannot be separated from the earlier expansions of various colonial powers. And yet the modern European colonialism ushered in new colonial practices which altered the whole globe in a way that the other colonialisms did not.[6] Marxist thinking on this distinction is that the earlier colonialisms were pre-capitalist whereas the modern colonialism was established alongside capitalism in Western Europe.[7] Modern colonialism not only extracted tribute, goods and wealth from the conquered countries but it also drew the latter into a complex relationship with their own. As a result, there was a flow of human and natural resources between colonized and colonial countries.

Thus, sugar was produced in the West Indian plantations for consumption in Europe, and raw cotton from India was exported to England for the manufacturing of cloth only to be sold back to India to the detriment of its own cloth production. The movement was in both directions. The colonized moved as slaves (from Africa to the Americas), indentured laborers, domestic servants and traders, whereas the colonizers moved as administrators, soldiers, merchants, writers, missionaries, teachers, and scientists. "In whichever direction human beings and materials traveled, the profits always flowed back into the so-called 'mother country."[8] This was necessary for the growth of European capitalism and industry. "Thus, we could say that colonialism was the midwife that assisted at the birth of European capitalism."[9]

2. Imperialism

The distinction between pre-capitalist and capitalist colonialisms is often made by referring to the latter as imperialism. Now colonialism is over. But the process which leads to the relations of dependence and control is not over. Sometimes words like 'neo-imperialism' or 'neo-colonialism' are used to describe these situations. In other words, power flows from the imperial country (or "the metropole") and it penetrates and controls the colony or neo-colony. "Imperialism can function without formal colonies (as in United States imperialism today) but colonialism cannot."[10]

3. Postcolonialism

Now the age of colonialism is over and the whole world has become postcolonial because the descendants of once colonized peoples live everywhere. This term 'postcolonialism' has been fiercely contested on many counts. The term itself is written sometimes with a hyphen (post-colonialism) and sometimes is left unhyphenated (postcolonialism). The hyphenated version denotes the period after colonialism.[11] The prefix 'post' in postcolonialism complicates the matter. It "implies an 'aftermath' in two senses – temporal as in coming after, and ideological, as in supplanting."[12] The temporal sense implied a chronological meaning, designating the post-independence period. However, now the term has been used by literary critics in the latter sense to discuss the various cultural effects of colonization and especially on literary production. It is the second implication which needs further discussion. "A country may be both postcolonial (in the sense of being formally independent) and neo-colonial (in the sense of remaining economically and /or culturally dependent) at the same time."[13] In the new global order the economic, cultural and political penetration of some countries by others continue to take place. Since the inequities of colonial rule live on in the contemporary imbalances between 'first' and 'third' world nations, it is perhaps premature to proclaim the demise of colonialism.

4. The oppressed within India's Postcoloniality

In India the postcolonial status is not usually contested. Yet, internal fractures still exist. "These internal fractures and divisions are important if 'post colonialism' is to be anything more than a term signifying a technical transfer of governance."[14] *Shishu* (Children) is a moving story in which the Bengali writer Mahasweta Devi describes how the tribal peoples have been literally and figuratively crippled in post-independence India.[15] As this story, the situation of the Dalits and the poor in India, too, reminds us that anti-colonial movements have rarely represented the interests of all the peoples of a colonised country. After independence, these fissures can no longer be glossed over. The independent India makes available the fruits of liberation only selectively and unevenly: the dismantling of the colonial rule did not automatically improve the status of women, the working class, the Dalits and the tribals.

Therefore, it has been suggested that it is helpful to think of postcolonialism more flexibly as the contestation of colonial domination and the legacies of colonialism than literally as coming after colonialism and signifying its demise.[16] Such a position would allow us to include people who are discriminated against on the basis of caste, color and gender. It also allows us to incorporate the history of anti-colonial resistance into the contemporary resistances to dominant cultures whether within or without.

B. Intellectual Inheritance of Postcolonialism

Postcolonialism starts to distil its particular provenance through both earlier and more recent 'Western' theories such as Marxism, poststructuralism, humanism and postmodernism.

1. Marxist Anti-Imperialist Thought

In the first decade of the twentieth century, Marxist thinkers such as Lenin, Bukharin and Hilferding "have been urging the Western World to concede that the story of colonialism is a necessary sub-plot to the emergence of market society in Europe and to the concomitant globalization of capital."[17] However, the subsequent Marxists in general have failed to critique comprehensively the colonial history and ideology.[18] Even those critics who continued their interrogation of empire are opposed to the prevailing postcolonial orthodoxy.

2. Poststructuralism

I. Poststructuralism and Deconstruction[19]

Poststructuralism emerged in 1970s and it displaced structuralism as the dominant body of thought regarding language and text. For structuralists such as Ferdinand de Saussure, language is a structure in which signs (composed of a signifier and a signified) are relational to other signs. The signified is the mental process that occurs when the signifier is read or heard and it is nothing but the mental picture produced in reaction to the signifier.

Poststructuralists, although accepting the structuralist notion that language is the site of meaning, view their above project as futile given the very nature of language. The poststructuralists say that when you read the word 'water' what comes to mind is not any definite signified or some quintessential picture of water but it can be of drops of water, of a lake, a puddle, a glass of water, or the chemical symbol H_2O. When any of the concepts called to mind by 'water' is considered, for example, 'puddle', we find that this process is continued and in that we may think of rain, thunderstorms, mud, or splashes, but we do not think of a definitive signified. Thus, signifiers lead to other signifiers, not to definite signifieds. This concept, known as 'deferral of the signifier' or 'the endless play of the signifier' is a key element of deconstruction, a type of poststructuralist criticism. This shows that the meaning of a word cannot be pinned down. Thus, no central meaning exists.

Deconstructive critics apply this theory of language to texts and show that the notion of a centre in a text (a definite 'meaning' of a text) is illusory. Thus, if one follows any thread of meaning within a text, one arrives not at the 'centre,' but is lead to other possible interpretations and meanings.

To further elucidate this point, consider the dilemma often faced by students of literature who attempt to write a coherent essay on a work. No matter how strong the argument made, there always seem to be details which don't fit in the thesis of the paper – elements of the text that "leak out" of the structure imposed on the work by one person's interpretation. Students are often encouraged to "ignore" this textual information, and to present only their strongest arguments, yet they often recognize the limits of the 'meaning' which they have found within the text.[20]

II. Postcolonial Theory in a Poststructuralist Climate

Edward Said's *Orientalism* published in 1978 is considered to be the point of reference for postcolonial theory. However, "insufficient attention is given to the fact that this ur-text (and its followers) evolved within a distinctly poststructuralist climate, dominated in the Anglo-American academy by the figures of Foucault and Derrida."[21]

Foucault's notion of a discourse, as elaborated in *The Archaeology of Knowledge* and in *Discipline and Punish*, for example, informs Said's attempt to isolate the principle and workings of Orientalism. In addition, Gayatri Spivak's translation of Derrida's *Of Grammatolgy* in 1977 gained recognition for her in the literary-critical world and "her subsequent work has been preoccupied with the task of dialogue and negotiation with and between Derrida and Foucault."[22]

Following the poststructuralist thought, "postcolonialism has inherited a very specific understanding of Western domination as the symptom of an unwholesome alliance between power and knowledge."[23] Thus, postcolonialism was able to make a shift from the economic paradigms of Marxist thought "to diagnose the material effects and implications of colonialism as an epistemological malaise at the heart of Western rationality. It has also learnt to be suspicious of the problem of Universalism/Eurocentrism that was inherent in Marxist (or for that matter liberal) itself."[24]

It is this recognition that led the postcolonialist historians to engage in Subaltern Studies.[25] Foucault equated Western rationality with the economic and political domination of colonialism[26] and Derrida suggested that the structure of Western rationality is racist and imperialist.[27] Although Foucault and Derrida challenged the universal validity of Western culture and epistemology, they hardly addressed the problem of colonialism directly. However, in their challenge postcolonial thought secured its intellectual moorings.

3. Humanism

It is a very contentious term pointing to Christianity, the critique of Christianity, science, anti-science, Marxism, existentialism and so on.[28] However these various humanisms are unified in their belief that in the midst of the varied human experience it is possible to discern a universal human nature which is revealed in the common language of rationality. In contrast, poststructuralist and postmodernist anti-humanists maintain that the ideas of 'rationality' and 'human nature' are historical constructions and that "any universal or normative postulation of rational unanimity is totalitarian and hostile to the challenges of otherness and difference."[29] This view appeals to the postcolonial concern with cultural diversity.

To understand the relationship of postcolonialism to humanism we must recognize two types of humanism which postcolonialism inherits. One is the Renaissance humanism which began in Italy as a cultural and educational program in the sixteenth century. The second one is the Enlightenment humanism which finds its flowering in the eighteenth century. The latter is the poststructuralist approach to humanism which is identified with the theory of subjectivity and knowledge inaugurated by Bacon, Descartes and

Locke in philosophy, and scientifically substantiated by Galileo and Newton.[30] In Renaissance humanism the human being is made human by the *content* of the things he/she knows. In contrast, Enlightenment humanism takes 'humanity' to be a function of the *way* in which one knows things subjectively emphasizing the structure of epistemology.[31]

While both humanisms assert that all human beings are, as it were, the measure of all things, they simultaneously suggest that some human beings are more human than others depending on their access to superior learning or to their cognitive faculties. The historical logic of such humanism is illustrated in Macaulay's infamous minute of 1835 with regard to the introduction of English education in colonial India:

> The intrinsic superiority of the Western literature is indeed fully admitted by those members of the committee who support the oriental plan of education...It is, I believe, no exaggeration to say that all the historical information which has been collected in the Sanskrit language is less valuable than what may be found in the paltry abridgements used at preparatory schools in England."[32]

Similarly the Reverend J. Tucker attributes India's civiliasational inferiority to the "dullness of their comprehension."[33] From the above reading of the nineteenth-century debate on colonial education one may say that "the underside of Western humanism produces the dictum that since some human beings are more human than others, they are more substantially the measure of all things."[34]

4. Postmodernism and Postcolonialism

Attempts are made to collapse postmodernism and postcolonialism into one but their differences are too many to be erased. It is true that both have their common origin. Modernistic thinking was known for its excessive reverence for reason and objective truth. It savagely controlled the environment and was less critical of institutions such as the nation-state.[35] Both postmodernism and postcolonialism are born out of discomfort over modernistic thinking. Both are offshoots of the crumbling of the Western political and cultural hegemony and its imperialistic tendencies.[36]

However, the alliance ends here and the differences between them are too many. Postmodernism is still seen as Eurocentric and is found wanting from a third world perspective. It lacks the theory of resistance and it fails to cultivate a transformative agenda due to its detached attitudes. Its celebration of differences alienates the subalterns. Postcolonialism, on the other hand, is recognized as a branch of cultural studies and is emerging as a distinctive discourse. It centers around a critique of Eurocentrism whether it is a state, a condition or a critical reading strategy and is emerging among the former victims of colonized "Others" who insist on taking their place as historical subjects. Thus, the postcolonial discourse is mainly about the colonized "Other" and not about the West, as is the case with other theoretical practices, such as feminism and structuralism.[37]

C. Biblical Scholarship & Postcolonialism

1. Applicability of the Postcolonial Method to the Bible

Biblical scholarship in our contemporary times acknowledges that "there is no interest-free interpretation"[38] Postcolonialism is a method which exposes such hidden interests in this field.

2. Biblical Interpretations in the Colonial India

The biblical interpretations which originated in the colonial era are neatly classified into three modes by R. S. Sugirtharajah: "Orientalist," "Anglicist," and "Nativist."[39]

I. The Orientalist Mode[40]

Orientalism was the cultural policy advocated by the Western scholars, known as the Orientalists, to study of India's ancient linguistic, philosophical and religious heritage. It is they who elevated Sanskrit to a venerable status. Such study helped the colonial rulers to control the Indian people. The Indian converts of the nineteenth century grabbed the knowledge of their past and interpreted the Bible demonstrating the similarities between biblical and Vedic texts.

Sugirtharajah sees in Krishna Mohan Banerjea (1813-85), a Bengali convert who wrote the book *The Asian Witness* (1875) an early pioneer. By showing the interconnections between the Vedas and the Bible, Banerjea strived to show that Vedas more than the Hebrew Scriptures, anticipated the coming of Christ. Such comparative hermeneutics with Sanskritic and brahmanical traditions to interpret the Bible is seen in the writings of T. M. Manickam, R. H. S. Boyd, Swami Abhishiktananda, M. A. Amaladoss and Wickremesinghe in the post-independent India.

We also have some who tried to enhance Indian biblical hermeneutics by borrowing critical tools from Sanskritic literary tradition. Paul Gregorios (tools from the three Indian philosophical schools: the Nyaya, the Vaisesika, and Sankhya), Thomas Manickam (tools from the three Indian classical schools: Mimamsa, Vyakarana, and the Vedantic school of Sankara), K. P. Aleaz who follows the *laksana* method (borrowing tools from the Indian Logic), Anand Amaladoss and Sister Vandana who initiated the *dhvani* method (worked out by Anandavardhana in the ninth-century) and Martin Kampchen (a German) and Jyoti Sahi who refined and applied the *rasa* method – are prime examples of this.

The above Sanskritic exegesis differs from the Western modes of interpretation in its effort to construct inner and mystical meaning rather than the historical and textual meaning. This Orientalist phase provided the educated middle class converts a sense of Indianness which saved their face from the colonial power's negative perception of India and the Hindu majority's skeptical view of the converts. At the same time the Orientalists' uncritical equation of India with Hindu-Aryan not only neglected the vernacular, the native and folk traditions, the materialistic and theistic lokayata and Sankhya systems and Islamic and Persian influences but also left unexamined the damage done to the Dalits and the tribal peoples. This Orientalist hermeneutics created a spiritual Hindu India and offered very little to alleviate the plight of the poor.

II. The Anglicist Mode[41]

It introduced Western modes of biblical investigation in Indian theological colleges mainly through the technique of historical criticism and the development of themes such as the uniqueness of biblical faith as different from others. Relying on modernism's recognition of objective reality, it strove to discover the single, original meaning of the text. Here the biblical faith became historical and objective while the Hindu faith became mythical and ahistorical.

Following this, two biblical commentary series were written by expatriate missionary teachers. One was "Indian Church Commentary," initiated during the colonial era and the other was "The Christian Student's Library," written soon after Indian independence. Here the missionary exegetes with their modernist ideas were looked upon as enlightened educators and mocked at the cultural heritage of India's past. Here English literature and European sciences came as an endorsement of Christian principles over against the Hindu Texts as a sign of error. "While the Orientalists endeavored to turn the Indians into "Vedicmen," the Anglicists tried to mould them into surrogate Englishmen."[42] Indian readers were encouraged to use the method of demythologization which was, in fact, aimed at Europeans who had lost the sense of awe and wonder as a result of the scientific mode of thinking. The Indian biblical quarterly *Bible Bhashyam* provides us with examples of Indians using such Western interpretative methods.

III. The Nativistic Mode

The search for models in the vernacular tradition is called nativism.[43] It refers to the revival of the regional language traditions to counter the double burden of Western and Sanskritic theories. In this mode, the hermeneutical enterprise takes place within a specific cultural and language matrix. There are various non-Sanskritic traditions in India.[44] Becoming aware of this, an attempt is made in this mode to animate *bhasa* or vernacular tradition. This has offered an alternative classical culture in Tamil and paved the way for a shift from a Vedantic to a bhakti type of religious experience.[45] In this mode, the hermeneutical enterprise is governed by rules set by a particular language and culture.

Borrowing largely from the vernacular mode of storytelling, Sadhu Sundar Singh (Pujabi), Mungamuri Devadas (Telugu), Vaman Tilak (Marathi), and H. A. Krishna Pillai (Tamil), interpreted the bible. Drawing inspiration from the Hindu pundits' way of teaching the intricacies of the *Vedas* to ordinary people through musical accompaniments and recitations, Iyadurai Bhagavatar, a Tamil Catholic, developed the *kaletchepam* method to expound biblical stories. Biblical ideas, in this mode, are described with vocabulary and concepts drawn from bhakti, the devotional writings. The works of H. A. Krishna Pillai, G. S. Vedanayagam Sastriar, and A. J. Appasamy[46] reflect such a category. Intertextual study also was done in this mode by Jaswant Raj who compares grace in the writings of Paul with the *Thiruvarutpayan* (The Gain of Divine Grace),[47] the twelve books of the hymns of the Tamil Saivite saints;[48] and by Corona Mary who compares the Johannine understanding of birth in the Spirit with another Saiva text, *Meikanda Sastram*.

Although this nativistic mode enabled interpreters to address audiences in a common language, its problem is its isolationism and apologetic tone. Any ghettoized theology stands in danger of becoming irrelevant to the majority outside its region. It idealizes local culture as static and unchanging. In the emerging complex of global interconnections, pure culture is an illusion. Besides, while Christians were trying to promote the idea of the distant past or in Fanon's term "mummified figments" as normative, other Asian religions were trying to modernize and accommodate themselves to meet the challenges of industrial development.[49]

IV. Critical Analysis and Viability of Postcolonialism

Sugirtharajah's critical analysis of these three methods[50] is very appropriate here. Western orientalists created an image of a glorious India of the past in which the brahmanical culture reigned supreme. In our desire to recover native characteristics we uncritically used the brahmanical discourse which kept the dalits, the indigenous people and women outside the mainstream and worked against our own people. Thus, the theories of interpretation worked out by Sanskritic theoreticians[51] in the ancient time and adopted by Indian Christian scholars[52] in an attempt to apply to the Bible waned and it contributed to the development of a new form of Orientalism this time by the natives themselves. Fanon cautioned us long ago that "the desire to attach oneself to tradition or bring abandoned tradition to life does not only mean going against the current history but also opposing one's own people."[53] Thus, in the postcolonial world of 'a single place' where 'boundaries between cultures blur' and where we have 'multiple belongings and multiple loyalties,'[54] we need to look for an appropriate method to interpret the Bible in India.

D. Three Authors & Three Concepts

There are three authors whose contributions have navigated the course of postcolonial studies. They are Edward Said, Gayatri Spivak and Homi Bhabha. Each will contribute one concept each to the study in which the fourth Servant Song in Deutero-Isaiah and the Dalit context will interact.

1. Said's Otherness

The perception of racial difference is a key to understand the phenomenon of the Other in the context of European colonialism and the vehicle for the dissemination of this perception is commonly referred to as colonial discourse.[55] The objective of colonial discourse is to "construe the colonized as a population of degenerate types on the basis of racial origin, in order to justify conquest and to establish systems of administration and instruction."[56] Said's main contribution to the postcolonial theory is the concept of otherness which opposes the Western way of looking at the world as divided into two opposites. Otherness is an ambiguous term that took its origin in the writings of H. W. F. Hegel (1770-1831) and was later developed in the psychoanalysis of Lacan.[57]

To support his argument Said draws on two principal methodological sources, Foucault and Gramsci. Said attempts to synthesize Foucault's thinking with the work of the Italian Marxist Gramsci. Like Foucault, Gramsci, too, is "less concerned with the repressive apparatuses of state power and more with the way that the consent of the subordinate (or 'subaltern') sectors of society is 'solicited' in the domain of 'civil society' through such channels as education and cultural practices."[58] Thus, his argument is that "one should not count only on the material force which power gives in order to exercise an effective leadership."[59]

In using this term, Said appropriates a label which had been used in two contexts.[60] It described first those officials of East India Company who opposed the programmes of the Westernizing radicals like T. B. Macaulay whose influence was dominant from the 1820s to the 1850s.[61] Secondly, it referred to the group of scholars who were at work in India between 1780-1830 and who were also known as Orientalists, with whom these opponents were closely associated.

Until Said's text appeared, these scholars were considered to be enthusiastic about Indian culture and learning. But Said shows that whether the orientalists are sympathetic towards Eastern culture or not, the fact is, as he sees it, that all Western discourse about the East is determined in the last analysis by the will to domination over Oriental territories and peoples. In the colonial domain, the pursuit of knowledge, for Said, cannot be 'disinterested,' owing to the fact that the relationship between cultures on which it depends is an unequal one and that such knowledge, whether of the language, customs or religions of the colonized is consistently put at the service of the colonial administration.[62]

Orientalism, for Said, is at the service of the West's hegemony over the East and produces the East discursively as the West's interior 'Other' and constructs the West's self-image as a superior civilization. It does this by distinguishing and then essentializing the identities of East and West. As a result, the East is produced in Orientalist discourse as voiceless, sensual, female, despotic, irrational and backward. The West, by contrast, is represented as masculine, democratic, rational, moral, dynamic and progressive.[63] Said is aware that at times the East is wanted in the West for its spirituality, longevity and stability. "In describing these qualities as 'overvalued,' however, Said suggests that the vision inscribed in such motifs is as distorted as its negative counterpart and similarly produced, above all else, by Western projections onto the Other."[64]

2. Spivak's Deconstruction

In the realm of literary studies 'structuralism' is appealing to some critics because it adds a certain 'scientific' objectivity. This scientific objectivity is achieved by studying the structure of a system in the abstract. In structuralism, the individuality of the text disappears in favor of looking at patterns, systems, and structures.

Structuralism represents a major challenge in literary criticism especially to the 'liberal humanist'[65] because it erases the author, the individual text, the reader, and history. My criticism of structuralism is this. Structuralists cannot account for change or development. They are uninterested in how literary forms may have changed over time. They are not interested in a text's production or reception/ consumption, but only in the structures that shape it.[66] It is here that deconstructionism appears necessary or attracts interest.

Deconstruction is a name coined by Derrida. It has subsequently become synonymous with a particular method of textual analysis involving the close reading of works of literature to reveal logical or rhetorical incompatibilities between the explicit and implicit planes of discourse in a text.

Spivak uses deconstruction as subaltern strategy. She interrogates the politics of culture from a marginal perspective. In her insightful article, "Can the Subaltern Speak?"[67] she concludes that they cannot. Speaking, for her, is a transaction between speaker and listener. Subaltern talk does not achieve the dialogue level of utterance.

To understand Spivak's point of view we need to understand the concept of "Representation." Spivak in her seminal essay, 'Can the Subaltern Speak,' emphasizes the fact that representation is a sort of speech act, with a speaker and a listener. Although the subaltern often times makes an attempt at self-representation, it is neither heard nor recognized by the listener and this makes representation by subaltern individuals almost impossible. In this essay Spivak encourages but also criticizes the efforts of the subaltern studies group that has re-appropriated Gramsci's term "subaltern" (the economically dispossessed) in order to locate and re-establish a "voice" in postcolonial India. She suggests that any attempt from the outside to ameliorate the condition of the subaltern by granting them collective speech will invariably encounter the following problems: a logocentric assumption of cultural solidarity among a heterogeneous people, and a dependence upon Western intellectuals to "speak for" the subaltern condition rather than allowing them to speak for themselves.[68] She proves her point in this essay by describing the circumstances surrounding the suicide of a young Bengali woman whose attempt at self representation ends in utter failure. She fails because her attempt "to speak" outside normal patriarchal channels was not understood or supported. Thus, Spivak concluded that "the subaltern cannot speak." Her point was not that the subaltern does not cry out in various ways but since speaking for her is transaction between the speaker and the listener, the subaltern talk does not achieve the dialogical level of utterance.[69]

3. Bhabha's Hybridity

Bhabha's contribution to the understanding of colonial culture is its hybridity, the "inbetweenness"of the two cultures, colonizing and colonized. Here there is mimicry and this mimicry repeats rather than re-presents. Postcolonial studies are preoccupied with the issues of hybridity which is an identity generated by colonialism. It is the nature of thought and logic to seek order and classification. The process of classification is done in viewing the world as either this or that, as for example, an object can be red or not red, action can either be good or bad.[70] Thus, binarism is intrinsic to thought itself. Now what about some identities that defy classification? Here comes Bhabha's notion of hybridity that expresses the intercultural encounter.

K. S. Singh points out that there are few persons in India who are not immigrants and that bilingualism characterizes 64.2 percent of all communities in India.[71] "Bhabha's work certainly lends the trajectory of identity an inherent elasticity hinting at the mixing and crossings of globalized cultures. For him the hybrid is the site of resolution of conflict. In fact, tensions are not always resolved and oppositions and tensions continue within."[72]

Technically speaking a hybrid is a cross between two different species. Therefore, Robert Young reminds us that the term 'hybridisation' evokes both the botanical notion of inter-species grafting and the vocabulary of the Victorian extreme right which regarded different races as different species.[73] Benedict Anderson cites the example of Pedro Fermin de Vargas, an early nineteenth-century Columbian who advocated a policy of interbreeding between whites and Indians in order to 'hispanicise' and finally 'extinguish' Indians, and though in this example he rightly characterizes those colonial educational policies which aimed to create Europeanised natives or to use Macaulay's famous words, 'a class of persons, Indian in blood and color, but English in taste, in opinion, in morals and in intellect.'[74] The underlying premise was that Indians can mimic but can never reproduce English values and that this perpetual gap between themselves and the 'real thing' will ensure their subjection.[75] Thus, colonial 'hybridity' is a strategy premised on cultural purity, and aimed at stabilizing the *status quo*.[76]

But in practice, it did not work in that way. Anti-colonial movements and individuals invoked hybridity self-consciously as an anti-colonial strategy. They hybridized Western ideas and vocabularies which they borrowed, by juxtaposing it with indigenous ideas and used it to assert cultural alterity or insist on an unbridgeable difference between the colonizer and the colonised.[77] We see this in Gandhi's notion of non-violence which was forged by reading Emerson, Thoreau and Tolstoy, even though Gandhi's vision of an ideal society evoked a specifically Hindu vision of 'Ram Rajya' or the legendary reign of Lord Rama.[78]

The concept of hybridity used by Homi Bhabha is the most influential in the recent postcolonial studies. It is he who coined, elaborated and popularized the term *hybridity* in postcolonial theory. Postcolonial discourse "locates, investigates, and celebrates such hybridity, such cross-pollination."[79] As for Fanon, for Bhabha, too, liminality[80] and hybridity are necessary attributes of 'the' colonial condition.[81] According to Fanon, the realization of the colonized that he can never attain the whiteness he has been taught to desire, or shed the blackness he has learnt to devalue results in psychic trauma. Amplifying this Bhabha suggests that colonial identities are always a matter of flux and agony. It is always in relation to the place of the Other that colonial desire is articulated, Bhabha writes.[82]

In "Signs Taken for Wonders," Bhabha shows how the authority becomes hybridized when placed in a colonial context and layered against other cultures. Here Bhabha illustrates how a Christian missionary when trying to teach about the Christian communion service to Indian Hindus is quite confounded by the reaction of the vegetarian Hindus for whom the idea of eating Christ's body and drinking his blood is appalling.[83] "Suddenly it is the white English culture that betrays itself, and the English missionary who is turned into a cannibalistic vampire."[84] The above example shows how the European colonial discourse is effectively decentred from its position of power and authority. This is an example of ambivalence, a concept taken from psychoanalysis to describe a continual fluctuation between wanting one thing and its opposite. In Bhabha it is a key word to show how the periphery has become the indeterminate ambivalence that characterizes the centre.

E. Marks of Postcolonial Scriptural Reading

Postcolonial Criticism brings marginal elements or voices which have been subjected to institutional and exegetical forgetting in the text to the front and, in the process, subverts the traditional meaning.[85] According to Stuart Hall, a cultural critic, a television discourse is embodied with four codes: hegemonic, professional, negotiated, and protest or oppositional.[86] He advocates that one should look for oppositional or protest voices in the text. Although biblical texts reflect all four codes, traditional interpretations generally paid attention to only the first three. Postcolonialism, in contrast, will look in the text for oppositional or protest voices. To illustrate this point Sugirtharajah explains the parable of the Tenants in Luke 20:9-18.[87] This parable is usually read from an overly Christological viewpoint or from the property owner's perspective. One seldom pays attention to the audience's shocking response "Heaven forbid!" (Lk 20:16; see for another example: Mk 8:24=Jdg 9:7-15). "What post-colonial criticism will do is to bring to the front such marginal elements in the texts, and in the process subvert the traditional meaning. It will engage in an archival exegesis as a way of rememorialising the narratives and voices which have been subjected to institutional forgetting."[88]

Postcolonial reading will not romanticize or idealize the poor.[89] Hegemonic readings, for example, tend to valorize the poor widow in Luke 21:1-4. Postcolonial reading would show how this woman is manipulated by the system into parting with what little she had.[90]

Instead of blaming the victims, postcolonial reading will direct attention to the social structures and institutions which spawn victimhood.[91] In the story of the woman caught in adultery in John 7:53-8:11, for example, poscolonial reading will not blame the woman but rather will draw attention to Jesus' critique of the system codified by the cultural norms.[92]

Postcolonial reading will advocate a wider hermeneutical agenda to place the study of sacred texts – Christian Hindu and Christian Buddhist – and will replace the totalitarian claims of biblical narratives with the claim that they have to be understood along with other communally inspired sacred narratives.[93] Such intertextual reading will provide a multiplicity of perspectives and can help us account for our collective identities.[94] R. S. Sugirtharajah cites the example of the article written by George Soares-Prabhu in which the author studies Matthew's missionary command alongside the Buddhist *Mahavagga* text.[95] Such intertextual reading is so vital because the various interpretative methods like Historical Critical Methods introduced by Western teachers are colonial in the sense that they were used to form a wedge between us and our neighbours in trying to show that the Christian texts are superior to the sacred writings of others and that these methods breathe an air of universal validity which other indigenous reading methods lack.[96]

Edward Said unmasked the coloniality of such methods and attitudes when he demonstrated that it was the intellectual and cultural control of the natives which was more effective in sustaining colonialism than mere territorial and political domination.[97] When the West, thus, sets the ground rules for interpreting the Bible it actually produces modern colonialism and eliminates non-Western interpreters as outcastes and outside the system.[98] Unfortunately to earn credibility in Biblical Exegesis many of the Asian theologians and colleges mimic the West in this respect. Postcolonial interpretation of the Bible comes as a corrective to such uncritical adaptation of Eurocentrism.[99]

Postcolonial reading will address the questions which affect people's lives. The purpose of its reading is not so much to produce subtle nuances of emotion and feeling in individuals but to help communities to face the problems of the contemporary world where people are thrown together more and more in multilingual, multiracial, and multifaith societies. Setting the agenda for any biblical criticism. Kaesemann says:

> I do not know Dom Helder Camera personally, and he – an out and out conservative in comparison with myself – will be unacquainted with my work. But were my work no possible help to him in his troubles, I will not want to remain a New Testament scholar. No real service is rendered to the Spirit by one who is unable to assist men under trial.[100]

Now I would like to conclude by saying that the postcolonial perspective is not entirely new for the religions. Within the Jewish and Christian religions parallels are perceived between the prophetic tradition of the Bible and the goals of the emerging postcolonial literatures in which both call individuals and societies to new ways of life and both proclaim the need for justice at all levels of society.[101] Although both of them emphasize that religiosity is worthless if one is unmindful of the sociopolitical implications of religion, they have their differences, too. One such difference is that while the prophetic tradition awakens the people to socio-ethical concerns, postcolonialism addresses the historical, textual, discursive and epistemological legacies of colonialism.[102]

Endnotes

1. H. Tiffin, "Post-Colonialism, Post-Modernism and the Rehabilitation of Post-Colonial History," *Journal of Commonwealth Literature* 20, No. 3 (1988): 170.
2. L. Hutcheon, "Circling the Downspout of Empire," *Ariel* 20, No. 4 (1989): 171.
3. This paper is an abridged version of the chapter on Postcolonialism in my doctoral dissertation.

4. A. Loomba, *Colonialism/Postcolonialism* (London: Routledge, 2001), 1-2.
5. Ibid., 2.
6. Ibid., 3.
7. T. Bottomore, ed., *A Dictionary of Marxist Thought* (Oxford: Basil Blackwell, 1983), 81-85.
8. Loomba, *Colonialism/Postcolonialism*, 4.
9. Ibid., 4.
10. Ibid., 7.
11. This version was first used by political scientists and economists and later by the literary critics.
12. Ibid.
13. Ibid.
14. Ibid., 10.
15. Mahasweta Devi, "Shishu,' in *Women Writing in India*, Vol. II, ed. S. Tharu and K. Lalita (New York: The Feminist Press, 1993), 236-250.
16. Loomba, *Colonialism/Postcolonialism*, 12.
17. Leela Gandhi, *Postcolonial Theory* (New York: Columbia University Press, 1998), 23-24.
18. Ibid., 24.
19. I basically follow here B. Catherine & T. Rachel, "Poststructuralism and Deconstruction," accessed 5 April 2002); available from http://educ.queensu.ca/~qbell/update/tint/postmodernism/postst.html; Internet.
20. Ibid., 2.
21. Gandhi, *Postcolonial Theory* 25.
22. Ibid.
23. Ibid.
24. Ibid., 26.
25. D. Chakrabarty, "Marx after Marxism: History, Subalternity and Difference," *Meanjin* 52, No. 3 (1993): 422.
26. M. Foucault, "George Canguilhem: Philosopher of Error," *Ideology and Consciousness*, No. 7 (1980): 54.
27. J. Derrida, "White Mythology: Metaphor in the Text of Philosophy," *New Literary History* 6, No. 1, (1974).
28. J. Bernauer & M. Mahon, "The Ethics of Michel Foucault," in *The Cambridge Companion to Foucault*, ed. G. Gutting, (Cambridge, Cambridge University Press, 1994), 141-142.
29. Gandhi, *Postcolonial Theory*, 27.
30. Ibid., 28.
31. Ibid., 29.
32. Cited in E. Said, *The World, the Text and the Critic* (Cambridge, Massachusetts: Harvard University Press, 1983), 12.
33. Cited in G. Viswanathan, *Masks of Conquest: Literary Studies and British Rule in India* (London: Faber & Faber, 1989), 6.

34. Gandhi, *Postcolonial Theory,* 30.
35. R. S. Sugirtharajah, *Asian Biblical Hermeneutics and Postcolonialism* (Maryknoll, New York: Orbis Books, 1998), 15.
36. Ibid.
37. Ibid., 16.
38. Brueggemann, 63.
39. Sugirtharajah, *Asian Biblical Hermeneutic,* 3. In the following pages I basically follow his trend of thought in explaining these three modes of interpretation in India.
40. See Sugirtharajah, 4-7 for this section and I follow his thought in this section.
41. See Sugirtharajah, 8-11 for this section and I follow his thought in this section.
42. Ibid., 9.
43. G. N. Devy, *After Amnesia: Tradition and Change in Indian Literary Criticism* (Hyderabad: Orient Longman, 1992), 119-120. This is quoted by Sugirtharajah, 132.
44. Students of Indian Culture draw a distinction between the *marga* (the high road) which refers to the spiritual path found in the sacred texts written in Sanskrit and the *desi* (the country road) which refers to the spiritual path found in the vernacular tradition.
45. P. A. Sathiasatchy, "Interactions between the Faiths of Tamils as Reflected in Tamil Literature with Special Reference to Christianity," *Arasaradi: Journal of Theological Reflection,* 4, No. 2 (1991): 82. Here he says, "It is high time that, instead of harping on about Indian Christian theology which is prejudiced in favor of Vedic philosophy, we thought in terms of Tamil Christian theology drawn from the context of Tamil culture and its literature and philosophy."
46. See the exegetical work of A. J. Appasamy on John's Gospel which appeared in two volumes, *Christianity as Bhakti Marga: A Study of the Johannine Doctrine of Love* (Madras: Christian Literature Society, 1926, reprint 1991). *What is Moksa? A Study in the Johannine Doctrine of Life* (Madras: Christian Literature Society, 1931).
47. The Saiva canonical poems composed by 63 leading saints scanning approximately 600 years were classified into 12 books (terms also *Thirumuraigal*) by Nambiandarnambi in the 11 C. E. according to the wishes of *Chozha* king Kulasekaran.
48. See Jaswant Raj, Joseph, *Grace in the Saiva Siddhantham and in St. Paul: A Contribution in Inter-faith Cross-cultural Understanding* (Madras: South Indian Salesian Society, 1989).
49. Sugirtharajah, *Asian Biblical Hermeneutics,* 134.
50. Ibid., 129-139.
51. See Sugirtharajah, 131 where he says, "we encountered the theory of *rasa,* propounded by the sage Bharata in the fifth century, which holds that poetry is essentially an emotive discourse. There was Ksehemendra's *auchita,* translated

as "propriety," a harmonious adaptation of language, figure, imagery, and so forth. Then there was *dhvani*, expounded by Anandavardhana in the ninth century, which stresses the suggestive possibility of a text, its evocative nature, and its emotional grip on the reader, hearer, or spectator."

52. Among whom Sister Vandana and Anand Amaladass came to be closely associated with the *dhvani* method in the late 1970s.
53. This is quoted by Sugirtharajah, 131. See F. Fanon, *The Wretched of the Earth* (Harmondsworth: Penguin Books, 1990), 180.
54. Sugirtharajah, *Asian Biblical Hermeneutics,* 138.
55. M. L. Raina, "Third World Literature: Making of a Canon," in *Post-coloniality*, ed. C.T. Indra and Meenakshi Shivram (Delhi: Vikas Publishing House , 1999), 3.
56. Homi K. Bhabha, "The Other Question: Difference, Discrimination, and the Discourse of Colonialism," in *Literature, Politics and Theory: Papers from the Essex Conference 1976-84*, ed. Francis Barker (London: Methuen, 1986), 154.
57. "Week Seven: Postcolonialism/Otherness/Alterity," (accessed 30 April 2004); available from http://www.eciad.bc.ca/~rcutler/cultnotes/week7.html; Internet.
58. B. J. Moore-Gilbert, *Postcolonial Theory* (London, New York: Verso, 2000), 37.
59. A. Gramsci, *Selections from the Prison Notebooks of Antonio Gramsci*, ed. and trans. Quintin Hoare and Geoffrey Nowell-Smith (London: Lawrence & Wishart, 1971), 59.
60. Moore-Gilbert, *Postcolonial Theory* 38.
61. To situate this historical context, a good source would be the book of G. Viswanathan, *Masks of Conquest.*
62. Moore-Gilbert, *Postcolonial Theory* 38.
63. Ibid., 39.
64. Ibid., 39.
65. The 'humanist' model proposes: that there is a real world out there that we can understand with our rational mind; that language is capable of depicting that real world; that language is a product of the individual writer's mind; that the 'Self' is center of all meaning and truth in which words mean what they say they mean, and truth is what I perceive as truth. This model is different from the structuralist model in which language speaks us and the structure of language which produces 'reality' is at the center.
66. See "Structuralism/Poststructuralism," 1 (accessed 5 April 2002); available from http://www.colorado.edu/English/ENGL2012Klages/1derrida.html; Internet.
67. G. Spivak, "Can the Subaltern Speak?" in *Marxism and the Interpretation of Culture*, ed. C. Nelson and L. Grossberg (Urbana: Univerisity of Illinois Press, 1988), 271-313.
68. "Can the Subaltern Speak" (accessed 22 March 2002); available from http://www.scholars.nus.edu.sg/landow/post/poldiscourse/spicak/spivak2.html; Internet.

69. "Representation" (accessed 6 December 2002); available from http://www.emory.edu/ENGLISH/Bahri/Glossary.html; Internet.
70. S. Mayaram, "Rethinking Meo Identity: Cultural Faultline, Syncretism, Hybridity or Liminality?" *Comparative Studies of South Asia, Africa and the Middle East* (formerly *South Asia Bulletin*) 17, No. 2 (1997): 36.
71. See K. S. Singh, ed., *People of India: An Introduction*, Vol. 1 (Calcutta: Anthropological Survey of India, 1992), 103.
72. S. Mayaram, "Rethinking Meo Identity," 36.
73. R. Young, *Colonial Desire: Hybridity in Theory, Culture and Race* (London: Routledge, 1995), 10.
74. B. Anderson, *Imagined Communities: Reflections on the Origins and Spread of Nationalism* (London and New York: Verso, 1991), 13 and 91. It is quoted by Loomba in *Colonialism/Postcolonialism*, 173.
75. Loomba, *Colonialism/Postcolonialism*, 173.
76. Ibid., 173-174.
77. Ibid., 174.
78. Ibid.
79. Homi K. Bhabha, *The Location of Culture*, 236. See also Boehmer, *Colonial and Postcolonial Literature; Migrant Metaphors* (Oxford: Oxford University Press, 1995), 7 in which the author talks about the cultural mix of the once-colonized Others and of the West in the former's entry into the latter.
80. See Mayaram, "Rethinking Meo Identity," where the author says that the liminal helps constitute a third space that does not presuppose binarism. The liminality of religion relates to the hybridity of kinship in terms of analogous metaphors such as of the staircase connecting two floors, the bridge between two shores and the harbor that links land and ocean.
81. Loomba, *Colonialism/Postcolonialism*, 176.
82. Ibid.
83. Homi K. Bhabha, "Signs taken for Wonders: Questions of Ambivalence and Authority under a Tree Outside Delhi, May 1817," *Critical Inquiry* 12, No. 1(1985): 145-146.
84. R. J. C. Young, "Colonialism and the Desiring Machine," in *Postcolonial Discourses: An Anthology*, ed. G. Castle (Oxford: Blackwell Publishers, 2001), 76.
85. Sugirtharajah, *Asian Biblical Hermeneutics*, 22.
86. H. Stuart, *Encoding and Decoding in the Television Discourse* (Birmingham, England: Center for Cultural Studies, 1973), 16-19.
87. Sugirtharajah, *Asian Biblical Hermeneutics*, 21.
88. L. E. Donaldson, "Postcolonialism and Biblical Reading: An Introduction," in *Semeia* 75, ed. L. E. Donaldson and R. S. Sugirtharajah (Atlanta: Scholars Press, 1996), 5.
89. Sugirtharajah, *Asian Biblical Hermeneutics*, 22.

90. Ibid., 23. Traditionally she is portrayed as a model for Christian discipleship (although no widow joined Jesus' group) or giving (overlooking the ultimate destiny of the money and Jesus' opposition to the temple and the Scribes in the context).
91. Ibid.
92. Ibid.
93. Ibid.
94. Ibid.
95. Ibid., 23-24. For the cited article see George Soares-Prabhu, "Two Mission Commands: An Interpretation of Matthew 28:16-20 in the Light of a Buddhist Text," *Biblical Interpretation* 2 (1994): 264-282.
96. Ibid., 125-127.
97. Said, *Culture and Imperialism* (London: Chatto & Windus, 1993), 131-132.
98. Sugirtharajah, *Asian Biblical Hermeneutics,* 126-127.
99. When I say 'uncritical adoptation' I do not mean that all Western reading methods are evil.
100. E. Kaesemann, "The Problem of a New Testament Theology," *New Testament Studies* 19, No. 3 (1973): 235-45. This quote is taken from Sugirtharajah, *Asian Biblical Hermeneutics and Postcolonialism,* 135.
101. S. V. Gallagher, "Introduction: New Conversations in Postcolonial Literature," in *Postcolonial Literature and the Biblical Call for Justice,* ed. S. V. Gallagher (Jackson, MS: University Press of Mississippi, 1994), 3-33.
102. L. E. Donaldson, "Postcolonialism and Biblical Reading", 1.

Chapter 5

Towards an Interreligious Dialogical Theologizing in India

Its Presuppositions, Prerequisites and Implications

Joseph Lobo, SJ

Introduction

At the outset I would like to make it clear that this essay is an enquiry into the presuppositions, prerequisites and implications of an interreligious dialogical theologizing process in India; and not the actual articulation of such a theology. The aim of this enquiry is to become aware of the necessary 'ground conditions' for fulfilling the prerequisites and the consequent implications. Therefore the form of the essay is more a tentative and open-ended theological exploration than a neatly concluded treatise.

The starting point of this enquiry is two-fold: a) A general feeling of dissatisfaction springing from the fact of a lot of "talk" about "Indian theology" right from the early decades of the past century and, at the same time, of not having made a real headway in its birthing. Presenting even a cursory survey of the authors related to this issue does not seem to be possible in this limited space.[1] b) A very heartening experience of praying together in a group consisting of Hindus and Christians on the occasion of Christmas, for the last six years.

While the second point will inspire the entire process of reflection with regard to the first, the questions that arise are: Have the methods proposed for developing Indian theology(ies) remained only theoretical? Have their practical prerequisites been met? Have their presuppositions really been taken seriously or is it too problematic to handle them? Three point blank questions: Are Indians in general and Indian Christians in particular ready for a truly indigenous theologizing process? To what extent such a process is theologically viable for Christians? Are there appropriate ground conditions for its sprouting in our land and among our people?[2]

In the following sections we shall briefly sketch the salient features of an effective Indian theologizing process. We shall, then, detail some important features of a method required for it; and then inquire into the prerequisites, presuppositions and implications of making such a process functional.

The aim of a theologizing process is to guide those involved towards integral liberation. Both the content of theology as well as the very process of theologizing itself are essential for achieving this goal. The context or 'situatedness'[3] describes the negativity from which an integral liberation is sought for. It indicates the types of sources of the theologizing process; and also determines the method or procedure towards such a liberation.

A. Some salient features of the situatedness of Indian people(s)

The general situatedness of the Indian people(s) can be seen as revolving around three interrelated axes: 1) ***The economic axis***: Coexistence of pockets of affluence and the poverty of the masses, which is further aggravated by an imbalanced integration of the Indian economy into the Global capitalism. 2) ***The political axis***: Coexistence of a constitutional democracy and the powerless masses. 3) ***Thereligio-cultural axis***: Coexistence of a religio-cultural plurality and recent efforts towards homogenization of cultures both at the global as well as the national levels. Some related factors are: a) Plurality of cultures, religious experiences and traditions and mushrooming of myriad new religious groups; b) Religion and culture based discrimination of various subaltern groups; and, c) Rising religious fundamentalism.

Obviously the third axis, being constitutive of meaning systems, operates in life at a level that is more fundamental than those which are related to the other two axes. However, we cannot deny the mutual link among the three of them and the necessity of referring to all of them while dealing with any attempt towards integral transformation.[4]

B. Some preliminary clarifications

1. *Who are the agents of the envisaged theologizing process?*

All who share the Indian 'situatedness' as described above, and desire to respond theologically to the related negativities can be understood as the agents of an Indian theologizing process. We shall explicate later how it is necessary for such agents to come together as "theologizing communities" in the very process of their theologizing. The membership of such communities in the context has to be multi-religious. Hence they can be called multi-religious theologizing communities (MTCs). However, forming of MTCs should not mean that specificity of different religions are sacrificed or emptied. MTCs have to be built on the open-ended specificities of different religions.

2. *What are the sources of the theologizing process?*

1. Primary sources: a) The experience of negativity, b) The religious experiences, spiritualities, religious traditions and the sacred 'texts' of the MTC, and, c) 'Wisdoms' of the MTC.
2. Secondary sources and means: i) Various linguistic facilities, ii) Cultural symbols, metaphors and narratives (mythic or otherwise), iii) Various art forms, iv) Various modes of interpretation, v) Philosophical concepts, vi) Fruits of research

in linguistics, hermeneutics, and humanities, and, vii) Western and Eastern religious insights and philosophical tools, to the extent they are helpful.

3. *Types of Indian theology*

In the Indian context we become aware of three possible basic theologizing processes. They are: a) A theology based on one particular religious tradition that has no positive reference whatsoever to other religious traditions – ***an exclusivist approach.*** b) A "theology of religions" based on one particular religious tradition – ***an accommodative or inclusivist approach.***[5] c) A theology based on the shared experience[6] of all participants from different religious traditions – ***an interreligious dialogical*** *(and* ***integrative)*** ***approach.***

In this essay we focus on the third type. This is because justice/ liberation related goals of any religion (including Christianity) in the Asian/ Indian context cannot afford to neglect the religio-cultural milieu of that religion.[7] In the Indian context it would mean that a theological enterprise of any one religious group cannot really be liberative for all, if it is pursued in a way that is unrelated to other religious traditions.[8] At once we are faced with the following questions:

a. Can the Christian revelation in the process of its appropriation and articulation (historicization) be tied to any single culture?[9]
b. Can the Christian revelation in its totality be unrelated to the manifestations of the Divine in other religions? Some significant Biblical texts seem to be answering this question in the negative.[10] According to R. Panikkar "there can be today no convincing Christian theology (nor any philosophical reflection on any religion) without taking into consideration the wider spectrum of the different religious traditions of the world."[11] This is because the historical context of the divine disclosure in a given religious tradition (including Christianity) is made up of, among other things, also other religious traditions. Hence,

they have to be considered seriously in order to make sense of the disclosure in a given religious tradition. Rightly then, in the spirit of the Vatican II (NA n.2; AG n.11) we need to affirm "the fact of God's communication to humanity, also outside the Church". "[It] is an important factor in developing a deeper insight into revelation and its implications for our life and world. Therefore, it is necessary to be sensitive not only to Sacred Scriptures and other inner Church resources, but also to God's presence and action in other religious and secular movements and events. To fail to do so would be to exclude a large part of what the Spirit is saying to the churches. This could only impoverish the Church's mission and grasp of revelation".[12]

c. Is a theology of religions based on Christian revelation alone meaningful for *all* in India? The current and emerging situation seems to indicate a negative response to this question. For, such a theological process at this point of history does not seem to have the potential to form communities of people belonging to different religious traditions.

d. From the perspective of the Reign of God to which the person, teaching, death and resurrection of Jesus Christ are intrinsic, is an interreligious dialogical theology more suitable to Indian peoples than a purely 'Christian theology'?[13] Can we have a meaningful co-existence of both? We shall reflect on these issues in the course of this paper.

e. Is a theology of religions based on a plurality of experiences of the Divine across religious traditions possible? This is the crux of the matter and we shall attempt to respond to this issue in the later sections.

f. Is a mutual reconciliation of diverse cosmologies and anthropologies depicted in various religio-cultural traditions possible and necessary for a viable interreligious dialogical theologizing process in India? Arriving at some agreeable anthropological and cosmological presuppositions seems to be necessary.

We shall attempt to reflect on these questions and issues in the course of this essay. Obviously, as far as the Catholic participant of the MTC is concerned, it is necessary that the final theological conclusions, have to be acceptable to the Magisterium and the whole Church.

C. Salient Features of a Relevant Theological Method for India

Instead of sketching a full-fledged, well-rounded method for theologizing in India, I would like to restrict this section to a discussion of some of its salient features. This is mainly because of two reasons: a) It is difficult to suggest a full-fledged method in an *a priori* fashion. All such attempts in human sciences fail. A method in human sciences in general and in theology in particular should rather be described *a posteriori* by reflecting on the way in which a community has actually theologized and come out with certain liberative responses to the context.[14] It may involve many ups and downs, and even errors but also very useful learning processes. b) There just doesn't exist the Indian context with certain fixed features. Though one can speak about such features in general, in concrete situations due to the various possible permutations and combinations in which these features get ordered, we can think of myriad shades of the Indian context. Accordingly a theologizing method has to make necessary adjustments.

With these preliminary clarifications I would like to present a few non-negotiable features of an Indian theological method.

1. The starting point of the theologizing process is the lived experience of the MTC in its entirety and in its concrete historicity, namely, a) Experiencing a common 'situatedness' and striving together towards a common (not necessarily understood identically in every detail) goal is constitutive of the experience of being a 'community'. b) Experience of the Divine, however differently thematized, yet something that truly promotes life and is opposed to all that is anti-life.[15] c) Experience of an existential drive in

the human that is aimed at harmony and unity (need not be uniformity).

2. Since an MTC consists of people from various religio-cultural and such other 'ideological' backgrounds, on the one hand, and from various socio-economic strata, on the other, the theological method envisaged is essentially dialogical and contrapuntal in its fundamental dynamics. a) An MTC has to encounter the richness of the Ultimate Mystery expressed in various religious traditions. This is possible only by means of engaging the actual (living) religions (as opposed to their romanticised and/or essentialised versions) and critical dialogue with their adherents, practices and texts.[16] b) In an authentic dialogical situation differences and the otherness are genuinely respected without any attempt to resolve them. At the same time such a dialogue does challenge all the participants and invites them towards a real *metanoia* towards life. c) The shared experiences of the negativities, on the one hand, and that of the Divine, on the other, are to be set in mutual dialogue.[17] As the shared religious experiences begin to act transformatively in the participants, they are enabled to act against the negativities, thereby making such praxis a real shared spirituality.
3. Such a dialogue has a wider 'back and forth' dynamic whereby each participant brings to the dialogue 'lights' and 'shadows' of his/her own living religious tradition to the MTC and in turn takes back to his/her religious group the fruits of the theologizing process. The following results are envisaged: a) The participants of the MTC have a dual or multiple membership: that of the MTC and of their original religious group. Albeit, all such memberships cannot be conceived as equally binding on the individuals concerned. The membership of the original religious group remains more fundamental than that of the MTC.[18] b) Life and spirituality of the original religious group and that of the MTC are enriched by the process. c) Those adherents of various religious groups who are

not directly involved in the theologizing process could also benefit from the fruits of the theologizing process. d) No one needs to abandon his/her original religion; unless prompted by the Spirit to do so. But by means of the interreligious theologizing process a facility is created for the gradual renewal and enrichment of all participating members and their respective religious traditions.[19]

4. A fruitful participation in this process itself is an experience of being a community. Such experiences need articulation and are to be made to promote concrete forms of liberative praxis.
5. The 'secondary sources' (cf. above) should be put to use as and when they are deemed helpful at any of the above stages.

D. Presuppositions, prerequisites and implications

Let us now examine some important presuppositions, prerequisites and implications of the type of theologizing method/process envisaged above.

(a) Socio-cultural and religious axes

Presuppositions and prerequisites

1. A genuine respect for the historicity of faith demands a due consideration for the religious and cultural plurality of India. It goes beyond a mere acknowledgement of the fact of such plurality and appeals for a more positive and constructive response on the part of all people of good will.
2. The theologizing process is a community exercise; perhaps facilitated by professional theologians and, hence, the existence of an MTC is a must. Forming such a community can be a part of the theologizing process itself and need not be totally prior to the process. Requirement of a community is essential because an effective theology emerges only from a shared life and is geared towards the transformation of that shared life. When such is

the case an individual theologian, left to himself/ herself can do mighty little.

3. An inculturation understood as 'conversion'[20] from a state of alienation to a state of at-one-ment (solidarity) in the shared situatedness of one's people is essential for the formation and effective functioning of an MTC.
4. Is a reconciliation of diverse 'theologies', cosmologies, spiritualities and anthropologies belonging to various traditions possible and necessary for the formation of an MTC? Individuals such as Swami Abhishiktananda[21], RaimundoPanikkar[22] and a few other Indian theologians and mystics of the early 20th century implicitly claim to have arrived at such reconciliation in their personal lives. Occasionally one comes across certain individuals and families especially in rural areas who are 'at home' with the "Gods" and worship practices of different traditions. Usually they are called 'syncretists'. However, there are types of syncretism that do not respect the precious specificity of different religious traditions. We certainly reject it.[23] In some places, on festive occasions, we witness "strange" events such as the following: Hindus singing Hindu devotional songs in the village mosque on a Ramzan day and participating in the related celebrations; Muslims offering prayers in a Hindu temple on the occasion of Ganapathi festival; Hindus and Muslims visiting Churches during Christmas and praying along with Christians, etc.[24] We do see such devotees going back with peace and serenity. But we hardly see 'multi-religious communities' as such who live a life of religious "dialogue" on a more regular basis.
5. The life and functioning of an MTC envisaged here do not demand any giving up or diluting of the fundamental dimensions of the faith on the part of the participants. However, one needs to keep in mind that in every religious tradition there is a 'hierarchy of truths'. This fact becomes helpful in differentiating what is central from what is peripheral in a given tradition. For a Catholic participant, what is affirmed in *Unitatis Redintegratio*is particularly helpful: "in Catholic doctrine there exists an order or a 'hierarchy' of truths, since they vary in their relation to the foundation of the Christian faith" (No. 11).[25]Life of the

individuals belonging to the theologising community aims more at commitment to each other, to the community, and to the wider society than at inter-faith conversion.[26] God alone is One and the only Absolute. Therefore, anything that can be of actual help to reach this Absolute can be integrated into one's own religious tradition, just as anything that goes contrary to this goal should be rejected even from one's own religious tradition. It means that the theologizing process envisaged here has the potential to bring necessary alterations in the original religious traditions of the participants. Such possibilities should be evaluated positively.

6. Is being a member of an MTC mandatory for all those who live in a pluri-religious society? It does not seem to be so. Just as vocation to a religious congregation is a unique calling, so is the membership of an MTC. It has a very unique mission to fulfill in God's plan of salvation; especially in multi-religious societies. For such a community interreligious theologising becomes a unique way of life.

Implications

1. The theologizing process envisaged here reduces the possibility of mistaking it for a survival tactic or for a strategy of imposing the perceptions and interpretations of one's own religious tradition on others.
2. Theologizing process can build a true community of individuals belonging to various religious traditions, based on mutual respect and understanding. Such a community truly points at the 'eschatological' unity or harmony that is envisaged in many religious traditions.
3. In the course of the theologizing process, all religious traditions can be purged of some of their respective non-liberative factors and dimensions.
4. The theologizing process envisaged here can give rise to new religious traditions based on new experiences of the Divine. But they are not given *a priori* nor do they attain an unchangeable fixed form. In other words, the theologizing community need

not be seen as practicing an altogether new religion (a sort of *Din-e-Ilahi*); though the theologizing process can make the participants look at their religious traditions with new attitudes, new insights and perspectives. An example would be Paul's cross-textual/cultural hermeneutics as reported by Luke in Acts 17:16-34. Here Paul's faith-vision is broadened to understand the "unknown God" of the Gentile tradition as having a resonance with his own Judeo-Christian faith.[27] For a Christian participant, for instance, the interreligious theologising process could give new perspectives on the Eucharistic celebration; a Hindu participant could begin to find new meaning in his/her offer of *pooja* and so on.

In fact, *Dei Verbum* 8 makes explicit reference to the "growth in insight into the realities and words that are being passed on [in Tradition]". It is because of this fact that we can say that "as the centuries go by, the Church is always advancing towards the plenitude of divine truth, until eventually the words of God are fulfilled in her."[28]

5. The German equivalent for "tradition" is *Ueberlieferung*. It literally means "handing over" (*paradosis* in Greek). Although there should be something (constant) to hand over, the process of handing over is affected by its context.[29] Such a phenomenon actually contributes positively towards the growth of a tradition. To the extent that a faith-community lives in a multi-religious/cultural milieu the handing over and the growth of its religious tradition is bound to get affected by it. The point, however, is to be aware of this fact and acknowledge it.
6. In general, along with caste, religion too seems to be the most fundamental identity marker in India. Such identities, indeed, cut across cultural and linguistic boundaries. However, in the formation and functioning of an MTC the order is reversed; namely, an MTC is basically some sort of a cultural and linguistic community, in whose formation and functioning, caste and religious boundaries are crossed over but not abolished. At the outset this seems to be an impossible task, for the simple reason

that a weaker or a more surface level identity marker cannot bridge the chasm created by a stronger or a more fundamental one. Is an MTC then only a figment of the imagination or a wishful thinking? Some examples in history seem to be answering this question in the negative.

We have an example of *anubhavamantapa* of the 12th century in Karnataka – a group of men and women belonging to various castes and outcastes came together and formed 'theologizing'groups. The factors that enabled them to cross over the caste barriers may have been multiple. But one glaring factor that stands out is *shivanubhava* – experience of *Shiva*.[30] We have individuals such as Swami Abhishiktananda crossing over Christian boundaries, as it were, due to his *advaitic* experience. Neither of these examples indicates any shedding of the original identities; they are rather extended or enlarged to accommodate the new experience. Perhaps it all begins with basic good will or even healthy curiosity to come together as an MTC. And the experience of the Divine facilitated in the very process of theologizing interreligiously enables the participants to transcend their original narrow religious and caste boundaries. In some cases, such experiences may even facilitate a transcending of the cultural and linguistic boundaries as at Pentecost (cf. Acts 2:6f). But under ordinary circumstances some sort of a cultural and linguistic homogeneity in the MTC may be helpful for better communication.

(b) Theological axis

Presuppositions and prerequisites

1. An interreligious theologizing process has to be seen more as a means that mediates between historically shaped cultural, socio-economic and political institutions, on the one hand, and religious experiences, on the other, rather than as something that concerns itself with a mere scrupulous transmission of the past religious articulations to the present generation.[31]
2. An effective theological method for India needs to be cross-cultural (and cross-textual), that involves a "multi-faith hermeneutics" as

KowkPui-lan terms it.[32]And, hence, the theologies that thereby emerge too are cross-traditional, capable of making liberative sense across traditions.[33] In such a theologizing process, first of all the participants need to have a deep rootedness in their own respective religious traditions. Being so rooted one reaches out in dialogue with the 'other'. In this context, **in the perception of the MTC as a whole**, no culture, no religious tradition and no religious text as such can take a 'superior position' over the others; although for a given participant his/her own tradition and texts are supremely binding. The CBCI has been very clear in its teaching regarding this matter.[34]

3. The Divine is encountered in all religious traditions.[35] Despite all the differences of such encounters, it is still possible to share them in meaningful ways across traditions at least partially.
4. The Ultimate Mystery is inexhaustible by any finite means. Therefore, the CBCI firmly affirms, "In whatever way one articulates one's understanding of dialogue and proclamation, the perspective should always be that of the Kingdom of God. We are all pilgrims towards that state where God will fully reign over all humanity."[36]
5. The main objective of the theologizing process is 'soteriological', which means a religious tradition has to make liberative sense in different historical epochs. Such an aim cannot be fulfilled by transmitting every single detail of a religious tradition in a static way. Fidelity to a religious tradition consists precisely in making it transmit God's liberative love in ever new situations. It entails openness to listen, learn, and be enriched, re-understood and ready to take up the enterprise of interreligious dialogue. Various aspects of the tradition have to be contextually reinterpreted and renewed precisely in order to make them effective mediations of God's salvation. In India such reinterpretations cannot afford to neglect the multi-religious and pluri-cultural context. Only in dialogue with other traditions can a religious tradition meaningfully share its salvific potential with others.
6. The inexhaustible nature of the Ultimate Mystery and the consequent incapacity of any human agency to grasp and transmit it in all its fullness have to be acknowledged. Under

such circumstances the dialogical method envisaged here can only broaden and enrich the participants' religious experience and insights.

7. Every religious Tradition in its formative stages borrows different elements from its surrounding traditions. Such factors, sometimes survive as distinct (but more or less harmonized) theological 'trajectories' within the tradition in question. We suggest that in an interreligious dialogical theologizing process the participants take advantage of such a diversity found in their own respective traditions in order to focus on those elements that are more conducive and beneficial to the theologizing process.

For example, in the Christian tradition, we have two distinct (but very much linked) depictions of God's activity: Creation and Redemption. Some scholars have pointed out how "creation" themes rather than salvation-history themes as the starting point for theology could be more helpful to integrate the histories of many peoples (especially in the Asian context) into Christian conception of God's salvific plan. The "salvation-history" themes as the starting point, on the other hand, could cause the Judeo-Christian history gain an undue preference over the histories of other peoples;[37] which in turn could result in making the history of ***a*** people normative for all others. The remedy, however, is not to ignore the "salvation-history" themes, but to interpret them within the framework of the more inclusive "creation" themes. In fact, we find a similar attempt in the Pauline depiction of the "new creation" (2 Cor 5:17; Gal 6:15). Such a preferential focusing needs to be done in the case of all the participating traditions in an MTC.

Implications

1. Anthropologies and cosmologies depicted in different religious traditions cannot be harmonized due to the presence of certain mutually irreconcilable elements in them. But in an interreligious theologizing process, one could focus on those elements that are mutually complementary. In the final analysis, it is possible that the presence of both mutually complementary as well as mutually irreconcilable elements across religious traditions, to

the extent that they spring from authentic Divine encounters (and not from human interests) point towards the unfathomable mystery of creation and of the Divine.

2. In a dialogical interreligious theologizing process, is it possible to hold onto the traditional Christian distinction between 'natural revelation' and 'supernatural revelation' as indicating the possibility of **separating** the latter from the former? Don't the non-Christian religions have something more than mere products of human contemplation on the created world? If we take NT texts(such as Jn 1:3; 1 Cor 8:6; Eph 1:10; Col 1:16.17) that depict a foundational relationship between creation and the Christ-Event, seriously, is it really possible to **separate** the 'natural revelation' from the 'supernatural revelation'?[38]
3. Each religious tradition has its own normative text(s) – written and/or oral, which witness the foundational events of the tradition in question. But the question is: What is actually normative: a text as such or the Divine encounter to which the text is a witness? If we agree that it is the Divine encounter that is primarily normative, then, in the theologizing process envisaged here, texts across religious traditions can bear witness to the unique disclosures of the Divine for the MTC. In this sense, though the normative texts of one's own tradition can continue to be normative to a given participant, nevertheless it is possible that some texts of another tradition too can facilitate a divine disclosure to the same participant within the shared context of the MTC. And if such revelatory disclosures can be considered normative to the MTC as a whole from that particular moment of its history, all the texts that are instrumental in providing such disclosures can be meaningfully considered as 'normative' to the MTC.

However a text of one religious tradition can facilitate a divine disclosure to an adherent of another religious tradition only in relation to the texts of his/her own tradition. But when such disclosure happens the texts of the 'other' religion are experienced as inspired/inspiring/revelatory by the individual in question. In this sense those 'other texts' can become normative to him/her. For instance, it is observed that there are various non-Jewish texts incorporated into the OT. Obviously such texts have been 'revelatory' to the OT communities who incorporated them into their own Scripture at various historical situations. For example, Ps 29. Also "from an internal analysis of the text and external comparison with ancient Middle Eastern literature we can deduce with certainty [...] that the Hebrews were actually using the ancient Canaanite law books in the covenant. The norms of justice accepted under the sacred covenant (Jos 24:25-26) and imposed under the divine sanction (Dt 16:19) were for the greater part *mishpatim* previously written down under Canaanitic religion. St. Paul's preaching too presupposes the active presence of Hellenistic exegetical texts (cf. 1Cor 15:45.54)."[39] The creation myths, the narratives about theFlood, dragons etc (Ps 74:13f), and marriage of gods (cf. Hos 2:4-17) are modified versions of the religious stories found among the Israel's neighbours which are integrated into the biblical texts.[40]

It should be acknowledged that to the extent that to a given individual, the membership of the MTC cannot be binding as rigorously as one's own original religion, to that extent the normativity of the 'other texts' too cannot be equally binding as that of one's own texts.

4. Is being a participant in an MTC mandatory for one's salvation? It does not appear to be so. One can accept God's free gift of salvation from within one's own religious tradition. However, a multi-religious context offers an opportunity to some to receive this offer of salvation in a unique way. For the ancient Israelites the gift of God's Rest came in and through the symbol of 'Promised Land'; for some in India it is the *advaitic*union with the Absolute that stands for *moksha*. For Christians in general, the gift of salvation is offered in and through the life, death and resurrection of Jesus of Nazareth. And it seems that at least some of those who live in a multi-religious context are called to receive the offer of God's salvation in a multi-religious way by means of sharing the life of an MTC, where one's own faith is not given up or diluted but enhanced and lived more radically in a broader context.

5. **Reflecting theologically** on the issues such as "unicity and universality of Christ", "unicity and universality of Church" etc., is to be understood as a typically 'Christian responsibility'. Such issues may be related to all but only a Christian is obliged to reflect theologically on them. There are such 'inner group issues' in other faiths as well. By their very nature, it is not possible to bypass them in any theological discussions and related praxes in the respective religious groups. In this context, the interreligious theologizing process envisaged here can give a further depth and width to such 'inner group' discussions and related praxes. For instance, in the context of an interreligious theologizing process, a Christian participant could be enabled to experience and articulate the Christic and/or ecclesial reality in hitherto unknown ways; so also could a Muslim/Hindu, regarding certain dimensions of his/her religious tradition.[41]While sharing such 'discoveries' with others in an MTC can be a fruitful activity, their integration into the participating traditions is subject to the established norms of each religious tradition.However, the whole process can also bring about a renewal of such norms.

(c) Hermeneutical axis

Hermeneutics is not only important but fundamental to human cognitive process. Hence, it is mandatory that the Indian theologizing process should become aware of its own hermeneutical presuppositions and their implications.

Presuppositions and prerequisites

1. Historical negativities provide special occasions for interpreting the sacred texts and traditions liberatively. Generally such negativities can also become occasions for Divine self revelation, which in turn can enable us to overcome the negativities.
2. A theological statement is a contingent expression of a historically experienced religious truth. It is relative on two counts: a) as an interpretation of some aspect of a sacred tradition (and text) it exists for the service of faith and not for itself, and, b) it has its own historicity.[42] In the Indian context a theological statement has

to interact with Indian historicity and, thereby, be contextually interpreted in order to be transformatively intelligible.

3. Our God-talk is essentially conditioned by our religious, historical and existential experiences. The existential and religious horizon of an MTC and its God-talk should not be unrelated to the factors that make its historical situatedness.[43] Hence, among other factors the multi-religious situatedness of India has far reaching implications for a truly indigenous theological enterprise.
4. The use of symbols, metaphors, narratives and various art forms becomes necessary in the Indian theologizing process envisaged here for the following reasons[44]: a) Due to their evocative power and their innate polysemous nature, they are better equipped to facilitate and transmit religious experiences than the rational philosophical concepts. b) 'Mythic' narratives abound in all religious texts. Their contextual retrieval has to take place in relevant 'mythic' forms. A mythic narrative cannot be retrieved in a rational-conceptual mode without the loss of its evocative power. c) *Pathos*is an intrinsic dimension of Asian life, religiosities and spiritualities. Therefore, an effective theologizing process in Asia cannot afford to neglect this dimension. It is the narratives and such other extended metaphors alone that can adequately maintain the power of *pathos* in a theologizing process.
5. Interpretation, indeed, is the essential dimension of any human knowing. The point however is to make this process more conscious in the 'transmission' of religious traditions. Secondly, fidelity to a given religious tradition is guaranteed not by its purist transmission, but by its faith-based historical and hermeneutical retrieval in each new 'historical' and 'existential' epoch. The FABC has enlightened us much with regard to this issue:

> By living within their particular context according to the "sense of faith aroused and sustained by the Spirit of truth" (LG 12), the faithful will learn to express their faith not only in fidelity to the Apostolic Tradition, but also in response to their cultural situations. This response is the responsibility of the whole community, which discerns God's Word and Spirit in its culture and history.[45]

In the Indian context such a process, among other things, could take the shape of a cross-cultural and cross-textual retrieval.

6. The radical historicity and historicality[46] of human experience and human cognition are not done justice to if we resolve the problem of hermeneutics of retrieval in theology by having recourse to 'essence-form' categorization; namely, by positing an unhistoricized 'essence' and a historically changeable 'form' of religious statements.[47] The only means to deal with the problem of change and continuity is a contextually faithful and responsible reinterpretation of the texts.[48]
7. If the Spirit of God is alive and active in diverse cultures through God's *Logos* and *Sophia*, encountering God in these manifestations becomes significant for any contextual encounter of and talk about the enfleshed *Logos* and his situated *Sophia*. The Word that was from the beginning and was heard (1 Jn 1:1-5) has to be heard afresh in a multi-cultural context, and the deeds of *Sophia* by which she is vindicated (Mt 11:19) have to be witnessed in the wisdom traditions and histories of many a people. It is only then that the radicality of Incarnation is affirmed and experienced in our context. Albeit, for the Christian participant of the MTC, the enfleshed and the risen Word in the person of Jesus of Nazareth remains the norm in all such activities. The other parties may have their own norms.

Implications

1. Contextual retrievals of several religious traditions in a theologizing process could lead to the emergence of new traditions of harmony and fellowship along with the renewal of the old. In this sense the 'handing over' of the tradition does not become a static 'relay act', but rather a living and liberating praxis.
2. Insights of thinkers such as H. R. Jauss, O. Rush and D. Tracy gain significance here. These thinkers speak of (in their own unique ways) the necessity of a certain 'otherness' or 'strangeness' of a text for it to be transformatively 'provocative' to the readers.[49] Such 'otherness' has to be maintained against a 'routinization' by

which the text ceases to be transformative. The MTC envisaged here due to its engaging with texts of diverse traditions, and especially due to its cross-textual and cross-cultural reading practices creates an overall hermeneutical milieu that promises to maintain the 'otherness' of the texts. Because of such a possibility the transformative 'provocation' of the texts becomes comparatively more intense and fruitful than if the texts were to be restricted to a mono-religious theologizing community.

3. Paul Ricoeur speaks of the *heretical imperative* in the process of interpretation. This concept denotes one's option or position from which one interprets; or due to such choices opts for one or a few of the possible interpretations. Whether or not one is conscious of it, anyone who interprets is necessarily governed by a *heretical imperative.* In the Indian theologizing process this imperative should emerge among other things, also from our option for the victims of Indian negativities. In fact such a choice imitates God's own option.
4. The historical facticity per se cannot serve as a foundation for faith since facts within a faith tradition are available only within a cultural and interpretative framework, as modern hermeneutics has demonstrated.[50] This consideration brings to our awareness two points: a) Those religious traditions which claim a historicity to their foundational events cannot ***by that fact*** claim superiority over those others whose foundational events seem a-historical or meta-historical.[51] Both types of claims have their own unique specificities. b) Every religious tradition can speak only of an 'event' which is the 'mythicised' (theologized) form of some historical 'occurrence'.[52] In this sense myth and history make the warp and woof of any religious tradition, be it Semitic or Indic.

(d) Praxical axis

A theologizing process should end up in liberating praxis. Hence, it is important to ask how such an aim has its bearing on the theological method followed, what presuppositions such a method makes and what their respective implications are.

Presuppositions and prerequisites

1. A fundamental requirement for being an MTC is a shared praxis. A shared praxis provides a shared context in which the members of an MTC have both – a shared experience of negativities as well as that of the Divine.
2. The truth and meaning of religious statements (texts) have an inseparable link in a theologizing process. Examining the truth of a religious statement essentially contains examining its salvific (transformative) meaning. In other words we need to affirm the fundamental soteriological (transformative) and ethical character of revelation-faith dynamic. Hence, one can speak about an ethical judgment on the authenticity and credibility of every religion. Indeed, religious sense does not dispense with ethical sense. What emerged from Moses' encounter with God at Sinai is the Law (prescription); what came through Jesus Christ was grace and truth (Jn 1:17). But that grace enabled a positive response (an ethical living) to God in those who received it.
3. The socio-economic and political issues and negativities such as hunger and poverty, caste and gender discrimination, socio-economic and environmental ramifications of some of the major political decisions taken at various levels, and myriad other struggles that an average Indian faces in daily life provide a praxical matrix for the theologizing process; religion(s) and culture(s) provide an 'ideological' one. Indeed, an MTC cannot afford to get stuck only in a faith-culture framework, though such a framework is operative at the most fundamental level of the human reality.

Implications

1. Generally all religious traditions relativize history, albeit in their own unique ways. But none of them can deny the fact of their cults, creeds and codes having very real consequences to the historical existence of their adherents and of others. Hence, the inquiry into the historical consequences of the beliefs systems, cults and teaching of the religious traditions gains significance.

2. The theologizing process envisaged here presupposes a 'theologizing community', a 'community' that has a shared 'situatedness'. In this context involvement in the justice related issues, issues related to authentic human development etc. can be envisaged as promoting the formation of such communities."Religious dialogue, therefore, does not mean that two persons [merely] speak about their religious experience, but rather that they speak as religiously committed persons with their ultimate commitments and religious outlook, on subjects of common interest".[53]
3. An eschatological hope that is in no way related to the present state of affairs should be looked upon with suspicion. Hence, it is mandatory to ask, what praxes do various 'eschatological' depictions and hopes across religious traditions promote in the here and now?
4. An Indian theologizing process should not fall victim to some of the world-negating spiritualities and religiosities prevalent in India. It is not enough to struggle to set one's mind free from whatever blurs the vision of the Ultimate Reality; it is equally important to set people free from those historical conditions that at least partially cause such blurring. One the other hand, it is true that the "liberation" envisaged in the Asian perspective is not only from external factors such as poverty and oppression but also primarily from the factors within, namely, greed, illusion and attachment.[54] Maintaining a healthy balance between these two dimensions is a must.

(e) 'Ecclesiastical' axis

Since the theological method envisaged here involves more religious traditions than just one, the process has a unique set of presuppositions, prerequisites and implications for the religious and spiritual systems of the respective religious groups that constitute an MTC.

Presuppositions and prerequisites

1. The MTC envisaged here requires a space that needs to be ensured by the 'ecclesiastical'/ 'governing' authorities of the respective participants.

2. The participants in the MTC need to come to terms with their 'dual' affiliation: at once adherents of the original religion and members of the MTC which is pluri-religious. Albeit, these cannot be conceived as equally binding on the individuals concerned. The membership of the original religious group remains more fundamental than that of the MTC.

Implications

1. For a Catholic, the teaching office of the Church (the Magisterium) is the supreme authority in the matters of faith and morals. However, an interreligious theologizing process envisaged here could give rise to such theological insights, statements, symbols and metaphors `that can be instrumental in enriching and expanding the current limits set by the Magisterium, especially, in matters theological. Under such circumstances a constructive dialogue between the Magisterium and the local theologizing communities at various levels is a must. In this connection it is significant to note that as early as 1970, the Asian Bishops' Meeting with Pope Paul VI passed a resolution to engage in "an open, sincere, and continuing dialogue with our brothers of other great religions of Asia, that we may learn from one another how to enrich ourselves spiritually and how to work more effectively together on our common task of total human development"[55]. Indeed the Magisterium has been showing such openness. The Vatican II documents such as *Nostra Aetate*, *Gaudium et Spes,* and *Ad Gentes*, and numerous such other gestures of openness[56] on the part of the Magisterium do indicate positive signs for the Catholic members of an MTC.
2. Can an MTC composed of members from diverse religious traditions be called a new way of being an *ecclesia*, a *sangha,* or an *anubhavamantapa*?[57] It will be a dialogical group, perhaps on experimentation. In fact the FABC envisions Church as a dialoguing community. "The Church is called to be a community of dialogue. This dialogical model is in fact a new way of being Church."[58]Such a community though composed of different 'tongues' can be united by one Spirit (Acts 2:6f.) and be inspired

to get involved in a single mission with multiple roles (1 Cor 12:4f).[59]

Conclusion

The awareness of the presuppositions, preconditions and implications of evolving a theologizing method and a process in India has made us deeply conscious of a Herculean task. One should definitely be careful while going to face an army of twenty thousand soldiers with one's own ten thousand (Lk 14:31), thereby, not to panic and give up but rather to have a better preparedness.

An Indian theological method(s) and the theology(ies) thereby emerging demand contemplation that reaches beyond the confines of any given religious tradition. A purely "Christian theology" for India (and for Christians in India) and/or a "theology of religions based on Christian revelation" alone do have their own respective significance. But the need of the hour seems to be an "interreligious dialogical theology" based on a shared situatedness, shared praxis and shared experiences of the Divine across religious traditions, to whatever extent such a sharing is possible. But the big question is – how far do the different religious traditions existing in India actually allow for and positively facilitate such a theology? Such verification with regard to each of the religious traditions, though necessary, falls beyond the scope of this essay.

A typically Christian engagement in history is not only the ***proclamation*** of the Reign of God that is experienced in and through the Christ-Event, but also has to do with its ***realization*** in various historical particularities– however partial it may be. In the Indian context, the existence of plurality of religions and cultures is one such fundamental particularity among many others. Hence, the need to recognize the coming of the Reign as related to all such particularities is not just important but fundamental.[60]

Endnotes

1. See Dan Cohn-Sherbok, ed., *Interfaith Theology: A Reader,* First South Asian Edition (Oxford: One World Publications, 2007). Excerpts of the writings on interfaith theology of about 117 authors belonging to different religions from 19th century to the present, both from East and West are presented in this

work. Also Robin Boyd, *An introduction to Indian Christian Theology* (Delhi: ISPCK, 1969).

2. It is very instructive to look at two parallel examples. The first is an attempt to imitate the Chinese Cultural Revolution in the Indian state of Kerala in the late 1960s; and the second, attempts at a blind borrowing of Latin American Liberation Theological models into the Indian scenarios in the 1980s. Both attempts experienced considerable failure not primarily because the models were developed in alien lands, but because the ground realities of our land were very different from those of China of Mao's times and of Latin American countries. Can we take a leaf out of such failures so that similar failures are not repeated in our endeavours in developing methods and models for an Indian theologizing process?
3. Under the umbrella concept of 'situatedness' we include all the external (socio-cultural, political, economic, historical, cosmic) and the internal (individual as well as collective psyche, all subjective experiences – religious and other), the positive as well as the negative factors that make up the historicity of a people.
4. For an excellent analysis of how the differences in the pace of changes in cultural, political and economic domains in India have produced unprecedented tensions and conflicts see Y. Singh, *Social Change in India: Crisis and Resilience* (New Delhi: Har-Anand Publications , 2009), chapters II, IV, V, and VII. Also see idem, *Social Stratification and Change in India*, 2nd rev. ed., (New Delhi: Manohar Publishers, 2006), chapter VII.
5. The latter connotes a one-way absorption of plurality into one; whereas the former indicates a certain space for maintaining the specificities of the individual items present in the plurality. However, even here a certain predominance of one religious tradition is maintained. For instance, 'A Christian Theology of Religions'.
6. By "shared experience" we mean the experience of the Divine that the members across the religious traditions can have in the context of a common engagement, which can be in the areas of religion proper (prayer, common celebration of festivals, theological dialogue etc.) so also in any other area related to day-to-day life; such as justice issues, cultural issues etc. The experience of the Divine had in such contexts can also vary according to the religious background of various participants. But the experience shows that such diverse experiences do have an overall harmonizing and liberating effect on the participants.
7. J. Berling, "Learning Asian Religions and Critical Engagement in the Asian Context", in *Critical Engagement in the Asian Context: Implications for Theological Education and Christian Studies*, ed. D. Preman Niles (Hong Kong: Asian Christian Higher Education Institute, 2005), 107.
8. Consider the following FABC recommendation: "The local church is a church **incarnate** in a people, a church **indigenous** and **inculturated.** And this means concretely a church in continuous, humble and loving dialogue with the living

traditions, the cultures, the religions - *in brief, with all the life-realities of the people whose midst it has sunk its root deeply and whose history and life it gladly makes its own.*" Gaudencio B. Rosales & C. G. Arévalo, *For All the Peoples of Asia: Federation of Asian Bishops' Conferences Documents From 1970-1991* (Maryknoll, New York: Orbis Books, 1992), 14. (Italics added). In order to make the history and life of people of various traditions its own it is necessary that their religious and cultural traditions are taken into a positive consideration in the Church's own theological reflections.

9. R. Panikkar's insights in this context are enlightening. He distinguishes between "Christendom" (political), "Christianity" (doctrinal) and "Christianness" (experiential). The last of these according to him can assume a variety of cultural forms. See R. Panikkar, "Words of Scripture, Universal Religious Categories? Christian Language for the Third Millennium", in *Going to the Roots: A Multi-Disciplinary Study*, ed. J. J. Puthenpurackal (Bangalore: ATC, 2005), 160-161.
10. For instance, Isaiah 44:48 calls Cyrus the Persian king the "shepherd" of the Lord, and Isaiah 45:1 names him "anointed one" (messiah!) of the Lord. Ps 87:4-6 mentions non-Israelite nations such as Ethiopia, Babylon, Tyre etc. as having their origin in Zion and that they know Yahweh (NRSV). Rev 21 visualizes nations bringing their "glories and treasures" to (new) Jerusalem. In Gal 3:28 Paul describes a new people in Christ, who transcend the categories of "Jew-Greek", "male-female", and "slave-free".
11. R. Panikkar, "Words of Scripture,"158. "The contemporary theological method", he says "if it has to be *catholic* (complete) cannot be solely '*ad usumnostrorum,*' only for the internal use." Ibid.
12. P. Puthunangady and others, ed., *Revelation and Faith* (Bangalore: TPI, 2009), 169-170.
13. The CBCI firmly affirms "in whatever way one articulates one's understanding of dialogue and proclamation, the perspective should always be that of the Kingdom of God. We are all pilgrims towards that state where God will fully reign over all humanity," *Guidelines for Inter-Religious Dialogue*, CBCI Commission for Dialogue and Ecumenism, 2nd rev. ed. No. 14, 41.
14. G. Soares-Prabhu, "From Alienation to Inculturation: Some Reflections on Doing Theology in India Today", in *Biblical Themes for a Contextual Theology Today: Collected Writings of George. M. Soares-Prabhu, SJ,* Vol. 1., ed. I. Padinjarekuttu (Anand: GujarathSahityaPrakash, 1999), 80.
15. In several pilgrimage centers in India we see people belonging to various religious traditions. They could be experiencing the Divine at such centers in their own unique ways. But the total effect seems to be harmony, peace, fellowship and other life-affirming values.
16. J. Berling, "Learning Asian Religions", 109.
17. FABC recommended that a network of centers of spirituality be developed where, "besides study and research, seekers of God and truth of all religious

affiliations could meet and share their spiritual experiences." BIRA IV/7, in *For All the Peoples of Asia: Federation of Asian Bishops' Conferences Documents from 1970-1991,* ed. G. B. Rosales and C. G. Arevalo (Maryknoll, New York: Orbis Books; Quezon City, Philippines, 1992), 311, recommendation 2.

18. I should like to clarify this point further: I am only suggesting that such a multiple membership, as described, is a necessaryprerequisite for the kind of theologizing method we are talking about. Much more study and discernment under the Spirit of Truth are needed before we can affirm its viability.
19. "When it is rightly said that dialogue does not aim at 'making converts' the meaning is that the intention of Christians or Hindus or any other participants in a dialogue activity is not to convince the others of their own beliefs or to bring them over to their communities, but rather in sincerity and disinterested love to give witness to their own faith and to be enriched by the religious values found in others". CBCI Commission for Dialogue and Ecumenism, *Guidelines for Inter-Religious Dialogue,* no 14.2nd rev. ed. (1989), 38.
20. Cf. G. Soares-Prabhu, "From Alienation to Inculturation".
21. Abhishiktananda claims to have had an *upanisadic-advaitic* experience. His effort was to speak about Jesus Christ in terms of this experience. His difficulty was to reconcile his *upanisadic* experience with some of the traditional Christian faith-articulations that held a clear distinction and duality between God and human being. He articulates his personal experience of the *Advaitc mystery* as follows:

    In the *advaitic* experience no one remains to say 'I have reached the plane of the Absolute'- still less to say: 'I have passed beyond, lost myself'. Nothing is left apart from that consciousness itself, pure and unalloyed: This (*tat*)...that which is (*Sat*) ... *OM* – 'OM *tat sat*', as the *Gīta*says (17:23). For men cannot see God and live (Deut5, 26).

    See Swami Abhishiktananda, *Hindu-Christian Meeting Point,* (Bombay: The Institute of Indian Culture, 1969), 64.
22. Panikkar confesses – "I 'left' [Europe] as a Christian, I 'found' myself a Hindu and I 'return' a Buddhist, without having ceased to be a Christian." R. Panikkar, "Faith and Belief", in *The Intra-Religious Dialogue* (New York: Paulist Press, 1978; Indian reprint, Bangalore: Asian Trading Corporation. 1984), 40.
23. In its call for a mutual dialogue, critique and enrichment between the Christian Gospel and culture, the FABC clarifies that what is "good, noble and living" in the Asian religio-cultural *Sitz-im-Leben* could be assumed into Christian life. It clarifies its stand on this matter by saying:

    "We are daily more convinced that the Spirit is leading us in our time, not to some dubious syncretism (which we all rightly reject), but to an integration - profound and organic in character - of all that is best in our traditional ways of prayer and worship, into the treasury of our Christian heritage. Thus is a fuller catholicity made possible in this age of the Church." - *FABC II*, article 31 in Gaudencio B. Rosales & C. G. Arévalo, *For All the peoples of Asia,* 35.

24. All these examples can be witnessed in different parts of Karnataka.
25. This is reiterated by Pope Francis in his *EvangeliiGaudium*, which he "holds true as much for the dogmas of faith as for the whole corpus of the Church's teaching, including her moral teaching." (No. 36)
26. Speaking about Ruth's commitment to Naomi, her widowed mother-in-law, H. Kinukawa in an insightful essay shows how the famous phrase "Your people shall be my people, your God my God" (Ruth 1:16) reflects more Ruth's commitment to widowed Naomi (despite running the risk of losing her religious identity) than her desire to convert to Naomi's religion as such. In fact such a commitment had been nurtured by means of practicing in a "multi-religious spirituality" ever since she (a Moabite) got married to a son of Naomi (a Judite). Cf. H. Kinukawa, "...and your God my God: How We Can Nurture Openness to Other Faiths – Ruth 1:1-19 Read from a Feminist Perspective of a Multi-faith Community", in *Scripture, Community, and Mission: Essays in Honor of D. Preman Niles*, ed. Philip L. Wickeri (Hong Kong: Christian Council of Asia, 2002; 2nd printing, 2003), 198-207.
27. See J. du Plessis, "ACTS 17:16-34 – The Resurrection of Jesus as a Crucial Moment in the Encounter Between Gospel and Culture," accessed 14 May 2006); available from http://www.academic.sun.ac.za/buvton/Vennote/GOCN/Bible%20 (Acts),%20culture%20and%20the%20resurrection%20of%20Christ. The author investigates the relationship between "a core religious belief and its cultural appropriation, between a first-century view of the resurrection of Christ and the Greco-Roman culture of Athens, according to Luke's construction of Paul's speech on the Athenian Aeropagus."
28. DV 8 mentions three sources of such a growth: a. contemplation and study, b. experience of spiritual realities and c. preaching by those who have received the sure charism of truth ensured by the apostolic succession. In the context of the essay we could perhaps consider the participation in an MTC providing unique dimensionsto the first two of these factors. For the Catholic participant, albeit, the *Magisterium* remains supreme authority in discerning the authenticity of the growth of his/her faith.
29. It is for this reason that Christianity (even of a given denomination) does not have identical incarnated forms in different parts of the world. This is true also in the case of any religion that has existed for sufficiently long period of time in various parts of the world.
30. Such experience was not identical for all the members of the *anubhavamantapa*. In fact each one of them had articulated it differently by means of addressing *Shiva* by different names. However, the fact that all of them formed a community shows that there was something in their experiences that enabled them to transcend the differences without necessarily negating them.

31. J. Putti, *Theology as Hermeneutics: Paul Ricoeur's Theory of Text: Interpretation and Method in Theology* (Bangalore: KristuJyoti Publications, 1991), 29.
32. Kwok Pui-lan, *Discovering the Bible in the Non-Biblical World* (Maryknoll, New York: ORBIS, 1995), 66. In this context J. Punt's conception of "a hermeneutics based on universal recognition of the sacred" suggests a broader theological basis for a cross-textual hermeneutics. See J. Punt, "Bible (Acts), Culture and the Resurrection of Christ in Religious Dialogue: A Response to J. du Plessis", accessed 14May 2006); available from http://www.academic.sun.ac.za/buvton/Vennote/GOCN/Bible%20(Acts),%20culture%20and%20the%20resurrection%20of%20Christ.
33. In connection with this issue I have specified elsewhere three possible ways in which a cross-textual interpretation can be attempted. They are: "Mutual critique and illumination" among the texts; "Arriving at a common horizon of meaning by means of a creative juxtaposition" of the texts, and "Superimposing an interpretive category or structure of one text on to another." See J. Lobo, "In Search of True Worship: A Cross-Textual Reading of Jn. 4:19-26 and *Vacana* 821:25", *Vidyajyoti: Journal of Theological Reflections* 70, No. 11 (November 2006): 827-844.
34. "Beyond the extremes of inclusivism and exclusivism, pluralism is accepted in resonance with the constitutive plurality of reality. Religions, as they are manifested in history, are complementary perceptions of the ineffable divine mystery, the God-beyond-God. All religions are visions of the divine mystery. No particular religion can raise the claim of being the norm for all others. We, religious believers, are co-pilgrims, who share intimate spiritual experiences and reflections with one another with concern and compassion, with genuine openness to truth and the freedom of spiritual seekers (*sadhakas*). In this process we become increasingly sensitive to human suffering and collaborate in promoting justice, peace and ecological wholeness... We walk together on the path of dialogue and service towards harmony as sisters and brothers bound in one Love and drawn by one Divine Truth." Bishops' Institutes for Interreligious Affairs on the Theology of Dialogue (*BIRA*) *V/3*, article 6.
35. Consider the following references:

    a. FABC – Theol. Consultation Statement, 1991, No. 43, holds that world religions "are expressions of the presence of God's Word and of the universal action of the divine Spirit".
    b. "World religions are significant and positive elements in the economy of God's design of salvation." (FABC, Plenary Assembly Statement, 1974, No. 12).
    c. A statement of the FABC, First Plenary Assembly, 1974 boldly claims, "Down through the centuries the ancient religions of the orient have expressed the noblest longings in the hearts of our people, our deepest joys and sorrows. They have shaped our history, and our way of thinking.

They are part of our culture. For us in Asia, they have been the doorway to God". (No. 12)

d. World religions "reveal the diverse ways of responding to God whose Spirit is active in all peoples and cultures." (FABC – BIRA IV/7, 1988, No. 12).

e. "We accept them [religions and their followers] as significant and positive elements in the economy of God's design of salvation" (FABC 1, 14 in Arevalo, C. *For All the Peoples of Asia,* 25-38.

f. "it is an inescapable truth that God's Spirit is at work in all religious traditions" (BIRA IV/12, No. 7)

g. The "great religions of Asia with their respective creeds, cults and codes reveal to us diverse ways of responding to God whose Spirit is active in all peoples and cultures" (BIRA IV/7, No, 12).

36. Guidelines for Inter-Religious Dialogue, CBCI Commission for Dialogue and Ecumenism, 2nd rev. ed. 41.
37. See C. S. Song, "Christian Mission in Reconstruction – An Asian Analysis" (New York: Orbis Books, 1975).
38. They are two distinct types of revelation. But the texts cited posit a sort of inseparable relationship between Christ and creation. From this perspective it seems difficult to ***separate*** the 'natural revelation' from the 'supernatural revelation.'
39. The above example and the quote are from the Statement of Research Seminar on Non-Biblical Scriptures (NBCLC, 11th-17th December 1974) in *Research Seminar on Non-Biblical Scriptures,* ed. D. S. Amalorpavadass (Bangalore: NBCLC, 1974), 673. This statement is made on the basis of the two articles – J. N. M Wijngaards, "The Integration into Scripture of Originally non-Jewish Religious Literature: (ONJRL)" and "The Co-existence of the Bible and the Non-Christian Sacred Scriptures", in *Research Seminar on Non-Biblical Scriptures,* 78-98.
40. For other such references see P. Puthunangady and others, *Revelation and Faith,* 171-172.
41. "In an authentic interreligious dialogue "each culture not only provides us with a new approach to the human, but also opens up new avenues for the understanding of the Gospel and its riches, When the Gospel encounters the tradition, experience and culture of a people, its hitherto undiscovered virtualities will surface; riches and meanings as yet hidden will emerge into the light. That is why it is so important to reinterpret the Gospel through the cultural resources of every people; this reinterpretation truly enriches the Christian tradition." - FABC Papers No. 60 (Hong Kong: FABC, 1991), 20-21

    "Only in dialogue with these religions can we discover in them the seeds of the Word of God (*Ad Gentes,* chapter I, 9). This dialogue will allow us to touch the expression and the reality of our peoples' deepest selves, and enable us to find authentic ways of living and expressing our own Christian faith. It will reveal to us also many riches of our own faith which we perhaps would not have perceived." First *FABC* Plenary Assembly, article 16, in *For All the Peoples of Asia,* 14-15.

42. See K. Rahner, Chalkedon – "Ende oder Anfang?", in *Das Konzil von Chalkedon: Geschichte und Gegenwart,* Band III, ed. A. Grillmeier & H. Bacht (Würzburg: Echter- Verlag, 1954), 3-49. Rahner opines that the Chalcedonian Christological formula needs interpretation in different historical epochs.
43. Rahner is critiqued for neglecting the historical dimension of human experience. His transcendental method is seen as prone to "run the risk of neglecting the Christian fact." J. Putti, *Theology as Hermeneutics,* 196. The relationship between the historical and the existential is not adequately brought out in Rahner's transcendental method. Therefore, his theology runs the risk of ignoring the social and the political implications of Christian faith. Incidentally one hardly finds any reference to the *holocaust,* which was so intrinsic to Rahner's socio-historical milieu, in his theological corpus. In this regard his theological enterprise stands in stark contrast to that of D. Bonhoeffer, J. B. Metz and J. Moltmann, who in turn have so explicitly historicised ('politicized') Christian faith.
44. I have dealt with this issue elaborately in my book *Encountering Jesus Christ in India* (Bangalore: ATC, 2005).
45. FABC Papers No. 60 (Hong Kong: FABC, 1991), 28. See also Gaudencio B. Rosales & C. G. Arévalo, *For All the Peoples of Asia,* 337
46. 'Historicity' refers to the fact of being in time and space; and 'historicality' connotes the effect of being in time and space.
47. See, for instance, J. S. Spong, "Transcending the Limits of Religion in Search of the Wonder of God" *QUEST: An Interdisciplinary Journal for Asian Christian Scholars* 3, No. 1 (April 2004): especially 84-85. Spong advocates such a method to arrive at the 'pearl' of one's own religious tradition by sifting the chaff of historical, political, military and such other human made compromises in its development. The question is whether one can find an unhistoricised 'pearl' in any religious tradition. In fact one of the FABC document clearly states - "given the historicity of human existence in a determined context and tradition, it is inescapable that our perception of truth, understanding and experiencing of reality – including the Gospel and faith – be bound up with a particular culture" See FABC Papers No. 60 (Hong Kong: FABC, 1991), 21. (Thesis 5, article 5.08)
48. J. Putti, *Theology as Hermeneutics,* 213.
49. For a comparative presentation of these authors with regard to the concepts of "provocation" and "otherness" see, A. C. Thiselton, *The Hermeneutics of Doctrine* (Cambridge UK: William B. Freedmans Publ. Co), 2007, Chapter 6.
50. J. Putti, *Theology as Hermeneutics,* 216.

51. In this connection F. X. D'Sa's insights on non-historical consciousness are especially enlightening. "To ignore the non-historical dimension of reality", he says, "is to reduce the whole of reality to the historical dimension...Krishna's birth, though not historical, is not less real. The language of myth and symbol is more, not less, real than the language of historical." See his "How is it that We Hear, Each of Us, in Our Own Native Language?: A Tentative Cross-cultural Reading of the Incarnation (John 1) and Avatara (Bhagavadgita 4)", in *Scripture, Community, and Mission*, ed. Philip L. Wickeri,137-138.
52. For the possibility of considering theologizing as mythicization of history and historicization of myth see, J. Lobo, "Mythicization of History and Historicization of Myths and Mythologies: Interplay of Religion and Politics and its Significance for a Liberative Religious Discourse and Praxis in Asia", *Vidyajyoti: Journal for Theological Reflection* 72, no.1 (January 2008): 22-37
53. *Guidelines for Inter-Religious Dialogue*, CBCI Commission for Dialogue and Ecumenism, 2nd rev. ed. No. 14 (1989), 35
54. G. Soares-Prabhu, "Inculturation- Liberation- Dialogue: Challenge to Christian Theology in Asia Today", in *Biblical Themes for a Contextual Theology Today*, ed. I. Padinjarekuttu, 56.
55. *Asian Bishops' Meeting*, resolution 12, in *For All The Peoples of Asia*, ed. Gaudencio B. Rosales & C.G. Arévalo, 9
56. For instance, consider the following:
    The *Magesterium* recognizes the "seeds of the Word" in other religions and the fact that they "often reflect a ray of that truth which enlightens all people" (NA 2)
    - "The Spirit of the Lord fills the earth … man is constantly worked upon by God's Spirit" (GS 11; 41)
    - "Christ is now at work in the hearts of people through the energy of his Spirit" (GS 38)
    - "...we ought to believe that the Holy Spirit is in a manner known to God offers to every person the possibility of being associated with this paschal mystery." (GS 22)
    - Religions do possess "the elements of goodness and truth which [they] possess by God's providence" (OT 16; LG 16)
    - "Truth and grace are to be found among the nations, as a sort of secret presence of God" (AG 9)
    - Action of the Holy Spirit "has been exercised in every place and at every time, indeed in every individual...whereby this action was to be closely linked with the mystery of the Incarnation and Redemption" (*Dominum et Vivificantem* 53)
    - The firm belief found in the adherents of other religions "is an effect of the Spirit of truth operating outside the visible confines of the Mystical Body" (*RedemptorHominis*, 6)

- The Spirit of God "Continually sows the seeds of truth among all peoples, their religions, cultures and philosophies". (*Ecclesia in Asia*, 15)

57. "A local Church comes into existence and is built up through a deep and mutually enriching encounter between the Gospel and a people with its particular culture and tradition. In current theological and magisterial language, this is known as inculturation. Inculturation consists not only in the expression of the Gospel and the Christian faith through the cultural medium, but includes, as well, experiencing, understanding and appropriating them through the cultural resources of a people. As a result, the concrete shape of the local Church will be, on the one hand, conditioned by the culture, and, on the other hand, the culture will be evangelized by the life and witness of the local Church." FABC Papers No. 60 (Hong Kong: FABC, 1991), 18. (Thesis 5)
58. BIRA IV/12, No. 48 in *For All The Peoples of Asia,* ed. Gaudencio B. Rosales & C. G. Arévalo, 332.
59. Tina Rendel presents an interesting description of various ways of being a church community (different from the traditional 'Christendom model') based on mission praxis. Such communities in Australia are often cross-denominational and even 'beyond-denominational'. What is instructive in her depiction is that the individual members have their own theological beliefs and spiritualities and yet come together and celebrate their faith(s) in common in the context of their mission among people who are in need. See "Post-Denominational Ways of Being Church and Doing Mission", *CTC Bulletin: Bulletin of the Program Area on Faith, Mission and Unity,* XXI, No.1 (April 2005): 45-49.
60. "The process of inculturation is no longer a question of a search for external adaptation to Asian reality and way of living, but a question of an existential nature: *being* and *living* in Asia and with Asians, becoming involved in all the aspects of life, collaborating with all the forces which are working actively to build up the Kingdom." L. Nemet, "Inculturation in the FABC Documents," *East Asian Pastoral Reveiw* 31 (1994): 93.

Chapter 6

Implications of People's History for a Theological Method in India

Thomas Kuriacose, SJ

Introduction

Theology, like every discipline, has its own characteristic methods. Examples of theological methods are the 'Transcendental Method' of Karl Rahner and Bernard Lonergan, the 'Existential Method' of John Macquarrie and Paul Tillich, the 'Empirical Method' of David Tracy and Bernard Meland, and the 'Socio-Phenomenological Method' of Edward Schillebeeckx and Jon Sobrino.[1] One could talk of the methods of different 'systems' of theology like 'Scholastic theology', and 'Analytic Theology';[2] or of methodologies of 'Confessional approaches' like those of Roman Catholics and Protestants, or of various contributions brought to theological method by individual theologians or groups of theologians.[3] Therefore, it is evident that theologizing in India can be done with different methods. Further, as Bernard Lonergan rightly reminds us, "Method is not a set of rules to be followed meticulously by a dolt. It is a framework for collaborative creativity."[4] So, one need not be under the tyranny of any theological method. Rather, it would be ideal to collaborate together and creatively work out, methods that would be best suited to the different contexts of India.

The theology that we desire for India, is not one which is totally theoretical and abstract, or far removed from the realities of the people of India. I am fully in agreement with Errol D'Lima when he says, "Many professional theologians have begun viewing theology less as an elucidation of doctrine and more as a prophetic and transformative exercise affecting persons or communities."[5] If theology has to be meaningful, appropriate, prophetic and transformative for a given community, then the method followed in theologizing must give due importance to the history of the people of that community. Some remarks on 'history' are, therefore, called for.

History in Theological Method

Any serious theology must give due importance to history because, as Gustavo Gutierrez so convincingly puts it, "If all that is human is illuminated by the Word, it is precisely because the Word reaches us through human history; von Rad comments that 'it is in history that God reveals the secret of his person.' Human history, then, is the location of our encounter with him, in Christ."[6] Therefore, theological method must include history in it.[7]

There has been, and there still is, a tendency among people to compartmentalize human life into the 'sacred' and the 'secular'. However, as Mathew Paikada rightly points out, there is only one human history. "There are no two histories for people, one secular history and another sacred or salvation history."[8] Further, the past seems to hold such a strong fascination for many people, that they glorify it as being so golden that they become overly critical of the present, and pessimistic of the future. On the other hand, as Mathew Paikada correctly reminds us, "At the same time the strength of history is in its orientation to the future."[9] In the context of postmodern theology, the importance of history for understanding the present[10] and being open to the future,[11] is also highlighted. Going further, Stephen Bevans highlights that which is theologically even more profound: "If the ordinary things of life are so transparent of God's presence, one can speak of culture and events in history — of contexts — as truly sacramental, and so revelatory."[12]

Jon Sobrino draws our attention to the great importance of the present: "Our theology takes the present moment very seriously as God's self-manifestation. This means that it pays great attention to the signs of the times."[13] The question arises as to how to understand this present 'now': Is this 'now' a single 'now' or a succession of 'nows'? Bernard Lonergan answers: "There results what is called the psychological present, which is not an instant, a mathematical point, but a time-span, so that our experience of time is, not of a raceway of instants, but a now leisurely, a now rapid succession of overlapping time-spans."[14]

Talking specifically of history, Lonergan draws our attention to important aspects of it. "Again, besides the memories of each individual, there are the pooled memories of the group, their celebration in song and story, their preservation in written narratives, in coins and monuments and every other trace of the group's words and deeds left to posterity."[15] And also that we have to see both the positive and the negative. "In literary terms history is concerned with the drama of life, with what results through the characters, their decisions, their actions, and not only because of them but also because of their defects, their oversight, their failures to act."[16]

Bernard Lonergan enlightens us further on the distinction between 'Critical History' and 'Precritical History' and some of its dimensions:

> A first step towards understanding critical history lies in an account of precritical history. For it, then, the community is the conspicuous community, one's own. Its vehicle is narrative, an ordered recital of events. It recounts who did what, when, where, under what circumstances, from what motives, with what results. [...] The function of precritical history is to promote such knowledge and devotion. So it is never just a narrative of bald facts. It is *artistic*: it selects, orders, describes; it would awaken the reader's interest and sustain it; it would persuade and convince. Again, it is *ethical*: it not only narrates but also apportions praise and blame.

> It is *explanatory*: it accounts for existing institutions by telling of their origins and developments and by contrasting them with alternative institutions found in other lands. It is *apologetic*, correcting false or tendentious accounts of the people's past, and refuting the calumnies of neighboring peoples. Finally, it is *prophetic*: to hindsight about the past there is joined foresight on the future and there are added the recommendations of a man of wide reading and modest wisdom.[17]

Bernard Lonergan highlights, within critical history, the heuristic, selective, critical, constructive, and judicial aspects, but also, what he calls an "ecstatic aspect that eliminates previously entertained perspectives and opinions to replace them with the perspectives and views that emerge from the cumulative interplay of data, inquiry, insight, surmise, image, evidence."[18] It is in this manner, continues Lonergan, that critical history of itself moves to objective knowledge of the past, though it may be impeded by such factors as mistaken views on possibility, by mistaken or misleading value-judgments, by an inadequate world-view or standpoint or state of the question.

There is often characterization of some understandings of history as 'cyclic', others as 'linear', and some as pre-determined by fate. I fully agree with Sebastian Painadath:

> Neither a historical process nor a dialogical interaction evolves according to a fixed pattern, because human freedom is at work there. History is nowhere a purely linear movement in the sense of a uniform way of launching ahead, nor can it be understood exclusively in terms of a cyclic process of constant repetition of the foregone. The image of a spiral movement is more suited to describe the process of history, because it involves both the aspects of repetition and progress. However, the historical evolution of humankind is more than that. It takes place with a lot of ups-and-downs, with several moments of setback and new breakthrough.[19]

Let us now turn our attention to 'People's History'.

The Term 'People's History'

'People's history', or as some would term it 'history from below' or 'subaltern history', is a type of historical narrative which attempts to account for historical events from the perspective of common people rather than political and other, often famous, leaders.

'People's history' includes the stories of mass movements and of those considered to be 'outsiders' to 'normal history'. It embraces individuals and groups who were not incorporated in the traditional type of writing about history. In fact, the primary focus of people's history is on the disenfranchised, the oppressed, the poor, the unnoticed, and the forgotten people.[20]

Some refer to this type of history-writing as a 'revisionist' approach to writing history. They argue that the driving factor of history is the daily life of ordinary people, and their concerns. Those who propagate this theory of history are of the opinion that it is from the 'pushes and pulls' of the ordinary lives of the common people that major historical trends develop, and not because of the initiatives of the famous or 'great' people.[21]

Whatever be the truth or impact of a revisionist approach to history, it is worth noting that Howard Zinn's *A People's History of the United States*, published in 1980, did cause much interest in 'People's History'. Similarly, in India, Irfan Habib's *People's History of India* in several volumes, has led people to take special notice of this type of writing of history. Specially worth mentioning over here is Ranajit Guha's series on *Subaltern Studies*.[22] Similar attempts have been made for 'People's history' of Christianity.[23] In this context, Felix Wilfred's remarks on the conditions to be kept in mind, and the usefulness of a 'People's history' of Christians in India, is worth referring to.[24]

The purpose in this essay, is not to enter into a debate on the issue of people's history in the realm of history *per se*. Rather, the aim here is to see its importance for theological method in India, and its implications for the same.

Methodological Importance of 'People's History' in Theology

Theology can be categorized into different types of theology. For example, theology as faith-reflection on reality; theology as theological anthropology; theology as critical reflection on Christian praxis; theology as interpretation of the Christian story.[25] Each of these has its own method, and in each of these, history can be an element, but serving slightly different purposes. The justification for this comes from the fact that "All theologies, for that matter all knowledge and its communication, are historically, socially and culturally situated."[26]

Among the functions performed, and purposes served by theology are that it explains, analyses, elaborates and systematizes the faith and, thus, helps to understand and assimilate it better and better. Further, theology has interpretative and prophetic roles. The pastoral role of strengthening the faith and empowering Christian life is another important goal of theology. The goal of theologizing is not only the transformation of individual Christians and the renewal or reform of the Church, but also the transformation of the whole world into the Kingdom of God.[27]

What is to be noted here is that while theologizing, one needs to make clear what are the purposes that are intended. The method used must be adapted to the purpose intended, and resources, then, need to be used accordingly. The methodological significance of people's history is clearly shown in the following statement: "However, as Asian Christians, we do theology together with Asian realities as resources in so far as we discern in them God's presence, action and the work of the Spirit. [...] The cultures of peoples, the history of their struggles, [...] stories of oppressed people crying for justice, freedom, dignity, life and solidarity become resources of theology and assume methodological importance in our context."[28] From this it can be seen that people's history will be used accordingly as a resource for theologizing.

> Movements for social transformation in different areas of human life constitute another resource. All movements for social change and events marking such a change can be considered *loci theologici* in so far as they embody the commitment of people to transform themselves and society. This commitment manifests the Spirit's presence. The saga of human struggles for liberation becomes a significant

> contextual resource. In liberation movements there is an awakened consciousness and commitment to justice, dignity, freedom, solidarity and for the transformation of life and society. Reflection on these movements give birth to new theologies. Examples of this are the Minjung theology in Korea, the theology of struggle in the Philippines, Dalit theology in India."[29]

It is worth noting that one need not limit oneself to a "Catholic" or "Christian" people's history alone. "One of the primary resources of theology is people and their experience. God's self-gift or self-communication or revelation is directed to all people, irrespective of caste, creed and nationality." In fact, the experiences of different peoples can enrich one another: "The different peoples in the world, the diverse ways God spoke to them, acted in their histories, and the diverse ways they responded to God's self-communication and actions are important resources of theology."[30] Further, some people think that only that history of people, which happened long ago in the past, as recorded in Scripture, is guided by God, and a resource for theology, and other histories of people cannot be used as a resource for theology. Such thinking is not theologically tenable: "If in the past God initiated and guided the people's movements for freedom, justice, equality and fellowship, He will do the same today also, because God is the same yesterday, today and tomorrow." The theological basis for people's history is clear. "These movements generally stand for freedom, justice, and equal dignity of all God's people and for the sustenance and protection of God's world. God's word resounds in a special way in the voice of the marginalized."[31] Further, as *Gaudium et spes* (GS) 4 points out, this becomes a duty for theologians: "the Church has always had the duty of scrutinizing the signs of the times and of interpreting them in the light of the Gospel."

Examples from people's histories, of 'Movements of Special Importance' serve as powerful resources in the methodology of theology. One clear example is from 'Women's Movements'. "They struggle not only for justice, equality and rights but also for a new vision of society, a wholeness in human relationships. This includes a critique of the existing society, its institutions and arrangements with a vision to move towards a just, humane, participatory, compassionate, peaceful world." Another clear example is from 'Tribal Movement'. "Another resource for theology is found in the various Tribal movements. Tribal peoples are struggling to protect their identity, their value heritage, and their rights in situations where they are exploited, displaced and marginalised [...]". Yet another would be 'Ecological Movements'.[32]

People's history, characterized by 'Peoples' Movements', is the indication of the presence and action of the Holy Spirit to bring about the Kingdom of God.

> Peoples' movements for human rights, workers' movements, etc., develop stories of people's struggles for a new humanity and are important signs of the times which we have to interpret theologically for the mission of God's Kingdom. [...] It is the liberating and transforming presence and action of God and His Spirit in the cosmos and in history that makes contextual realities theological resources. [...] Christians affirm that God is the Lord of history. This means that God, who created the universe and humankind, is present and active in and through His Spirit in the whole gamut of human history leading all to the eschaton of God's kingdom.[33]

Within people's history, the poor have a special place. This must be given due importance in the methodology for theology for the following reason: "Liberation theologians today speak of the *epistemological privilege of the poor*. It means that as God is present and active in a special way among the poor and that they are the beloved of God, and as the poor totally depend on God's benevolence, they have a better chance to know more about God."[34]

Further, history must by "reread" from the point of view of the poor: "The locus of our encounter with the Father of Jesus Christ is the concrete history of men and women. And in Jesus Christ we proclaim to all men and women that Father's love. We have called this history one of conflict. But there is more to it than that. We have also to insist that history—where God reveals himself, and where we proclaim him—must be reread from the viewpoint of the poor [...]" The main reason for this is that up to now, history has not been seen from their view-point, but from the standpoint of the powerful, because the oppressor has a hidden agenda: "History has been written from the viewpoint of the dominating sectors. We have a clear example of this in the history of Latin America and Peru. The perspective of history's vanquished is something else again. But history's winners have sought to wipe out their victims' memory of the struggle, so as to be able to snatch from them one of their sources of energy and will in history: a source of rebellion."[35]

The consequence of this will be a new way of living Christian lives, which is more true to what Jesus Christ intended. "For many a Latin American Christian, new involvement in the popular struggles for liberation has been, and is, the beginning of a new way of living, sharing, and celebrating the faith."[36] This now brings us to a practical question, as to who theologizes, especially where people's history is concerned.

Who Theologizes?

Traditionally it has been professional theologians who have been theologizing. The reasons for this have been that theology requires specialized knowledge, long training, skills of philosophy and other disciplines, etc. On the other hand, simple logic would dictate that methodologically it seems natural that the people most affected, and who are the principal stake-holders, must be the ones to theologize. What then of the professional theologian? His or her role will largely be that of a facilitator. Stephen Bevans has put it very aptly:

> If theology is truly to take culture and cultural change seriously, it must be understood as being done most fully by the subjects and agents of culture and cultural change. The process of contextualization, says Peter Schineller, is too complex and important to be left to professional theologians. The role of the trained theologian (the minister, the theology teacher) is that of articulating more clearly what the people

> are generally or vaguely expressing, deepening their ideas by providing them with the wealth of the Christian tradition, and challenging them to broaden their horizons by presenting them with the whole of Christian theological expression.[37]

The question then arises as to whether a rank outsider, one who may have had no personal experience of the situation, be part of the theologizing process. From one point of view, the answer would be 'no', because the person does not fully share the experience of that context. On another level, to some extent, and in limited ways, people who do not fully share the experience of the other can contribute to the development of a contextual theology. For example, an outsider can see things which an insider may not see. Sometimes the outsider can provide a kind of counterpoint by his or her critique of a particular culture or situation. Further, a non-stake holder is sometimes better able than the people involved, to see the weaknesses or negative elements present in the context. Also, the person from outside can stimulate people to do their own theological thinking, especially when he or she thinks so differently, that this difference itself is striking for the people concerned.[38]

In a multi-religious context like India, especially when the stake-holders include people of different religions it is imperative that theologizing be done by people of all the faiths involved.[39] Depending on the context, the theologian can play different roles of facilitator, interpreter, stimulator, reviser, challenger, supporter, insight-provider, and so on. This now brings us to several implications that people's history has for a theological method in India.

Implications For Theological Method in India

Taking off from where the previous section had ended, it is necessary that 'who' theologizes be made clear in any theological method for India. In fact, the problem gets compounded by those who insist that it is impossible to have an "Indian" theological method, given the sheer diversity of India. The only viable answer seems to be: the stake-holders, the community involved, and competent professional theologians together. If the professional theologians are not stake-holders themselves, then their role will be mainly as facilitators, not principal agents. If this be the case, one could ask, whether one could have an "Indian" theological method, because there are so many varieties of stake-holders. The answer would be clear if one homogenous group were involved, for example, Dalits alone of a particular place. However, this is not the case most of the time. Even Dalits of the whole of India is not a homogenous category, because the situation of Dalits varies from place to place in India. Further, people's history involves many different types of stake-holders.[40] It is clear from all this that it is not possible to have one single "Indian" theological method. Yet it would be 'Indian' as it is 'by, of and for Indians'.

Related to this is the question of pressure upon Indians to conform to standards set from outside India, especially Western standards of theologizing, or criteria imposed which are alien or inimical to the Indian context, with all the more reason when our people's history is a constitutive element of our theological method. Our theological methods should not be determined or pressurized in any way by the West[41] or anybody or anything else. By extension, pressure groups even within India, which are detrimental to the welfare of India as a whole, are to be exposed and resisted.

People's history brings very powerfully to the fore the millions who suffer, and who are either totally ignored, or given mere lip service, very specially those who have been disregarded by 'traditional' history. Some of these can be identified in 'groups' like slum dwellers, child laborers in production centres, exploited factory workers, etc. There are others who are so scattered and alone that it is almost impossible to even contact them. These include domestic workers, non-school going children, migrant laborers, etc. There are millions of people in India who are hungry, undernourished, without basic necessities like drinking water, and primary medical care. There are millions of women who have to carry water for very long distances every day, blow into smoke-choking cooking fire-places day-after-day for years on end. Our theologizing must look into how all these people can be helped in their needs, and shown they are equally loved children of God as other persons. Questions must also be raised as to why history has been silent about them so long and what this silence conveys, why these people have been neglected for so long, what keeps them ignored, what needs to be done to reverse this and see that in the future this will not happen. They must be given a chance to speak, to change their horrible situation in ways that maintain their human dignity and self-respect. Further, groups that work with them and for them, must be part of the theologizing process. There is also need to look into 'micro histories', oral histories, and traditions which have no written records. Greater place must be given to what affects the 'common' man, woman and child. Due consideration must be given to those who are exploited, terrorized, cheated and victimized in any way.

Methodologically speaking, people's history (as enunciated above in this paper) has been given pride of place by liberation theology, more than any other type of theology. It must continue to be so. In India, one could speak of liberation for women, Dalits, Tribals, etc., as coming within the ambit of Indian liberation theology. As theology, liberation theology has come under severe attack, but on many counts this attack was unjustified, as George Soares-Prabhu so brilliantly points out: "Liberation theology is an instructive example. When it first appeared it was dismissed by theologians in the West as theologically inadequate". Reasons given were: its inverted method, where theology follows praxis; its unashamed bias for the poor; its strong pastoral orientation, a theology of the people, by the people, for the people; and a dangerous liaison with Marxism. "Since then it has developed into one of the most consistent, effective and influential systems of Christian theology existing in the world today. Liberation theology has achieved a rigour and a hermeneutical self-awareness that far exceeds anything found in the West."[42]

Our theological method must make clear our orientations and purposes; become aware of our biases and prejudices; etc. There are other questions to be asked as well: Are we being prophetic? Supportive to those who need our support? Is our theologizing aware of all the necessary elements of our context? Is it relevant, adaptive as needed? Any theological method must have the elements mentioned in this paragraph. With added reason, in the context of people's history these elements get sharpened even more, because these people have been neglected up to now.

Another dimension that any methodology must cater to, is the question of criteria to judge the correctness of a local theological expression. Robert Schreiter gives five criteria for this. One, inner consistency; two, to be able to be translated into worship; three, orthopraxis; four, open to criticism from other churches; five, able to challenge other theologies.[43] From the Indian context one could add other criteria like: there must be openness, in fact, positive attitude towards all people, religions, cultures, diversities; and in the context of people's history, priority to the poor, the marginalized, the exploited and the voiceless.

GS 40 puts before us the task of humanizing not only our own country, but the whole of humankind – "Thus through her individual members and her whole community, the Church believes she can contribute greatly toward making the family of human beings and its history more human." Therefore, our theological method must be a factor in this task. People's history reminds us that there are many things in our country that need to be made more human. We need to respond to our context of so much discrimination, of caste, gender, etc.; marked by colonialism, and the vestiges that still remain; in the ambit of globalization; etc. Further, we need to check whether our theologizing is marked by too much apologetics or self-defence in the face of threats of all kinds.

Sensitivity to people's history, reminds us of the type of response we have to make within the Indian context. To illustrate with an example: to respond to the need of greater spiritual awareness, and contemplation in particular, ashram life, for example, may be suitable, and even necessary, for some. This however, cannot be generalized for all. For those who need to maintain the liberative and prophetic dimensions of their life, ashram life may blunt, not help these dimensions.[44]

As Errol D'Lima rightly points out, "Such theologizing will include – among other prophetic actions – *Chipko*-style pressure group, demonstrations, *dharnas*, Gandhian-style fasting and non-cooperation, sit-ins and strikes coupled with prayer and discernment." And also that: "Peoples' theology has to do with the events of daily life that shape peoples' expectations and hopes that encourage introspection and suggests change. In short, peoples' theology does not require high-level speculation that is often found in classical theology."[45]

In the context of people's history, our theologizing must give priority to the present, as Jon Sobrino so aptly points out: "To accept the signs of the times as the basis of one's theology means that theology, in its role as *theory*, must give priority of the present over the past, to reality over texts, although one must understand this well." The reason for giving priority to the present is to avoid fixating God's action only in the past: "as if God had been acting at the origins alright, but would thereafter ignore his creation."[46]

The following caution of Jon Sobrino would be valid in our theological method as well: "This leads us to a theme that is not often treated in theological reflection: the sinfulness of theology and its need of conversion. [...] The most fundamental sin of the intellect is to imprison or suppress the truth."[47] We need to ask often enough whether we are consciously or unconsciously ignoring or omitting important dimensions. This is pertinent in the light of people's history where millions have been neglected for centuries.

Conclusion

It would be good to end this paper by reminding ourselves of Jon Sobrino's exhortation that our theology has to be '*intellectus amoris*', or understanding of love, along with being an understanding of faith.[48] Probably the biggest incentive for us to include people's history in our theological method is the presence of the Lord in the very least, the so-called lowliest in human society, who is hungry, sick, lonely and in most need of our attention, care and above all, actually manifested loving concern.

Endnotes

1. J. J. Mueller, *What Are They Saying About Theological Method?* (New York/Ramsey: Paulist Press, 1984). Mueller gives a separate chapter on each of these four methods in this book.
2. Oliver D. Crisp, "On Analytic Theology," in *Analytic Theology: New Essays in the Philosophy of Theology*, ed. Oliver D. Crisp and Michael C. Rea (Oxford: Oxford University Press, 2009). On page 33 Crisp writes, "However, there is also a preponderance of work dealing with questions of theological method,

one central aspect of traditional theological prolegomena". On page 35 Crisp talks of "scholastic theological method".

3. Fernando Canale, "Interdisciplinary Method in Christian Theology? In Search of a Working Proposal," *Neue Zeitschrift Für Systematische Theologie Und Religionsphilosophie* 43, No. 3 (2001): 366-367. "Some of the more notable contributors to the current debate on theological method are John Macquarrie (1966), Thomas F. Torrance (1969), Rene Latourelle (1969), Jose Miguez Bonino (1975), Gerhard Ebeling (1975), Gordon D. Kaufman (1975), Wolfhart Pannenberg (1976), Bernard Lonergan (1979), Randy L. Maddox, (1984), David Tracy (1988), a group of Evangelical theologians (1991), Oswald Bayer (1991) and Avery Dulles (1992)" [references are provided for each of these] ... "Among the confessional approaches it is possible to recognize the Roman Catholic and Protestant views on theological methodology."
4. Bernard Lonergan, *Method in Theology* (New York: Herder and Herder, 1972), xi.
5. Errol D'Lima, "Doing Peoples' Theology," in *Indian Theology Seeking New Horizons,* ed. Kuncheria Pathil and Mathew Paikada (Mumbai: The Bombay Saint Paul Society, 2007), 64.
6. Gustavo Gutierrez, *A Theology of Liberation: History, Politics and Salvation,* Trans. and ed. Sister Caridad Inda and John Eagleson (Maryknoll, New York: Orbis Books, 1973), 189. The entire chapter ten of this book is on "Encountering God in History".
7. Lonergan, *Method in Theology*. Lonergan devotes the whole of eighth chapter of this book to history.
8. Mathew Paikada, "Memory of Suffering – A Theological Investigation from the Subaltern Perspective," in *Indian Theology Seeking New Horizons,* ed. Pathil & Paikada, 286.
9. Ibid., 287.
10. Mieke Bal, "Postmodern Theology as Cultural Analysis" in *The Blackwell Companion to Postmodern Theology*, ed. Graham Ward (Oxford: Blackwell Publishing Ltd, 2005), 5. "The importance of history lies not in attempts to reconstruct the past but in understanding the present".
11. Stanley Hauerwas, "The Christian Difference, or Surviving Postmodernism" in *The Blackwell Companion,* ed. Graham Ward, 157. Fn. 15: "Boyle suggests that in postmodernity a history that refers to the past has come to an end in favor of history that only names an unrealized future".
12. Stephen B. Bevans, *Models of Contextual Theology* (Maryknoll, New York: Orbis Books, 1992), 9.
13. Jon Sobrino, "Theology in the Third World – Reflections from El Salvador," in *Bread and Breath: Essays in Honour of Samuel Rayan, SJ*, ed. T. K. John (Anand: Gujarat Sahitya Prakash, 1991), 30.
14. Lonergan, *Method in Theology,* 177.
15. Ibid.

16. Ibid., 179.
17. Ibid., 185.
18. Ibid., 195.
19. Painadath, "Dynamics of a Culture of Dialogue," 281-282.
20. Sathianathan Clarke, "Subalterns, Identity Politics and Christian theology in India," in *Christian Theology in Asia*, ed. C. H. Kim (Cambridge: Cambridge University Press, 2008), 279. "In a sense the Subaltern Collective engenders an alternate perspective that puts common people back into historical narratives. Subalterns 'constitute the mass of the labouring population' as distinguished from the elite in India." Sathianathan Clarke gives reference to Ranajit Guha, 'Introduction', in *A Subaltern Studies Reader: 1986–1995,* ed. Ranajit Guha (New Delhi: Oxford University Press, 1998), xiv-xv.
21. *The Encyclopedia Britanica* (Deluxe Edition 2007) in its article on "Revisionism" states that this term was applied at the end of the 19th century to revise Marxist doctrine. The *Wikipedia* website gives details about 'historical revisionism' and 'revisionist historians'.
22. Ranajit Guha, ed., *Subaltern Studies: Writings on South Asian History and Society.* Vol. 1 (Delhi: Oxford University Press, 1982). Guha edited seven volumes in this series.
23. Denis R. Janz, general editor, *A People's History Of Christianity: The Lived Religion of Christians In the First Two Thousand Years*, Vols. I-VII (Minneapolis: Fortress Press, 2005-2008).
24. Felix Wilfred, "Historiography of Indian Christianity: Some Reflections", *Vidyajyoti: Journal of Theological Reflection,* 73, no.10 (October 2009): 739. "A reconstruction of the history in relation to the life of the people in its diverse dimensions is a challenging but a very rewarding task. This will bring about a history of Christianity in its context, and the context is much wider than the Church-context."
25. Kuncheria Pathil and Dominic Veliath, *An Introduction to Theology* (Bangalore: Theological Publications in India, 2005), 14-20.
26. Ibid., 26.
27. Ibid., 34-37.
28. Franz-Josef Eilers, ed., *For All the Peoples of Asia. Federation of Asian Bishops' Conferences Documents from 1997 to 2011*, Vol. 3 (Quezon City: Claretian Publications, 2002), 355.
29. Ibid., 359.
30. For this quote as well as the previous one, see, Kuncheria Pathil and Dominic Veliath, *An Introduction to Theology,* 73-74.
31. For this quote as well as the previous one, see, Ibid., 80.
32. For all the quotes in this paragraph, see, Franz-Josef Eilers, ed., F*or All the Peoples of Asia,* 359-360.
33. Franz-Josef Eilers, ed. , *For All The Peoples of Asia,* 362-364.
34. Kuncheria Pathil and Dominic Veliath, *An Introduction to Theology*, 81.

35. Gustavo Gutierrez, *A Theology of Liberation*, 20. The quotes in this paragraph are from this page.
36. Ibid., 169.
37. Stephen B. Bevans, *Models of Contextual Theology,* 13.
38. Ibid., 13-16.
39. Errol D'Lima, "Doing Peoples' Theology," 68. "A peoples' theology must be pursued in a community that is (religion-wise) pluriform."
40. George Soares-Prabhu, "From Alienation to Inculturation – Some Reflections on Doing Theology in India Today," in *Bread and Breath*, ed. T. K. John, 91. In a context involving Catholics alone, George Soares-Prabhu's solution seems the most viable one, when he says that the locus "will be the 'local church', which I understand not in the juridical sense of a diocese, but in its proper theological meaning of a Christian community with a cultural identity of its own. With its many sub-cultures (a tribal culture, a dalit culture, a Westernized urban culture) all existing under the over-arching unity of their 'Indianness', the Church in India might have several such related 'local churches'."
41. Ibid., 92: "Theology in India, then, must distance itself from the West. It must resist the temptation to imitate accepted Western models of theologizing and refuse to be intimidated by Western expectations of what theology should be." And speaking of the Indian theologian, "It is the people's concerns that he voices, their problems that he takes up. Not only his theology, then, but his theologizing too must be Indian. That is, its Indianness must show itself not only in its content but in its method as well." On page 95 he says, "Theology in India must be careful not to be led into the wilderness of such academic irrelevance by hearkening to the repeated demands for professionalism and academic excellence addressed to it by its Western overseers."
42. George Soares-Prabhu, "From Alienation to Inculturation", 93. The previous quote is also from here.
43. Robert J. Schreiter, *Constructing Local Theologies* (Maryknoll, New York: Orbis Books, 1985), 117-121.
44. George Soares-Prabhu, "From Alienation to Inculturation," 96.
45. Errol D'Lima, "Doing Peoples' Theology," 72-73. Both quotes in this paragraph are from here.
46. Jon Sobrino, "Theology in the Third World – Reflections from El Salvador," in *Bread and Breath: Essays in Honour of Samuel Rayan, SJ*, ed. T. K. John (Anand: Gujarat Sahitya Prakash, 1991), 34-35. Both quotes in this paragraph are from here.
47. Ibid., 49.
48. Ibid., Pages 37 to 45 are on the sub-heading "Theology as an '*intellectus amoris*'".

Bibliography

Bevans, Stephen B. *Models of Contextual Theology.* New York: Orbis Books, 1992.

Clarke, Sathianathan. "Subalterns, Identity Politics and Christian theology in India." In *Christian Theology in Asia.* ed. C. H. Kim. 271-290. Cambridge: Cambridge University Press, 2008.

D'Lima, Errol. "Doing Peoples' Theology." In *Indian Theology Seeking New Horizons.* ed. Kuncheria Pathil and Mathew Paikada. Mumbai : The Bombay Saint Paul Society, 2007.

Eilers, Franz-Josef, ed. *For All the Peoples of Asia: Federation of Asian Bishops' Conferences Documents From 1997 To 2011.* Vol. 3 (Quezon City : Claretian Publications, 2002).

Guha, Ranajit. ed. *Subaltern Studies: Writings on South Asian History and Society.* Vol. 1. Delhi: Oxford University Press, 1982.

Gutierrez, Gustavo. *A Theology of Liberation: History, Politics and Salvation.* Trans. and ed. Sister Caridad Inda and John Eagleson. New York: Orbis Books, 1973.

----------. *The Power Of The Poor In History.* Trans. Robert R. Barr. London: SCM Press, 1983.

John, T. K., ed. *Bread and Breath: Essays in Honour of Samuel Rayan, SJ,* Anand: Gujarat Sahitya Prakash, 1991.

Lonergan, Bernard. *Method in Theology.* New York: Herder and Herder, 1972.

Mueller, J. J. *What Are They Saying About Theological Method?.*New York/Ramsey: Paulist Press, 1984.

Paikada, Mathew. "Memory of Suffering – A Theological Investigation from the Subaltern Perspective." In *Indian Theology Seeking New Horizons.* ed. Kuncheria Pathil and Mathew Paikada. Mumbai: St. Paul's, 2007.

Painadath, Sebastian. "Dynamics of a Culture of Dialogue." In *Bread and Breath: Essays in Honour of Samuel Rayan, SJ,* ed. T. K. John. Anand: Gujarat Sahitya Prakash, 1991.

Pathil, Kuncheria and Dominic Veliath. *An Introduction To Theology.* Bangalore: Theological Publications in India, 2005.

Pathil, Kuncheria and Mathew Paikada. ed. *Indian Theology Seeking New Horizons.* Mumbai: St. Paul's, 2007.

Rahner, Karl. *Foundations of Christian Faith: An Introduction to the Idea of Christianity.* New York: Seabury Press, 1978.

Schreiter, Robert J. *Constructing Local Theologies.* New York: Orbis Books, 1985.

Soares-Prabhu, George. "From Alienation to Inculturation – Some Reflections on Doing Theology in India Today." In *Bread and Breath: Essays in Honour of Samuel Rayan, SJ,* ed. T. K. John. Anand: Gujarat Sahitya Prakash, 1991.

Sobrino, Jon. "Theology in the Third World – Reflections from El Salvador." In *Bread and Breath: Essays in Honour of Samuel Rayan, SJ,* ed. T. K. John. Anand: Gujarat Sahitya Prakash, 1991.

Wilfred, Felix. "Historiography of Indian Christianity. Some Reflections." *Vidyajyoti: Journal of Theological Reflection.* 73, No.10 (October 2009): 737-751.

Chapter 7

A Feminist Theological Method for India

Dance of Emancipation, Empowerment and Enabling

Evelyn Monteiro, SCC

Introduction

Echoes of feminist theological voices have been heard since, at least, the late 1960s in North America and Europe. Since then, there has been a development of a steadily growing field of feminist theology in Africa, Asia and Latin America. To date, Asian feminist theology has advanced considerably and strong evidence of this is provided by the existence of the Asian feminist theological journal *In God's Image*, which is more than 25 years old. But the emergence of feminist theology in India is of more recent origin and Indian women's theological work is generally less known than that of other Asian feminists, such as Kwok Pui-lan (Hong Kong), Marianne Katoppo (Indonesia), Chung Hyun Kyung (Korea), Virginia Fabella (Phillippines) and of Latin American women like Ivone Gebara

(Brazil) and of Africa, Mercy Amba Oduyaye (Ghana) who have long been associated with liberation theology.

While several Indian women theologians like Aruna Gnanadason, Evangeline Anderson-Rajkumar and others have contributed towards Indian feminist theology, and in spite of the existence of the Indian Women Theological Forum (IWTF) since 2000, we have still not arrived at articulating a feminist theological method for India. This paper is an attempt to present one. The purpose of developing a feminist theological method for India is to include the feminist perspective as an integral and not *ad hoc* or secondary perspective in theological studies. Its inclusion will help construct a new way of being a participatory Church of equal discipleship and build a new society of integral human relationships.

This paper has four parts: The first deals with clarification of terms and traces the emergence of feminist theology in history. The second prepares the ground to articulate a feminist theological method for India. It begins with a brief explanation of critical pedagogy and its concerns, followed by a description of the characteristics common to most feminist theological methods. Features that are particularly distinct for Indian feminist hermeneutics are then underlined in the third part. Finally, the Dance of Emancipation, Empowerment and Enabling, a proposed feminist theological method for India is developed.

1. Clarification of Terms: Feminine/Femininity

Femininity (also called **womanliness**) refers to qualities and behaviors judged by a particular culture to be ideally associated with or especially appropriate to women and girls. Distinct from femaleness, which is a biological and physiological classification concerned with the reproductive system, femininity/womanliness principally refers to secondary sex characteristics and other behaviors and features generally regarded as being more prevalent and better suited to women, whether inborn or socialized. In traditional Western culture, such features include gentleness, patience, sensitivity and kindness. Femininity should not be confused with feminism, which is a movement aimed at establishing equal rights and legal protection for women.

Feminism

"Feminism," writes Evangeline Anderson-Rajkumar, "is that consciousness and sensitivity, which is developed within a man or a woman, to realize that "women" – as a class, caste, race and sex – have been discriminated, suppressed, denied of equal opportunities in life."[1] The term 'feminism' is used to describe a political, cultural or economic movement aimed at establishing equal rights and legal protection for women. Feminism involves political, cultural and sociological theories, as well as philosophies concerned with issues of gender difference. "Feminism is a critical stance that challenges the patriarchal gender paradigm that associates males with human characteristics defined as superior and dominant ... and females with those defined as inferior and auxiliary," affirms Rosemary Radford Ruether.[2]

Emergence of Feminist Theology

Feminists like Maggie Humm and Rebecca Walker situate the development of feminism in history in three waves. The first feminist wave saw its beginnings in the nineteenth and early twentieth centuries. It envisioned women as capable of participating in the public polis by voting responsibly. Facism and Stalinism stopped its spread during the 1930s. The second strong wave that emerged in the 1960s and 70s in the Western capitalist countries[3] sought civil rights and equality for women. The third wave of feminism that began in the 1990s considers seriously the differences in women's experiences and emphasizes justice for all women across the globe in order to reconstruct the gender paradigm and include women in full and equal humanity.[4] Feminist theory emerged from these feminist movements. It is manifested in a variety of disciplines such as feminist geography, feminist history, feminist literary criticism, and feminist theology.

Although the terms "feminism" and "feminist" did not gain widespread use until the 1970s, they were already used in public parlance much earlier.[5] With the collapse of European colonialism in Africa, Latin America and Asia, women in former European colonies and the Third World have proposed "Post-colonial" and "Third World" feminisms.[6]

Feminist

Who is a feminist? One who is ideologically and existentially committed to women's issues in society is a feminist. This implies that both men and women, irrespective of class, caste, creed, culture and race can be feminists. A feminist makes concerted and consistent efforts to eradicate patriarchy, prevalent in various forms and expressions as a gender discriminatory system in order to build an egalitarian society.[7]

Feminist Theology

Feminist theology is a movement found in several religions, including Buddhism, Christianity, Judaism, and Islam to reconsider the traditions, practices, scriptures, and theologies of those religions from a feminist perspective. Some of the goals of feminist theology include increasing the role of women in the clerical and religious hierarchical order, reinterpreting male-dominated imagery and language about God, determining women's place in relation to career and motherhood, and studying images of women in the sacred texts of religions.[8]

Feminist theology attempts to consider every aspect of religious thought and practice. Some of the questions that feminist theologians raise are:

- **How do we do theology?** Many feminist theologians assert that personal experience can be an important component of insight into the divine, along with the more traditional sources of holy books or received tradition.
- **Who is God?** Feminist theologians have supported the use of non or multi-gendered language for God, arguing that language powerfully impacts belief about the nature and essence of God. They also seek to reconstruct the basic theological symbols of God, creation, sin and redemption,

and the church, in order to define these symbols in a gender inclusive and egalitarian way. They recognize that symbols are social constructs and not eternally disclosed from beyond.

- **Where are women in religious history?** Feminist historical theologians study the roles of women in periods throughout history that have impacted religion. The work of these scholars has helped feminist theologians claim historical figures as their predecessors in feminist theology. Elizabeth Cady Stanton produced *The Woman's Bible* (1895), excising the traditional Christian text of all references she thought contradicted the positions of women's rights.

Emergence of Christian Feminist Theology: A Brief Historical Overview

In the Developed Countries

The major emergence of feminist theology dates back to the late 1960s in the United States.[9] Two developments supported the emergence of a more fully developed feminist theology: First, the civil rights and anti-war movements brought a wide-ranging critique of racial, class and militarist patterns. Secondly, women in the Christian Churches, particularly in liberal Protestantism, gradually acquired access to theological education and ministry from the late 19th century. By the 1970s, the opening of ordination to Christian women increased the number of women students in theological schools. The increasing number of women as students, ministers and teachers in Christian Churches paved the way for feminism to be translated into feminist theology. During this period Catholic feminist theologians such as Mary Daly, Rosemary Radford Ruether, Elisabeth Schüssler Fiorenza, Mary Jo Weaver, Elizabeth Johnson and Susan Ross also emerged as equal participants in feminist theology.

By the late 1970s and early 80s, an adequate number of feminist theologians were established on teaching faculties of theological schools.[10]American feminist theology was gradually diversifying as African American, Hispanic, and Asian women also engaged in theological pursuits. African American, Hispanic and Asian women began to articulate their distinctive theological voices. African American women have claimed the name of 'Womanist theology' for their theological perspective, rooted in sexism and racism of the American society. Hispanic women also began to claim their theological voice out of their cultural context, coining the name 'Hispanic women *mujerista*' theology. Many Hispanic and Asian women have become 'cross border' theologians. Mexican Maria Pilar Aquino calls herself Latina Feminist and Asian-American feminist theologians, Kwok Pui-Lan (Hong Kong) and Chung Hyun Kyung (Korea), teach and write more from their Asian contexts.[11]

Feminist theology of the 60s increasingly reflects cultural diversity and new dimensions of social concerns. Ecological crisis reshaped the way feminists look at human-nature relations, causing many feminist theologians to write from an eco-feminist perspective. Ruether and Daly had such concerns already in the early 1970s.

Feminist Theology in the Third World

The 1980s saw a vigorous development of feminist theology in Latin America, Asia and Africa. Latin American feminism focused on issues of sexuality, civil and reproductive rights and violence against women. It had a secular and anti-clerical stance against Roman Catholic dominance. In the late 1960s, Latin American theologians like Gustavo Gutierrez, Jon Sobrino and Leonardo Boff developed a liberation theology that centred on poverty, economic dependency and neo-colonial domination. These liberation theologians ignored gender issues and were oblivious to racial and caste subcultures, indigenous peoples, and Africans and Asians.

African and Asian theologians questioned the Latin American emphasis on class analysis and economic exploitation and argued for the need to discuss religious and cultural plurality. Women theologians like Mercy Amba Oduyoye, Virginia Fabella and Mary John Manazan, Marianne Katoppo, Sun Ai Park and Ivone Gebara challenged the lack of attention to gender issues in liberation theology. In 1983 at a joint meeting of the Ecumenical Association of Third World Theologians (EATWOT) and First World liberation theologians in Geneva, women theologians from all continents supported the demand of Third World women for attention to gender issues. Thus, the Women's Commission of EATWOT was founded. It supported the Third World Women to contextualize their own theological reflections in their national and regional situations.[12]

In their struggle against Western neo-colonialism in the 1960s, African and black theological movements focused on integrating values of traditional African cultures into biblical hermeneutics and Christian theology. However, as in Latin America, women and gender issues were ignored.

African women theologians have claimed their distinctive voice on the themes of inculturation and liberation. They question the romanticisation of traditional African cultures that oppress women and critique traditional practices such as polygamy and menstrual taboos, the women's work-roles, sexuality, reproduction and family life. Other areas of concern that have also dehumanized women are the treatment of widows and inheritance, belief in evil spirits and the use of women as witches in times of misfortune. They also critique the sexism of Christian tradition and its alliance with colonialism, but find positive resources in it for women's emancipation. African women attempt to recover areas of empowerment for women in traditional culture, as cult leaders and healers, as liberators in myth and folklore. They reread Christian themes of Jesus, the liberator of the poor and oppressed and the Church as redemptive hope for a new era of justice from an African women's perspective.[13]

Asian Women's Theology

Asian women theology has a history that goes back to the early 1980s. Many Asian women theologians prefer to call their work Asian women's theology instead of feminist theology because of its negative connotations of a militant, separatist and man-hating stance. Asian women's theology is understood not only as a form of theological reflection but also as a political movement to transform the church and society by fully recognizing women's freedom and dignity.[14]

Asian women's theology that is shaped by its fascinating multilingual, multireligious and multiracial context is pluralistic and multivocal, woven out of many distinct strands. There is no one way of doing Asian women's theology and today, increasing attention is given to both the commonalities as well as the distinct differences in the Asian contexts. Asian women have strong networks in several countries, especially in the Philippines, Korea and India and their valuable contribution to Asian theology is globally recognized.

The struggle against dictatorship in Korea sparked the Korean liberation theology movement, '*Minjung*' (People's) theology in the 1960s. Male *Minjung* theologians ignored gender issues which the Korean women addressed by developing their own networks for theological reflection and action. Korean Christian women have taken up several issues specific to their history: the reunification of North and South Korea and the abuse of women as sex-tourist trade. The well known Korean feminist theologian, Chung Hyun Kyung particularly focuses her writings on the theme of *han* (repressed anger emerging from unjustified suffering) and the healing of women from their particular suffering. Sun Ai Park, an ordained Korean woman started the first Asian women's theological journal, *In God's Image* in 1982. In 1988 she founded the Asian Women's Resource Center for Culture and Theology for publication and the organization of conferences.

In the Philippines, feminist theologians have developed a feminist reading of the theology of struggle that emerged in the people's fight against decades of dictatorial regime and economic oppression. They reclaim pre-colonial Filipino myth and stories that empower women.

In 2002, Ecclesia of Women in Asia (EWA), a forum for Catholic women doing theology in Asia was founded.[15] Catholic women theologians, both grassroots and academic, meet every two years for the EWA conference and four volumes of the conference papers have already been published: *Ecclesia of Women: Gathering the Voices of Women in Asia,*[16] *Body and Sexuality: Theological-Pastoral Perspectives of Women in Asia,*[17] *Re-imagining Marriage and Family in Asia: Asian Christian Women's Perspectives,*[18] and *Practicing Peace: Towards an Asian Feminist Theology of Liberation.*[19]

Feminist Movements and Feminist Theology in India

It would be helpful to trace the origin of the phase of women's movement in India to understand the development of feminist theology in India. The women's movement in India can be traced to the 1940s and the Telungana Peasant uprising in British India. Women organized themselves to fight against the triple oppression they experienced – economic exploitation, bonded labour they shared with the men in their communities and sexual violence they were particularly vulnerable to. The British suppressed the Telungana Movement and with it any revolt by women.[20] The policies of the so called 'moderates' in the Indian National Congress had tried some social reforms for women, and later Gandhi himself rallied women to the national cause. After a brief spell of organized strength by middle and upper class women, during the freedom struggle, women retreated to the hidden life of their homes till the 1970s.[21]

The present phase of women's movement was sparked off with the rape of a 14 year old girl by two policemen in a lockup in Maharashtra in 1978. Since then, what began as an urban/middle class movement has now moved into rural India. In 1982 and 1986, there were strong protests by rural women in Madurai and Patna (Bihar) against issues such as unequal wages, violence against women, women and health. The anti-Brahmin movements in Maharashtra and Tamil Nadu linked women's liberation with anti-caste struggles. The Marxists also endeavoured to integrate women into the class struggle.

Today women movements have gone far beyond traditional women's issues and are concerned about issues such as the impact of religious fundamentalism and communal violence, negative forces of science and technology and ecological destruction on women. Various feminist theories that have emerged in India recognize that the system of oppression and patriarchy is not just androcentricism or sexism. It is also a system of graded subjugation and hierarchical relationships which specifies women's oppression in terms of class, caste, race, religion and gender. The interlinking of all forms of oppression that women face within patriarchal structures is the basis of women's movement in India. The new feminist paradigm also takes into account the need to be in solidarity with all oppressed groups and to work with all progressive forces – peace movements, ecology movements, human rights groups and others.[22]

Feminist theology in India grew from women's movements in society and from a commitment to articulate the faith experience of Indian women as lived in the realities of their life. Female foeticide, dowry deaths and honour killing, sexual abuse and rape, domestic violence and wife battering, illiteracy within the complex framework of India's patriarchal and caste systems and its many religions and cultures have been particular concerns of Indian feminist theology. Feminist theology in India is supported by both women's movements at the grassroots level and women's studies in sociological and historical issues at universities.

While it is true that Indian women have not worked out a clearly defined Indian feminist hermeneutic, their contribution to theological development cannot be denied. Networks of feminist theology have developed among Catholics and Protestants in India. The All India Christian Women's Council and WINA (Women's Institute for New Awakening) have held conferences on feminist theology and sponsored research and publication. For the first time in its history, the Indian Theological Association focused on "Concerns of Women: An Indian Theological Response" as the theme of its annual seminar in 2004.[23]

The Indian Women Theological Forum (IWTF) meets every year to share experiences and discuss theological issues. Local groups, such as Satyashodak (Searchers for Truth) in Mumbai work on issues of women in the Church and society. The Lutheran Seminary in Gurukul has made both women and Dalit theology areas of particular attention. The United Theological College, Bangalore, has published several books on Feminist issues and concerns. The task of Indian women is to search for an Indian feminist hermeneutic that will enable the Church to become a new community in India.

This brief overview of the emergence of feminist theology in the last 50 years affirms that feminist theology has become global. Christian women theologians across the world are conscious of the need to critique common themes of sexist symbols in Christianity and to reconstruct the symbolism for God, Christ, humanity and nature, sin and salvation in order to affirm women's full humanity. Women theologians in each context are also attempting to develop a method to theologize on women's experience unique to their respective situations.

2. A Feminist Theological Method for India

Feminism and Critical Pedagogy

What is critical pedagogy? Critical pedagogy is "an effort to work within educational institutions to raise questions about inequalities of power, and about the way belief systems become internalized to the point where individuals and groups abandon the very aspiration to question or change their lot in life," explains Pushpa Joseph.[24] Some of the authors associated with this tradition include Paulo Freire, Peter Mclaren and Ira Shor.

In critical pedagogy, the critical person is one who seeks justice and emancipation. Following Marx's principle, the critical person not only seeks to recognize injustice but also works towards changing it. Critical pedagogues support those groups who are deprived of social, economic, and political possibilities. The emphases on change and on collective action to achieve it are primary concerns of critical pedagogy.[25]

Concerns of Critical Pedagogy

The major concern of critical pedagogy in Women's Studies is the development of a feminist critical consciousness. All feminist pedagogy and analysis, begins with the recognition of the oppressive relations in the patriarchal system, and one's own place in that system. The task of critical pedagogy is to make the members of the oppressed groups of women consciousness of their patriarchal[26] situation as a starting point of their liberative process. Changes in consciousness and concrete action are closely linked for feminists. The greatest barrier against the possibility of liberation is an ingrained belief and passive acceptance of the unjust status quo generated by male dominated structures.

For critical feminist pedagogy, critical reflection and interpretation of the world are not sufficient. One must also be willing and able to act to change that world. In feminist pedagogy changing thought and practice must occur together. Critical thinking requires reflection and action, interpretation and change. Critical consciousness in feminist parlance is brought about not through intellectual effort alone but through *praxis* – through the authentic union of action and reflection.[27]

Feminist critical pedagogy addresses two significant concerns affecting the lives of women – patriarchy and androcentrism. Patriarchy designates a gender biased social structure in which power is always in the hands of the dominant male and others are ranked in a descending graded series of subordinations. Religious patriarchy that is one of the strongest forms of this sexist graded structure claims to be divinely established. Consequently, it is claimed that the power of ruling men is delegated by God and exercised by divine mandate.

Androcentrism is a personal pattern of thinking and acting that makes the characteristics of ruling men the norm for all humanity. In theology, androcentrism ensures that ruling men determine the language not only about human nature, but also about God, sin and redemption. Androcentric thought legitimizes patriarchy and constructs the world in terms of language, mindset and imagery so as to marginalize women and justify structures that exclude them from full and equal participation.

Patriarchal ways of constructing power structures have ignored women's contributions in the academia, and society and the Church have repressed their authentic wisdom in patriarchal controlled communities. Feminist critical pedagogy aims to transform societal structures and androcentric linguistic patterns. It uses the tools of feminist hermeneutics to rediscover the lost literary, historical, cultural, religious and philosophical traditions of women.[28]

Some Common Characteristics of Feminist Theological Method

Feminist theology that originated in the First World is now taking roots in different countries and growing in different soils, all producing rich harvests of their own. While Indian feminist theology is diverse and distinct from the feminist theology of the West or any other feminist theology, it also shares a number of aspects with them. Some of the common elements are the following.

The Omni-relevance of Gender

Feminist pedagogical strategies focus on the significance of gender and gender asymmetry as a basic feature of all social life and texts. The dichotomies of the public and private realms have influenced our way of interpreting gender. The public world is associated with men, which is the world of activity, logic, reasoning, leadership, authority and culture. The private world of the home is associated with women and regarded as a place of reproduction, emotion, intuition and dependency.

Feminist pedagogy questions this dichotomy of private/public and reason/intuition that has influenced our interpretation of gender. Feminist interpreters of the Bible, for instance, affirm that every human is 'whole' before God and that both male and female are created in the image of God with the common mandate to multiply, fill the earth and care for it. Feminist theological method considers it mandatory to question those ideas and structures that impede the full humanity of all.[29]

Emphasis on Women's Experience

Feminist pedagogy challenges male viewpoint and masculine assumptions about the world. It questions the male experience as the defining experience of what it means to be human. All feminist hermeneutics have an experiential quality about them and affirm the unique experience of women as an important source of feminist theology. But feminist theologians have debated on how experience, given its diverse and changing nature, can be normative in feminist theology.

Rebecca Chopp distinguishes two epistemological approaches based on women's experiences: standpoint theory and social constructionism.[30] The stand point theory posits that women's knowing is ontologically different from men's and the social constructionist approach advocates that "knowledge is itself always historical, always related to power and interests, and is open to change and transformation."[31] The latter position does not universalize women's experience but rather emphasizes the diversity of their experiences.

Since women's experience is a social construct and is shaped by a complex interaction of factors, such as class, caste, race, ethnicity, culture, religious traditions and political systems, a woman's viewpoint always reflects her situation and perspective.[32] Because of the uniqueness of women's experience, feminist hermeneutics brings up the issue of women's voice, agency, identity and power in regard to every academic discipline.

Doing Theology from Below

Traditional hermeneutics is committed to being scientific and objective. Feminist scholars have recognized androcentric biases and patriarchal interests in such neutral interpretation. They have recognized that the classical, Western, colonial, feudalistic, elite and patriarchal theologies have inflicted much violence on women's life. Furthermore, these theologies have separated intellectual discipline from dehumanizing experiences of people and rational reflection of Christian faith from social action for justice. Feminist scholars challenge the norm of objectivity in such theologies which assume that the subject and object of research can be separated.

Embracing the relationship of mutuality and favouring the most oppressed and silenced in society, lead to replacing the 'view from above' with a 'view from below' that includes both scientific and ethical dimensions. Since feminist theology emerges from the womb of life, from the wounds that hurt, from stories that have no ending, feminist theologians learn to look at history from the underside. They find that neither Aristotelian logic, Aquinas' dialectics nor Tillich's method of correlation are adequate to articulate the theological aspirations of women. Analyzing symbols and concepts, feminists insist, is not sufficient. One must question their impact on the historical reality of women in the past, present and future.[33] Creative ways of networking, innovative communicative styles and community building will facilitate the participation of grassroots women in theologizing and will bring in new voices on to the theological front.

Deconstruction and Reconstruction

Masculine pedagogical models have always favoured a hermeneutics based on the principle that meaning is either author or text or context centred. Feminist models of interpretation are concerned with questions such as: How meaning is constructed? Who constructs meaning and for whom? What are the power dynamics associated with meaning-making? Whose meaning becomes part of tradition? Why? Questions such as these become a deconstructive process of interaction, both with texts and traditions.

When reading a biblical text, for instance, the following questions may be raised: What does the text say about women? From whose point of view was the text written? Are there hidden implications about women suggested in the texts? These questions are engendered by the presupposition that "biblical texts and their interpretation are androcentric and serve patriarchal functions."[34]

The presuppositions, models and unarticulated interests of the androcentric texts are questioned in order to surface the liberating elements of women hidden in these texts. A historical-critical reconstructing of texts from the women's perspective will not only yield a feminist meaning of the texts but also reclaim women's history.

Em-body-ing theology[35]

All gender issues are based on what we believe about the body. Women have been largely objectified as bodies: bodies to be taken in sex, bodies to bear children, bodies to work in households and fields. Patriarchy is most dominating over the realm of women's body and sexuality. With globalization, women as both consumer and consumed end up being sacrificed even more at the altar of greed. History will also vouch that religious and philosophical traditions have greatly contributed to the devaluation of women's bodies through their doctrines and practices.

Feminist hermeneutics focuses upon the body as the locus for human experience, reflection and action because body is inextricably bound up with the self and identity of a woman. It also aims to change unjust structures and distorted symbol systems that deny the full humanity of women. Em-body-ing theology and celebrating the sacredness of the body in theology is a crucial task for feminist theology. The female body has to be liberated from the multiple layers of suppression and violence it has been subjected to. Em-body-ing theology implies according the female body the beauty and integrity that have been denied it.

3. Indian Feminist Hermeneutics

Indian feminist hermeneutics has its own distinct features and is more complex since Indian feminist consciousness emerges from Indian women's struggle against the many and varied oppressive systems and structures. Indian feminist theology must be understood within the larger context of both feminist theology and liberation theology as well as of the distinct Indian theologies. Its emphasis is on doing theology from within the context of women's experience and of their struggle for liberation. It is doing theology as an ongoing process rooted in praxis, interdependent with and compassionately committed to life, justice and freedom from oppression. It is not an academic theology with watertight categories, clear boundaries and sharp intellectual definitions totally separate from people's experience. It includes intellectual effort and creative thinking, but this is part of and arises from the realities of life as lived, experienced, struggled through, wrestled with and celebrated.

Some Distinct Features of Indian Feminist Hermeneutics

Some of the essential and distinct features that must be taken note of while designing a feminist theological method for India are the following:

Indian Women's Experience is Diverse

The situations of Indian women can be broadly categorized as urban/rural; tribal/non-tribal; caste/Dalit/subcaste; educated/illiterate; rich/poor, and each situation determines and shapes the experience and status of women differently. Moreover, the multiple forms of oppression and discrimination that Indian women are subjected to within the multi-layered socio-cultural order of the Indian society also impacts their experience. Since women's experience (*anubhava*) varies from context to context, no uniform feminist methodology is possible or even recommended for India.

India's Multi-Religious Traditions

India is a mosaic of religions and religious traditions. It is undeniable that religions have legitimized the subjugation of women, and today religious fundamentalism is reinforcing gender discrimination. It is, therefore, essential to re-read and re-interpret from the perspective of Indian women the Sacred Scriptures of different religions that have sanctioned and perpetuated the silence and submission of women. It is also imperative to unearth the spiritual riches of indigenous traditions and popular folklore, and de-mythologize the Marian cult and the goddess cult in Hindu mythology.

This process will enable us to retrieve the empowering elements of the goddess-cult and remember the significant contributions of our foremothers like Sarah, Judith, Esther, Vashti and others in salvation history. Furthermore, the liberating elements found in the sacred texts and traditions can be transformed into a challenge that will give new meaning and power (*sakti*) to women to participate in God's design of co-creating a new humanity.

Indian women – Poorest of the Poor

A majority of the poor in India is women and children dependent on women. Indian women are deprived of economic power because of unjust wages and job opportunities, unequal property rights in many cultures and rampant female illiteracy. The capitalist system and today globalization have reinforced the economic exploitation of women. Situations such as wars, communal/ethnic clashes, terrorism, migration and displacement further inflict an economic burden on women (widows, mothers, daughters). Restoring economic power to women through just systems will safeguard women's freedom, individuality and dignity.

India's Social and Cultural Structures

The patriarchal caste system has cast women in the bottom rung of its social structure. Her status as 'Dalit of the Dalits" deprives her of freedom and opportunities for education. The various cultures in India with their gender-biased oppressive customs and traditions deny women the dignity of their womanhood and humanhood. For instance, an analysis of the religious ceremonies and symbols used on occasions of birth, marriage and death reveal startling and subtle indications of gender discriminatory practices. Women are indoctrinated through such practices to internalize their subjugated status. The patriarchal social and cultural traditions of India stereotype the role of women as mother, wife, daughter and sister. Their stereotyped roles restrict their 'space' to the home, common village well and village bazaar, which in turn subjugates their status and reduces their identity and dignity to that of a non person or even a commodity.

Indian Women – Victims of Violence and Death

In spite of our booming economy, advance in science and technology and increase in literacy rate, women are still victims of violence and death. There is an increase in female foeticide, infanticide, dowry deaths, bride burning, maternal mortality and other forms of physical and sexual abuse. There is also a disturbing slide in the sex ratio.

1901	-	972 females	-	1000 males
1981	-	933 females	-	1000 males
1991	-	927 females	-	1000 males
2001	-	933 females	-	1000 males

4. A Proposed Feminist Theological Method

Against the backdrop of the characteristics that are common to all feminist theological methods and those that distinguish Indian feminist hermeneutics from the others, I shall now attempt to articulate a feminist theological method for India. I have developed this based on insights from Elisabeth Schüssler Fiorenza's Dance of Liberation and Transformation, A Feminist Critical Interpretation of the Bible.[36]

Four basic structural elements in this model

1. Hermeneutics of Suspicion and Critical Analysis
2. Hermeneutics of Proclamation
3. Hermeneutics of Remembrance
4. Hermeneutics of Creative Actualization

Hermeneutics of Suspicion and Critical Analysis

Feminist biblical interpretation involves asking lead questions: What does the text say about women? From whose point of view was the text written? Are there hidden implications regarding women suggested in the texts? These questions are engendered by the fact that "biblical texts and their interpretations are androcentric and serve patriarchal functions;"[37] therefore, they reflect only the masculine perspective. There is need to "search for lost traditions and visions of liberation"[38] of women in these androcentric biblical texts.

Hermeneutics of Proclamation

It involves asking further questions like, "How does the idea or biblical teaching function for men and for women? For example, not all stories in the Bible are liberating for women, hence, they have to be interpreted in the light of liberative semantic axes of the whole Bible before the truth is proclaimed. Eph. 5:21 – 6:9: "Wives, be subject to your husbands, as to the Lord. For the husband is the head of the wife as Christ is the head of the church, his body, and is himself its Saviour...." is a point in case.

Hermeneutics of Remembrance

Deconstruction is needed before reconstruction and remembrance. There is a need for a historico-critical reconstruction from women's perspective of all biblical traditions whether patriarchal or not. With such analysis, we can move beyond the androcentric texts and allow feminist reading to recall and reclaim the history of women.

Hermeneutics of Creative Actualization

This is necessary to make sure that we create alternative memory – a memory of resistance rather than just a memory of victimhood. It challenges women's creativity and imagination to retell the biblical stories.

Dance of Emancipation, Empowerment and Enabling Indian Women: A Feminist Theological Method for India

Feminist theology in India, as in any other Third World context, is theology from the perspective of women in struggle. It is women's struggles against the systemic sin of patriarchy in society and the Church. The expression 'women's perspective' underlines the distinctive character of women's experience as a methodological tool.

Stories of Women's Experience

The first step of the dance is a warming-up phase that will instill confidence in women to stand tall and speak-up. It includes sharing of women's experiences of struggle, suffering, pain, hopes and aspirations through narratives, songs, dance, myths, folklore, and popular proverbs.

Some specific areas of women's experience in India that are significant for the process of theologizing are: The social preference for the male and the increase in female foeticide and infanticide, the dowry system and its implications, caste system and honour killing, unjust property rights, job opportunities and wages.

Consciousness-Raising: Critical analysis and reflection from an inter-disciplinary perspective

A critical analysis of women's experience from socio-cultural, politico-economic and religious perspectives will create a consciousness of the enslaving systems and structures in India that dehumanize women on their "womb to tomb" journey of life. A feminist critical awareness will lead us to raise fundamental questions concerning the humiliating and oppressive situations women are subject to and the adequacy of any theological system that does not take women's issues seriously. For instance, a critical analysis of why a dalit girl from a remote village in North India was prevented from pursuing her studies because she cycled through a high caste village on her way to school will throw light on the gender-biased oppressive systems in India.

Feminist questioning and deconstruction

This entails a feminist questioning of androcentrism and patriarchial overtones prevalent in the Sacred Scriptures of different religions, in religious mythology and legends, in indigenous belief systems and popular folklore and proverbs. It searches for hidden traces of suffering and protest struggles of our foremothers and sisters against gender oppression. It also raises questions like, "What do the texts of Sacred Scriptures or popular belief systems say about women? By whom were they written and for whom? Who determines the locus of power and powerlessness in the Church and society? It is imperative for Indian feminists to deconstruct and demythologize gender discriminatory and oppressive texts and "search for lost traditions and visions of liberation"[39] of women.

Changed and New Consciousness

To re-read the Sacred Scriptures and religious traditions or history requires an awareness of different hermeneutical approaches to contend with the patriarchal past. For a changed and new consciousness, it is necessary to use our imagination, intuition and creativity to reconstruct the discriminatory experiences of women in the Sacred Scriptures and history, redeem those texts with hidden oppressive elements and remember the forgotten women and articulate a new vision for women.

The story of the murder of Jephthah's daughter (Judges 11) in striking contrast to God's intervention to save Isaac from being sacrificed (Gen 22) and the missing mothers and daughters in the Matthean and Lucan genealogies that trace the ancestry of Jesus are some such examples of discrimination. Feminist hermeneutic enables us to see how women have overcome patriarchal barriers and emerged as "victors and voices of resistance."[40]

Daring to Dream, Act and Network

The steps of the dance now changes and gathers momentum as it moves towards emancipating and empowering women. A reconstruction of androcentric texts and narratives creates an alternative memory of resistance and strength. With creative imagination, feminists dare to articulate dreams and new visions for the emancipation and empowerment of women through theological writings, poetry, music, art and painting; organize theological consultations to share and stimulate creative theological thinking and build solidarity and support among feminist theologians through a networking system.

In order to communicate their rich and varied theological voices, Indian feminist theologians will have to make imaginative use of the cultural resources of Indian people in order to engage in new myth-making, symbol-creating and story-telling. They will have to create new styles of expressing their faith experiences and proclaiming their spirituality of life.

Vision and Goal

The new consciousness of women, the ability to articulate their pain and suffering, analyze their oppressive situations, express their protest and seek radical change have given them the possibility of envisioning different ways of being for their communities and for themselves. Women are birthing a new vision and nurturing new hope, strength and courage. This inspiring vision is an imaginative leap forward into alternative possibilities and forms of existence born out of the determination to dream.

An Indian feminist theological method puts forth a new challenge. It demands a new way of looking at reality, at ourselves, at power, at life. Women develop a new sense of empowerment. This implies a new understanding of power, where power is not exercised in a dominant hierarchical mode as "power over" but as enabling power, as power that can be shared so that all who participate in it are strengthened and affirmed without excluding or diminishing anyone.

Indian feminist theological hermeneutics is not an antagonist approach that draws clear dividing lines between the male and female.

Rather it is an invitation to be human and recognize God's image in each other. It is a project where emancipated, empowered and enabled women work in partnership and mutuality of relationship with men for the transformation of society and for building a just and life-giving human and cosmic order for all.

Feminist Theological Method for India

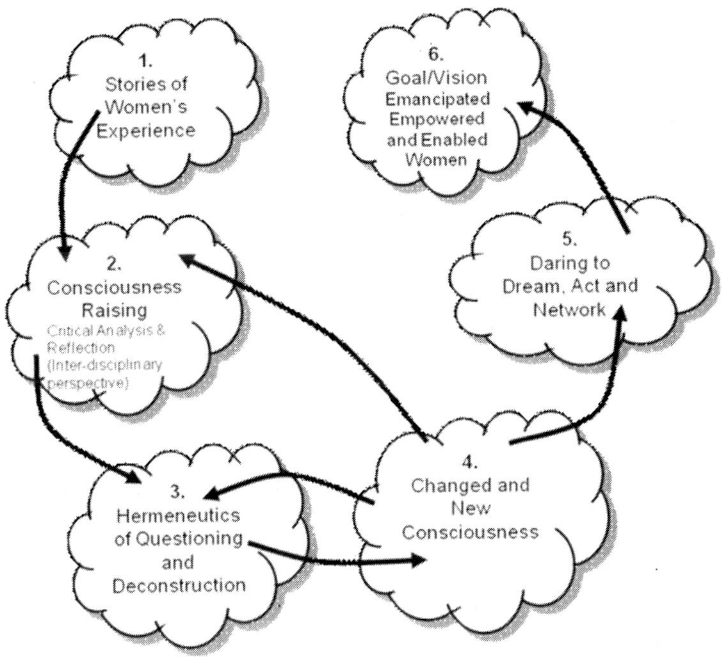

Conclusion

Humanity can be healed from the distortion of its true image and be restored to its original inclusive image only through an appropriate paradigm shift from the prevailing worldviews and value systems. It will also need the interventions of prophetic religious agencies. The contemporary liberation movements among the Dalits, Tribals, and women show hopeful signs for a transformation that privileges the powerless peripheries.

The feminist and other subaltern awakenings are the silver lining on the horizon. These give hope that humankind will be spared of any lopsided growth so that a holistic humanity can be re-constructed by conscious and concerted human efforts. The task before Indian theologians is to reconstruct a humanity that reflects the image of God. It will succeed when women are restored to their true humanhood. We are challenged to weave new patterns into our theological imagination that compel us to be "friends of God and Prophets" in the daring adventure of articulating the knowledge of God with a new vision.

Endnotes

1. Evangeline Anderson-Rajkumar, "New Eyes, New Reading, New Vision," in *Feminist Hermeneutics*, ed. Lalrinawine Ralte and Evangeline Anderson-Rajkumar (Delhi: ISPCK, 2002), 102
2. Rosemary Radford Ruether, "The Emergence of Christian Feminist Theology," in *The Cambridge Companion to Feminist Theology*, ed. Susan Frank Parsons (Cambridge: Cambridge University Press, 2002), 3.
3. This wave started in the US, swept through Western Europe and by the end of the 70s a new thrust of Feminist Movement evolved in the Soviet Union.
4. For more details on the development of feminism and feminist theology refer to Anne M. Clifford, *Introducing Feminist Theology* (New York/Maryknoll: Orbis Books, 2002); Susan Frank Parsons, ed. *The Cambridge Companion to Feminist Theology*; Ursula King, ed. *Feminist Theology from the Third World* (Maryknoll, New York: Orbis books, 1966).
5. For instance, Katherine Hepburn speaks of the "feminist movement" in the 1942 film *Woman of the Year*.
6. Some Postcolonial feminists, such as Chandra Talpade Mohanty and Black feminists like Angela Davis and Alice Walker are critical of the ethnocentric slant of Western feminism.
7. It is important to note that feminism does not advocate the understanding that all women are feminists and all men are perpetrators of patriarchy. In fact, every theologian, whether male or female should be a feminist because women comprise almost 50% of the Church, Indian and world membership/population.
8. Feminists have attempted to counter perceptions of women as morally or spiritually inferior to men; as sexual commodities, as dedicated only to childbearing, their homes, and husbands; and as having a lesser role in religious ritual or leadership because of such inferiority or dedication.
9. Feminist theology was not born *ex nihilo*. Some of the conditions for feminist theology also existed in earlier eras. In the Middle Ages, for instance, there were

women spiritual writers such as Hildegard of Bingen and Julian of Norwich, women theologians, teachers and preachers. R. R. Ruether, "The Emergence of Christian Feminist Theology," 4.

10. They were able to initiate the new generation of students to study and write from a feminist perspective.
11. R. R. Ruether, "The Emergence of Christian Feminist Theology," 10-11. American women from other religious traditions have also begun to find their feminist voice. Judith Plaskow pioneered Jewish feminist theology and American Buddhist women began to examine both the religious practice and the teachings of Buddhism from a feminist perspective.
12. This resulted in a series of consultations of women theologians of Asia, Africa and Latin America at national, continental and intercontinental conferences.
13. See, Mercy Amba Oduyoye and Musimbi Kanyoro, ed., *The Will to Arise: Women, Tradition and the Church in Africa* (Maryknoll, New York: Orbis Press, 1992).
14. Kwok Pui-Ian, *Introducing Asian Feminist Theology* (Sheffield: Sheffield Academic Press, 2000), 10.
15. I am the co-founder of EWA along with Annette Meuthrath (Missio-Germany) and Edmund Chia (US).
16. Evelyn Monteiro & Antoinette Gutzler, ed., *Ecclesia of Women: Gathering the Voices of Women in Asia* (Delhi: ISPCK, 2004).
17. Agnes M. Brazal & Andrea Lizares Si, ed., *Body and Sexuality: Theological-Pastoral Perspectives of Women in Asia* (Manila: Ateneo de Manila Press, 2007).
18. Sharon A. Bong & Pushpa Joseph, ed., *Re-imagining Marriage and Family in Asia: Asian Christian Women's Perspectives* (Malaysia: Vinlin Press, 2008).
19. Astrid Lobo-Gajiwala & Judette Gallares, ed., *Practicing Peace: Towards an Asian Feminist Theology of Liberation* to be published in 2011.
20. Aruna Gnanadason, " Towards an Indian Feminist Theology," in *We Dare to Dream: Doing Theology as Asian Women*, ed. Virginia Fabella, M. M. and Sun Ai Lee Park (New York/Maryknoll: Orbis, 1990), 117
21. Gabriele Dietrich, *Women's Movement in India: Conceptual and Religious Reflections* (Bangalore: Breakthrough Publications, 1988), 1.
22. Aruna Gnanadason, " Towards an Indian Feminist Theology," 117-118.
23. Evelyn Monteiro & Kochurani Abraham, ed., *Concerns of Women: An Indian Theological Response* (Bangalore: Dharmaram Publications, 2005).
24. Pushpa Joseph, "Critical Pedagogy and Feminism," (Unpublished), 1.
25. Ibid.
26. Today feminists are reluctant to use the term 'patriarchy'. They prefer expressions like "male domination" and "male dominated society" for the patriarchal system of the ancient world does not exist today. Patriarchy has taken different forms due to the impact of various forces.
27. Elisabeth Schüssler Fiorenza, *Wisdom Ways: Introducing Feminist Biblical Interpretation* (Maryknoll, New York: Orbis Books, 2001).

28. Pushpa Joseph, *Critical Pedagogy and Feminism*, 2.
29. Ibid., 7.
30. Rebecca Chopp, "Eve's Knowing: Feminist Theology's Resistance to Malestream Epistemological Frameworks," in *Concilium* 1996/1: *Feminist Theologies in Different Contexts*, ed. Elisabeth Schüssler Fiorenza and Mary Shawn Copeland (Maryknoll, New York: Orbis Books, 1996): 116-23.
31. Ibid., 120.
32. Kwok Pui-Ian, *Introducing Asian Feminist Theology*, 39.
33. Ibid., 32.
34. Elisabeth Schüssler-Fiorenza, *Bread Not Stone: The Challenge of Feminist Biblical Interpretation* (Boston: Beacon Press, 1984), 15
35. Gemma Tulud Cruz, "Em-body-ing Theology: Theological Reflections on the experience of Filipina Domestic Workers in Hong Kong," in *Body and Sexuality: Theological-Pastoral Perspectives of Women in Asia,* ed. Agnes M. Brazal & Andrea Lizares Si (Manila: Ateneo de Manila University Press, 2007), 69.
36. Schüssler-Fiorenza explains the theological method of feminist hermeneutics in the book, *In Memory of Her: A Feminist Theological Reconstruction of Christian Origins* (New York: Crossroad, 1984).
37. Schüessler-Fiorenza, *Bread not Stone*,15
38. Ibid., 16.
39. Ibid., 16.
40. Evangeline Anderson-Rajkumar, "New Eyes, New Reading, New Women," 107.

Chapter 8

Relevance of Oriental Theological Method

For Developing an Inculturated Indian Theological Method

George Thomas Kallunkal, OIC

Introduction

'Faith seeking understanding' (*fides quaerens intellectum*) is the traditional definition of theology proposed by St. Anselm, which became almost a universally accepted definition. This definition appeals to the understanding of theology and doing theology in the West. The understanding of the faith of the community is the essential aspect of theologizing. This process of understanding of faith happens not in a vacuum but in the concrete existence of people in their cultures, thought patterns and conditions of life.[1]

Now it is the fundamental mission and challenge before the Oriental Churches in India with their own liturgical, theological, traditional, spiritual patrimony to imbibe and express their understanding of faith through the medium of Indian cultures and values and in the context of the complex religious and social situations of this country and its people. Only through such an authentic process of inculturation can the Church in India become more effective for the people among whom she lives and works to spread and give witness to the gospel values and the Kingdom of God. Pope John Paul II has highlighted this point in his Apostolic Exhortation *Ecclesia in Asia* (*EA*) [2] which could be very well applied to the Indian context.

> Through inculturation the Church, for her part, becomes a more intelligible sign of what she is, and more effective instrument of her mission. This engagement with cultures has always been part of the Church's pilgrimage through history. But it has a special urgency today in the multi-ethnic, multi-religious and multi-cultural situation of Asia, where Christianity is still too often seen as foreign (*EA 21*).

The process of inculturation has to involve the entire people of God, "since the life of the Church as a whole must show forth the faith being proclaimed and appropriated" (*EA 21*). The Fathers of the Synod in Asia stressed the need of an appropriate theological vision in the area of inculturation and theologians have a significant role to play in this regard.

> The Synod expressed encouragement to theologians in their delicate work of developing an inculturated theology, especially in the area of Christology. They noted that "this theologizing is to be carried out with courage, in faithfulness to the Scripture and to the Church's Tradition, in sincere adherence to the Magisterium and with an awareness of pastoral realities." (*EA 22*).

In this respect, especially in the context of inculturation and an inculturated theology, the Oriental Churches in India, whose origin goes back to the arrival and evangelizing activities of Apostle St. Thomas in this country, have a vital role to play. The *Asian Synod*, while acknowledging the great spiritual resources and experience of these Churches, underlines the fact that they are born of a deep inculturation of the Christian faith in the soil of many Asian countries. Their experience and compatibility in the area of ecumenical and inter-religious dialogue is also specially mentioned:

> The situation of the Catholic Eastern Churches, principally of the Middle East and India, merits special attention. From Apostolic times they have been the custodians of a precious spiritual, liturgical and theological heritage. Their tradition and rites, born of a deep inculturation of the faith in the soil of many Asian countries, deserve the greatest respect ... It is clear that the Catholic Eastern Churches possess a great wealth of tradition and experience which can greatly benefit the whole Church (*EA 27*).

Having said this, Pope John Paul II, "calls upon everyone to recognize the legitimate customs and the legitimate freedom of these Churches in disciplinary and liturgical matters, as stipulated by the Code of Canons of the Eastern Churches" (*EA 27*). From this it is clear that the Oriental Churches in India, having close affinity to the culture and traditions of this land from the time of their origin conserve many important elements for the development of an indigenous theology.

1. The Strong Semitic Imprint of Oriental Theology

'Oriental theology' here refers to the theology and theological methods evolved and being applied among the Oriental Christian Churches, especially the Oriental Syrian Churches in India. According to Dr. Sebastian Brock, one of the greatest contemporary scholars in Syriac language and literature as well as Syrian Churches as a whole, these Churches and their theology are representatives or to some degree direct heirs of the Semitic world out of which Christianity itself sprang.[3] Church history witnesses to the fact that the Syriac Christianity came under the influence of Greek speaking Christianity. In spite of this influence the earliest literature of the Syrians is usually experienced in a manner much more characteristic of the Semitic and biblical world out of which it grew.[4] These Syrian Churches were the most flourishing Churches among the Eastern

Churches. "In the formative period of Christianity no other group of Churches can prove a more dynamic and creative record of service to Gospel and to human culture."[5]

The Syriac Christianity is Asian Christianity and Christianity in India clearly illustrates this reality. Before the arrival of the Portuguese, Christianity in India was represented by the Syrian Orient, i.e. the native Asian Christianity. According to Sebastian Brock, the Syriac Orient represents indigenous Asian Christianity which took root very easily in India and it is blessed with the absence of any association with European colonialism. Those Indian Christians portray particularly an Asian mold of Christianity with its own uncommon spiritual and cultural heritage, a heritage truly to be proud of.[6]

The history of Christianity in India shows clearly how the early Christians in India, who were known as Thomas Christians (after Apostle Thomas), came into contact with the Syrian Churches of the East and established liturgical and hierarchical linkage with them. The Thomas Christian tradition in India constitutes an essential sector of this Syriac heritage. The Church of Thomas Christians produced a style of life which was shaped by the social, cultural, political and religious background of that period of history.[7]

2. Sources and Methods

With regard to the sources and methods of Oriental theology, we could say, in general Oriental theology is grounded on the sources of faith, namely, sacred scripture, tradition, sacred liturgy, monasticism, mysticism and asceticism. Theology comes from prayer, meditation, contemplation, fasting, abstinence, etc.[8] A contemplative experience of the Divine mysteries and a life accordingly are essential aspects of Eastern theological traditions. The *Decree on Ecumenism* has very well pointed out this fact in the following words: With regard to the authentic theological traditions of the Orientals we must recognize that they are admirably rooted in holy scripture, are fostered and given expression in liturgical life, are nourished by the living traditions of the Apostles and by the works of the Fathers and spiritual writers of the East; they are directed towards right ordering of life, indeed toward a full contemplation of Christian truth.[9]

This Conciliar statement is repeated and further explained in the *Instruction: For Applying Liturgical Prescription of the Code of Canons of the Eastern Churches.*

> The Eastern rites trace their origins to the Alexandrian, Antiochene, Armenian, Chaldean and Constantinopolitan traditions. These Churches have jealously retained the symbolic biblical theology, explained at great length by the Fathers. They preserve the sense of the awesome and inexpressible mystery which surrounds and connotes the celebrative act. In the texts and in their whole spirit, they maintain the sense of liturgy with formulas that are both rich and meaningful as unceasing doxology, as petition for forgiveness and as uninterrupted epiclesis. These Churches boast of a spirituality drawing directly from sacred scripture and consequently a theology less subjected to strictly rational categories. For historical and cultural reasons, they have maintained a more direct continuity with the spiritual atmosphere of Christian origins, a prerogative that is ever more frequently considered even by the occident not as a sign of stagnancy and backwardness but of special fidelity to sources of salvation.[10]

These two historical documents give enough evidence regarding the sources and methods of Oriental theology. In this paper, I would like to reflect upon the sources and methods and show to what extent they are relevant and compatible with the sensibilities of Indian mind and culture and are suitable for the development of genuine theological methods in the Indian context.

3. Relevance of the Sources and Methods Towards an Inculturated Theology

3.1. Scripture Rootedness

Oriental theology is always portrayed as an output of a creative and fecund meditation on sacred scripture.[11]Therefore, the most fundamental tenet of Syriac theology is its rootedness in the Bible.

Theology is the interpretation of the Bible and, hence, it is considered as the best means for propagating the Christian faith. The teachings and writings of the Syriac Fathers clearly show how the Syriac tradition is soaked in the Bible and their writings are full of verbal allusions as well more direct biblical references.[12] It is said about St. Ephrem, the great representative of Syriac mysticism and theology, that even while living in the midst of doctrinal controversies involving Arianism, Manichaeism, Marcionism, as well as the still powerful pagan tradition and Judeo-Christian polemics, Ephrem was always able to transcend the existing frozen formulae and to maintain that extraordinary biblical freshness that gives the early Syriac Christian tradition a flavor of true universality. This is particularly true of Ephrem's theology of Incarnation, his sacramental typology and his understanding of ethical issues.[13]

The biblical rootedness is very conspicuous in the Eastern liturgies. Sacred scripture is most powerfully presented and authentically interpreted in the liturgy. What is presented in the Bible is retold and paraphrased in the liturgy. There is mutuality between Bible and liturgy.[14] There is a rich narrative tradition with different narrative methods, used by the Oriental Fathers, especially by the Syrian Fathers, to interpret the OT and the NT events of salvation history and to expose the life and teachings of Jesus Christ. According to Fr. George Ayyaneth, who is doing his doctoral research on biblical narratology in the Indian context, there is a rich narrative tradition in the Orient which has been the carrier of religious experience from time immemorial.

> Even at the time of Christological controversies and polemics in the first centuries of Oriental Christianity, there had always been the dynamism of narrating the religious experience with all its aura of literary richness, whether it was prose or poetry. This aspect is being best illustrated in the Oriental liturgy. The narration took diverse forms and literary genres like *Anaphoras, Hoosoyos, Promion-Sedros, Kolos* etc. The content of such narration was not in any propositional truths or principles of systematic form. They were genuine attempts to find meaning in story, to

> relate to God and to play our part in the mega narrative of salvation.[15]

The theology of the Syriac Fathers show great passion for the OT and the NT stories, myths, imageries, typologies to portray the Christ event. These Fathers and most of the theologians were literary geniuses or poets who realized the strength of narrating and who explained the full potential of narrating.

When we analyze the Indian system of belief, we see how Indian sages and spiritual leaders have taken narrative methods seriously in building up and structuring their belief system. The *Vedas*, which are primarily hymns, lyrical in form and devotional in content, are the best representatives of this kind of narrative. Fictional or encrypting narrative is a common devise in folklore which is used in *Ramayana* and *Mahabharata*. In the words of Fr. Ayyaneth:

> The great seers, monks and exponents of ancient Indian Hindu tradition were not primarily systematic theologians who articulated the belief system in propositions and principles. But they were great story-tellers and narrators and they made use of the existing narrative devices and went on exploring new devices. Even in this post modern era, stories in various forms of narratives function as main carriers of religious experience and ethos of Hindu tradition. What they believe they narrate in stories and what is narrated in stories they believe. This kind of narrative approach to religious experience, belief, ethos and life is a common patrimony of the Orient.[16]

The traditional Indian narrative art has been inspiring and evoking the indigenous and world narrative for centuries by contributing many models, patterns and practices.[17]

3.2. An Indigenous Narratological Approach

We are living in an era in which traditional dogmatic and metaphysical approach to theology is slowly losing its relevance and giving way to the path of transforming God experience. This is very well noticed in the Asian context. The religious experience of a person is always culturally conditioned and its narrative form also is culture bound. Therefore, an indigenous narratological approach to the Bible and liturgy, the two basic sources of theology, is an urgent need of our times.[18]

This is an important area of inculturation and theologizing in India. The Oriental theological method of narratology can contribute much to the process of developing an indigenous narrative system. This can become a true meeting point of Oriental Christianity and Indian traditions.

The *Asian Synod,* while speaking about the need of making sacred scripture known among the followers of other religions, pointed out that the narrative styles used in Asia have to be adapted to explain sacred scripture to them, because "the narrative style found in many books of the Bible has an affinity with the religious texts typical of Asia."(*AE* 22). Again, while proposing a pedagogy for presenting the mystery of Christ to the people of Asia, the Synod gives preference to the narrative methods akin to Asia's cultural forms. The Synod recommends "an evocative pedagogy, using stories, parables and symbols so characteristic of Asian methodology in teaching. (*AE* 20).

In initial proclamation, for example, "the presentation of Jesus Christ could come as the fulfillment of the yearnings expressed in the mythologies and folklore of the Asian peoples." In general, narrative methods akin to Asian cultural forms are to be preferred. In fact, the proclamation of Jesus Christ can most effectively be made by narrating his story, as the Gospels do. (*AE* 20).

3.3. Liturgy Centered

Oriental theology is liturgical and it has a deep liturgical character. It implies that worship conceived broadly is what gives rise to theological reflection rather than the other way around.[19] It is the law of worship which establishes the law of belief (*lex orandi, lex credendi*).[20] *Lex orandi statuit Legem Credendi* (Irenaeus). Dr. Sebastian Brock, commending on this subject in the background of the Malankara Catholic Church, writes:

> Following the familiar adage *lex orandi, lex credendi*, it is these *Anaphoras, shehimo, Fenquitho* and the Syrian Fathers and the other main liturgical books (notably baptism, marriage and burial) which will contribute the most obvious and immediate sources of theological reflection within the Malankara Catholic Church.[21]

Theological thinking in the Church should be verifiable in the liturgical texts of the Church. The liturgical texts, writings of the Fathers and that of the spiritual writers constitute the various sources of theology.[22] The liturgical tradition is not merely one of the theological sources among others, rather it is the original condition within which theological reflection is done and within which the Word of God is appropriately understood.[23] Liturgy is the *locus theologicus*. Liturgy has pre-eminence in the Eastern Churches. All the other aspects of theology are related to liturgy. The basic source of the identity of the Eastern Churches is their liturgical heritage.[24]

This strong liturgical character, liturgy centeredness, of the Oriental Churches and theology has special relevance in the Indian context because the liturgy, "is a decisive means of evangelization, especially in Asia where the followers of different religions are so drawn to worship, religious festivals and popular devotions." (*AE 22*). The inculturated nature of the liturgies of many of the Oriental Churches through their interaction with the surrounding culture for many centuries (*AE 22*), is of great advantage for the Church in India in her mission of evangelization. The obvious reason is that "the liturgies become an ever greater source of nourishment for the people through the wise and effective use of elements drawn from the local cultures." (*AE 22*).

3.3.1. Inculturation of Liturgical Music

Chants and hymns are essential aspects of Oriental liturgies. The Oriental liturgical music, especially of the Oriental Churches in India, has strong affinity with Indian music which has spiritual and mystical nature. Fr. Philip Vysaneth OIC, an expert in Indian music, who has made a comparative study on liturgical music and Indian music in the background of Malankara liturgy, scientifically shows the close affinity between the Oriental liturgical music and Indian music.[25] According to him:

> The basic principle of music in the Malankara liturgy and in Indian music is the same. When one compares Indian music with the liturgical music of Malankara it can be noticed that the basic nature of both the Indian music system and the musical nature of the Malankara liturgy is the same. The comparative study will be based on the concepts namely, *sruti, laya, raga, kalpita manodharma sangeeta* and the oral tradition or the *gurukula sampradaya* that is the Indian concept, God as *Nada Brahma*.[26]

The Second Vatican Council's *Decree on Liturgy* has already underlined the need of adapting liturgical music to the native genius of the people.

> In certain countries, especially in mission lands, there are people who have their own musical tradition and this plays a great part in their religious and social life. For this reason, their music should be held in proper esteem and a suitable place is to be given to it, not only in forming their religious sense but also in adapting worship to their native genius.[27]

This close affinity of the liturgical music of the Oriental Churches and the Indian music is an area of inculturation and theologizing in the Indian context.

3.3.2. Towards a Theology of Symbolism in the Indian Context

Oriental theology with its focus on liturgy is basically symbolic. According to Dr. Sebastian Brock, this is a different approach to theology and also is a unique approach. This approach to theology, "employing symbols and images rather than carefully defined terminology is an equally valid one, and it is this approach that can justly be seen as one of the distinctive features of Syriac tradition in general."[28]

Symbolism by nature is didactic.[29] Symbols are to be interpreted and this interpretation is always didactic and it is always dynamic. The meaning of a symbol is not restricted. The most prolific and adequate means by which one can create the symbolic language is the language of poetry. The hymns and poems of the Syriac Fathers make free use of typology, word play, paradox, repetition and metaphor to convey to the listener or reader the richness of the reality hidden in the visible symbols.[30]

> In India's cultural and religious world symbols and symbolism has acquired a very important place. There are so many symbols embedded in the Indian psyche, eg., the river, the tree, the *bhoomi*, the sun, the *thrishool*, the *swasthika*, the snake, the cow, the moon, etc. for which people give various and varied interpretations.[31]

The intense symbolic character of Oriental theology, especially of Syriac theology, can make a major contribution to the Church in India for the development of a theology of symbols and symbolism in the Indian context. The *Asian Synod* also speaks of the importance of symbols and symbolism as a means to create an evocative pedagogy which is so characteristic of Asian methodology in teaching. (*EA*20).

3.3.3. Adaptation of *Dhvani Siddhantha*

Through the application of *dhvani siddhantha* of the East on the meditation of words (*vacana*) which are symbols in themselves or the application of this age old system to the interpretation of the celebration of the sacraments (mysteries), one can transform them into a living experience of the manifestation of God, which is the core of the celebration. *Dhvani siddhantha* makes the brooding over (meditation) on the word (*vac*) easier and help the performer of the mysteries (sacraments), both the minister and the recipient encountering Christ in the mysteries.[32] Fr. Placid calls *dhvani* as the gateway to the Kingdom and to the Word and God.[33]

3.4. From Worship to Social Commitment

The liturgy centered theology of the Oriental Churches in India has to be in a position to attend to the social problems of the country such as poverty, oppression, injustice, corruption, illiteracy, gender discrimination, caste system, fundamentalism, communalism, ecological degradation etc. Participation in the liturgy should evoke in the worshipper a sense of prophetic commitment to propose and promote solutions to these problems. Then only liturgy becomes a sign and sacrament of Jesus' mission of love and service to the world imparting fullness of life to all.

Oriental liturgies, especially the Eucharistic liturgy, are the representation and celebration of salvation history.[34] Liturgical celebration is not merely heaven oriented. It is equally oriented to human persons which brings an existential transformation in the life of the worshippers challenging them to commit themselves to the life and needs of their brethren and to the establishment of a better society. The worship in the liturgy should disturb and challenge the worshippers through a transforming experience to give themselves to transform this world and to stand for the values of the kingdom like justice, love, equality, fellowship and reconciliation.[35]

Therefore, the liturgical inculturation in India by the Oriental Churches should not confine merely to a cultic or ritualistic view of inculturation. The *Asian Synod* clearly points out that inculturation of liturgy should also give sufficient attention to the genuine social concerns of the people. Otherwise liturgy will become meaningless.

> Liturgical inculturation needs to take account of the shifts in consciousness and attitudes caused by the emerging secularist and consumer cultures which are affecting the Asian sense of worship and prayer. Nor can the specific needs of the poor, marginalized, migrants, refugees, youth and women to be overlooked in any genuine liturgical inculturation in Asia. (*EA* 22).

This situation offers a great challenge before the Oriental Churches and their attempt of theologizing in India, where the above mentioned social issues are very active and seek immediate attention everywhere.

3.5. Mystical Dimension

For the Easterners, God is basically a mystery and the mystical approach is a long established method of the East, especially among the Syrians. Contemplation of God is the means for the knowledge of God. Scholars would agree that the works of St. Ephrem fall under the section of mysticism rather than theology. The Eastern tradition has never made a sharp distinction between mysticism and theology. There is no Christian mysticism without theology and no theology without mysticism.[36] The use of symbolic language in poetry, as well as paradoxes and allegorical imagery are the most precious tools in the hands of the mystic to express his/her immense vision of God, truth and God-experience. The analytic method is not the mode of a mystic. The Syriac approach as a whole is a mystical approach.[37]

In the Indian context, people's religiosity is experiential and spontaneous in spite of India's rich philosophical traditions. Whether one has experienced God? Which are the ways of experiencing God? These are the basic questions asked and answered in the Indian religious circles. This quest for God-experience brings thousands of people to this land and to its sages and gurus. Therefore, the emphasis in India has been on religious experience rather than on well systematized and presented dogma. Christ is better communicated in India not at the purely theoretical or verbal level or in an orderly presentation of doctrines but through sharing personal experiences. It is religious experience that transforms one's life and gives credibility to what one says and does. The mind of the *Asian Synod* in this matter is very clear: "In Asia the medium of approaching the divine is not speech but silence. The most effective and credible proclamation of the Risen Lord is the outspoken witness of a person who has undergone a deep God-experience and whose life transformed accordingly."[38]

In this regard, the mystical theology of the Oriental Churches has a very significant role to play in the development of a mystical theology, which is closer and endearing to the Indian mind.

3.6. *Apophatic* Character

Theoretical and purely rational approach is foreign to Syriac theology. When we are defining theological realities we are putting limits on them. Theology is the field of paradoxes and symbolisms.[39] It is the field of synthesis. The Eastern tradition is marked by a very lively sense of the impossibility of knowing God and, hence, its *apophatic* character. God is not only the revealed, but also the *apophatic*, the silent, the unspeakable, the ineffable God. Such a God can never be systematized.[40] The Eastern thought is pleased with synthesis. The overwhelming sense of mystery, God's transcendence, majesty and holiness are strongly emphasized all through the liturgical celebrations. The Syrian fathers were always aware of the mysteriousness and inaccessibility of God.[41] "They always assert that it is impossible to know who God is. One can only know that God is, since God has revealed God's self in the history of salvation as the Father, the Son and the Holy Spirit".[42]

The sense of wonder, awe and emptiness before the Divine Mystery is a strong characteristic of Indian thought and religion. Indian sages have shown an attitude of *neti, neti* and silence before the Divine Mystery which evoked an attitude of self surrender before the Divine and the acceptance of the Divine will. This *apophatic* character of the Oriental theology is yet another relevant subject in the context of evolving an Indian theology, giving priority to symbolic and synthetic approaches based on a deep God experience.

3.7. Contemplative Character

The Oriental theology bears also a strong contemplative character which leads to mysticism. Theology (*theologia*) is contemplation of a higher level or a superior form of contemplation that is contemplation of the *Logos*. This form of contemplation is preceded by natural contemplation or *theoria physike* or contemplation of nature.[43] The contemplative experience of God in prayer is a fundamental aspect of Oriental theology. That is how the saying of Evagrius, "if you are a theologian you will pray truly and if you pray truly you are a theologian" [44] has become famous in the Eastern theological circles.

The mission of a Christian in this world is the sharing of one's contemplative experience of Jesus Christ, the God made man. "*Contemplata aliis tradere*" – 'give what you have contemplated' – is the traditional maxim. The experience of God in prayer and contemplation is the basis of authentic and fruitful missionary action. "Mission is contemplative action and active contemplation." (*EA* 22).

In a land like India, that gives primacy to God-experience, "experiencing God in the cave of the heart," a missionary or a theologian needs to be rooted in the contemplative experience of God in order to be relevant, effective and influential. Pope John Paul II, from his contact with representatives of other non-Christian religions and traditions confirms, "the future of mission depends, to a great extent, on contemplation."[45] The *Asian Synod* also has strongly presented this subject.

> In Asia, home to great religions where individuals and entire peoples are thirsting for the Divine, the Church is called to be a praying Church, deeply spiritual even as she engages in immediate human and social concerns. All Christians need a true missionary spirituality of prayer and contemplation. (*EA* 23).

The Synod Fathers go on insisting that, "the work of justice, charity and compassion is interrelated with a genuine life of prayer and contemplation, and, indeed, it is this same spirituality that will be the wellspring of all our evangelizing works." (*EA* 23). In spite of the rising waves of materialism, commercialism, consumerism, hedonism, the Indian society shows an outstanding sense of the divine and spiritual values and upholds them in a striking manner.

> Moreover, despite the influence of modernization and secularization, Asian religions are showing signs of great vitality and a capacity for renewal, as seen in the reform movements within the various religious groups. Many people, especially the young, experience a deep thirst for the spiritual values, as the rise of new religious movements clearly demonstrates. (*EA* 6).

In this context, the Church in India has a special duty to fight against the evils of modernization and secularization and protect the traditional and cultural values like prayer, contemplation, simplicity, detachment, harmony, non-violence, discipline, spirit of hard work, etc. and foster these values in society. The Oriental Churches with their contemplative bend of liturgical spirituality and theology are in a unique position to defend and foster this contemplative attitude in the contemporary Indian society.

3.8. Monastic and Ascetic Character

Monastic life and spirituality are integral parts of the Oriental Churches' life and theology. "Being always at the very heart of the Church, monasticism is of vital importance in the Oriental Churches in the formation and development of their spirituality, liturgy and theology."[46] The *Decree on Ecumenism* gives emphasis on the need and unique place of monasticism in the Oriental Churches. "Moreover in the East are to be found the riches of those spiritual traditions which are given expression in the monastic life especially."[47] Pope John Paul II in his Apostolic letter, *Orientale Lumen* presents monasticism as a "reference point" for all the baptized according to the gifts offered to each by the Lord" and " a symbolic synthesis of Christianity. "[48] And he continues to emphasize that, "monasticism has always been the very soul of Eastern Churches and was an integral part of the Eastern *lumen* passed on to the West by the great Fathers of the undivided Church."[49]

With their life of prayer, worship, contemplation, life of simplicity, austerity, renunciation, ascetical practices, fraternal love and charitable works the monks gave valid testimony to the eschatological dimension of the Church and to the Christian faith in its purity. The life and teachings of the monks have played a crucial role in the molding of the Church's spirituality, theology and tradition in the East as well as in the West. Many of the Eastern Churches were deeply nourished and strongly supported by monastic life in various aspects and monasticism has always been the carrier and guarantor of the living faith and traditions. Because of this great influence some of the Eastern Churches are called 'Monastic Churches'.[50]

The Oriental Churches and theology, especially the Syrian Christianity, is distinguished by a strong ascetic character. They are described as ascetically oriented or ascetically colored Christianity. The ascetical works originated from *Doctrina Addai*, Tatian's *Diatesseron*, Aphraht's *Demonstration*, Ephrem's writings, the Apocryphal books, Acts of Thomas and so on, give witness to this fact. This spirit was manifested in their practice of evangelical poverty, virginity, fasting, vigil, and abstinence. The ascetical spirit was expressed in a radical manner of living the gospel precepts and other Christian ideals. The Sons and Daughters of the Covenant or the Covenanters were a special group of ascetics emerged among the Syrians by the 4th century. They were considered as the forerunners of monasticism in Syria.[51] The strong ascetical tradition of the Syrians has come down to the life and practices of the present day Syrian Christians in India and is well manifested in their liturgy, theology and day-to-day Christian life. Though the ascetic spirit is applicable to all Christians, we find its best expression in the monastic form of life.

India is known as the land of sages, *Rishis* and *Sanyasis* and Indian culture is *Arsha Bharata* culture. It is said that without reference to Indian *Sanyasa*, which is the fundamental characteristic of her religious attitude, we can neither understand nor enjoy the religious mind of India.[52] *Sanyasa* has influenced all the levels of Indian life, be it religious, cultural, social or political. "It is to the ascetic that India owes largely all that is valuable and enduring in her cultural and spiritual life."[53] The ideals of renunciation, asceticism, *tapas*, prayer, contemplation *ahimsa*, fraternal love and charity upheld by the Indian *Sanyasis* still command respect and influence in the Indian society. The Indian mind still perceives in the *Sanyasi* the spiritual and moral values embodied in ancient India.

3.8.1. An Indian Christian *Sanyasa*

Christianity in India, for her effective presence and the ministry of evangelization, has to give great attention to this status of life in India. Monastic life with its different derivations of Consecrated Life is the most suitable agent of inculturation because as we have seen India has a very ancient tradition of *Sanyasa*, even thousands of years before

Christ. Also, there is a close affinity between the Christian and the Indian forms of monastic life in their ideals, ascetical practices and life style. The Oriental churches and monasticism are in a privileged position in India to evolve an Indian **Christian *Sanyasa*** which will be the most potential agent of evangelisation in India.

The *Asian Synod* urges the members of Consecrated life "to become leaders in the search for God", and "to give witness to the primacy of God and eternal life" and "to keep their spirituality and life sensitive to the religious heritage of the people among whom they live and whom they serve" and "to make Consecrated life a privileged means of effective evangelization." (*EA* 44, 349-349). The *Asian Synod* eloquently speaks about the influence and persuasive power of the presence of the Consecrated people in Asia, especially in India.

> In the numerous religious traditions of Asia, men and women dedicated to the contemplative and ascetical life enjoy great respect, and their witness has an especially persuasive power. Their lives lived in community, in peaceful and silent testimony can inspire people to work for greater harmony in society. No less is expected of consecrated men and women in Christian tradition. Their silent example of poverty and abnegation, of purity and sincerity, of self-sacrifice in obedience, can become an eloquent witness capable of touching all people of good will and leading to a fruitful dialogue with surrounding culture and religions and with the poor and defenseless. (*EA* 44, 348).

3.8.2. Agent of dialogue and unity

Eastern monasticism is a powerful agent of unity between the Churches of the East and the West. "It was considered as a bridge between Eastern and Western Churches and one of the most efficient and enduring agents of universal church unity." [54] The reason is that there are many common elements in the monastic system of different Churches which will give a platform for communion and dialogue. As a universal phenomenon founded on human being's search for God and a practical life founded on prayer, contemplation, asceticism, simplicity of life, moral integrity and social concern, monastic life also can become a bridge between Christian and non-Christian monastic forms of life, like Hindu, Buddhist, Islamic etc.

The *Asian Synod* gives special attention to the extreme need of dialogue at the ecumenical and inter-religious levels for the mission of evangelization in Asian countries. (*EA* 226, 29-31). The Synod also makes special reference to the experience and relevance of the Oriental Churches in this important area.

> These venerable Churches are directly involved in ecumenical dialogue with their sister Orthodox Churches, and the Synod Fathers urged them to pursue this path. They also have valuable experience in inter-religious dialogue, especially with Islam. This can be helpful for other Churches in Asia and elsewhere. (*EA* 26, 326).

The strong Trinitarian dimension of Oriental theology and liturgy celebrated in India also challenges one to commit oneself to intra-ecclesial and inter-ecclesial communion in India and also calls for dialogue with other religions.[55] Eastern monasticism which is an integral part of the Oriental Churches, can contribute significantly to the development of a theology of ecumenism and dialogue especially in the pluralistic religious and cultural context of India.

3.9. Cosmic Dimension - Towards an Ecotheology

The cosmic dimension of the Oriental theology is well echoed in the spirituality of the Eastern Christians. The human-world (cosmos) relationship was an important theme of the Eastern Fathers. They have very clearly taught on the basis of the sacred scripture that this universe was created for human beings and human beings dragged nature down with them in their Fall. But the righteous prepare a profound renewal also for the world. "The aim and ideal of Christian asceticism is not the contempt of the world but a joyful acceptance of it. This can enrich the world by raising it to a higher plane, even to the fullness of a transfigured life."[56] This rich and scripture-based cosmic vision of the Oriental Fathers and theology could give a good foundation for the development of an ecotheology in the

Indian context.[57] The Indian religious traditions also possess a sound cosmic vision as manifested in the sacred books of *Vedas, Upanishad, Mahabharatha, Ramayana* and *Bhaghavad Gita*. Ecological degradation is a serious concern for a developing country like India.

3.10. Christological Dimension – A Balanced View

It is a real challenge before the Eastern Churches in India to present before the people of this country the image of Jesus and the mystery of Christ according to their cultural pattern and ways of thinking and, in a way, appealing to the sensibilities of these people and at the same time remaining faithful to the sacred scripture and the Tradition. The *Asian Synod*, while discussing the different aspects of a pedagogy of evangelization, has presented some images of Jesus Christ, such as the Teacher of Wisdom, the Healer, the Liberator, the Spiritual Guide, the Enlightened One, the compassionate Friend of the Poor, the good Samaritan, the Good Shepherd, the Obedient One etc. (*EA* 20). The development of a Christology in the Indian context is a basic need of the time because of its sensitive importance in the proclamation of Jesus and the Kingdom of God. [58]

The Oriental liturgy and theology very strongly express all the above mentioned images of Jesus in different contexts. The liturgical prayers during the administration of the sacraments, great Feasts of the Lord and the daily prayers strongly portray these images of Christ which bring Him closer to the day today realities of our life situations. But these images and titles are used only in relation to his divinity. The liturgy and theology do not allow in any way to down play the divinity of Christ through these images. It is a descending Christological approach emphasizing 'The Word became flesh', 'God becoming man'. The humanity of Jesus and all his events in history, all his human images become meaningful and salvific in relation to his divinity.[59]

Some of the contemporary Christologies give emphasis only to the social dimension of the Christ event. The mission of Jesus is associated only with some social problems downplaying the spiritual dimension of the soteriological mission of Jesus and his divinity. In this situation, the Oriental Christology can make a balancing act.

In a country like India, where people still uphold the importance of God experience, spiritual values and moral integrity, one has to emphasize correctly the divine dimension of Christ's personality.

Conclusion

This paper was an attempt to identify some of the relevant aspects of Oriental theology, especially that of Syriac theology, in view of developing an inculturated theology and theological methods in the Indian context. The *Asian Synod* has sufficiently highlighted the crucial need of inculturation for the effectiveness of evangelization in India and other Asian countries. The Oriental Churches generally have close affinity to Asian cultures and realities and these Churches in India have close affinity to Indian cultures and its realities because of their origin and growth in this soil. They have also acquired an inculturated character because of their close interaction with these cultures for a long period.

From our analysis of some of the conspicuous characteristics of the Oriental theology and its methods and the Indian cultural and religious ethos, we have underlined the acute need of evolving an indigenous narratology for an intelligible interpretation and communication of the sacred scripture for the people of India. The inculturation of liturgy, the *locus theologicus*, or the '*the gold mine*' of Eastern theology should aim at the existential transformation of worshippers and their consequent prophetic commitment for the values of the kingdom and the liberation of his fellow human beings from the clutches of oppressive and unjust human structures. Inculturation of Oriental liturgies in India has to take into serious consideration the field of liturgical music and the use of images and symbols. Application of Indian methods of interpretation like *dhvani siddhantha* to liturgical texts and ceremonies will make the participation more experiential.

The mystical, apophatic and contemplative character points to the primacy of deep personal experience of God and to the different methods of achieving it; for, it is the core of Indian spirituality. They also point to the need of developing a synthetic and symbolic approach to theology which is closer to the Indian mind than too much of rationalization and systematization. Oriental monasticism with different forms of consecrated life has to become the primary agent of inculturation in India considering the strong and widespread influence of *Sanyasa* in the contemporary Indian society and culture. In this respect monasticism is also an important agent of Inter-religious dialogue. The cosmic dimension of Oriental theology is a solid basis for evolving an eco-theology for India.

This is a unique and privileged task before the Oriental Churches in India which is a challenging one that involves the entire people of God. It needs a proper theological vision and an appropriate action plan. Theologians have to do it with courage and faithfulness to the sacred scripture, the Tradition and the Magisterium and with the awareness of and sensibility to the pastoral realities of the place and time. Proper formation of future priests, members of consecrated life and the laity is highly important. No one can question the relevance of Oriental Churches and theology in this process of theologizing in India. Already some attempts have been made by different people at different places and times. But a concerted effort is still in the offing.

Endnotes

1. Bishop Thomas Dabre, "Towards an Indian Christian Theology", in *Theologizing in the Malankara Catholic Church*, ed. James Puthuparampil OIC (Pune: BVP Publication, 2007), 26; Errol D'Lima, SJ," Theologizing in the Indian Context" in *From Streams to Source: Essays on the Foundation of Malankara Theology*, ed. Mathai Kadavil OIC et al. (Pune: BVP Publication, 2010), 46-64.
2. Pope John Paul II, *Apostolic Exhortations: Ecclesia in Asia* (Trivandrum: Carmel International Publication, 2005).
3. S. Brock, *The Syriac Fathers on Prayer and Spiritual life* (Michigan: Cistercian Publications, 1987), xxxiii.
4. Dr. Joseph Kallarangatt, "Dimensions and Perspectives of Oriental Theology," in *Eastern Theological Reflections in India,* ed. Xavier Koodapuzha (Kottayam: OIRSI, 1999), 87.
5. Robert Murray, "The Characteristics of East Syariac Christianity," in *East of Byzantine, Syria and Armenia in Formative Period*, ed. N. C. Garsoian et al. (Washington: Dumbarton Oaks Pub Service, 1982),14.
6. S. Brock, "Relevance of Syriac Studies", *The Harp*, I (1988): 11-12.
7. Joseph Kallarangatt, "Dimensions and Perspectives", 88.

8. H. J. D. Drijverse, "East of Antioch: Forces and Structures in the Development of Early Syriac Theology", in his *East of Antioch*, (London: Variorum, 1984), 18.
9. Vat. II, UR., 17
10. *Instructions: For Applying the Liturgical Prescriptions of the Code of Canons of the Eastern Churches*, (Vatican:1996), 11
11. S. Brock, *Syriac Fathers on Prayer*, xxxiii
12. Ibid.
13. K. E. McVey, *Ephrem the Syrian* (New Jersey: Paulist Press, 1989), 90.
14. Fr. John Berchmans OIC, "Doing Theology in the Malankara Catholic Church: Some soundings of Methodology" in *From Streams to Source*, 68
15. George Ayyaneth OIC, "A Narratorial Overture to Liturgical Theology" in *From Streams to Source*, 211
16. Ibid., 212
17. For some Narratological devices and models of Indian narrative system, see, K. Ayyappa Panicker, *Indian Narratology*, (New Delhi: Sterling Publishers, 2003).
18. Ayyaneth, "A Narratological Overture," 212
19. Aidan Kavanagh, *On liturgical Theology*, (Minnesota: Pueblo Publishing Co., 1992), 73.
20. For a theological study on this subject in the background of Malankara Catholic Church, see, John Berchmans OIC, "Doing Theology in the Malankara Catholic Church: Some Sounding on Methodology," in *From Streams to Source*, 65-88.
21. S. Brock,"Some Reflections on the sources for theologizing in the Malankara Catholic Church" in *From Streams to Source*, 38.
22. A. Kavangh, *On Liturgical Theology*, 73.
23. Joseph Kallarangatt, "Dimensions and Perspectives", 93.
24. Instructions: *For Applying the Liturgical Prescriptions*, 16.
25. Philip Vysaneth OIC, *Musicality makes the Malankara Liturgy Mystical* (Kottayam: SEERI, 2004); See also his, "Cultural commitment of Malankara Liturgy" in *Streams to Source*, 311-332 and "Relevance of the Malankara Hymnology in the Celebration of Faith and in the Interpretation of the Signs of the Times," in *Theologising in the Malankara Catholic Church*, 216-232.
26. Philip Vysaneth," Cultural Commitment", 313
27. Vat. II, SL.119
28. S. Brock, "Some reflections on the sources of theologizing," 41
29. R. Murray, *Symbols of Church and Kingdom* (Cambridge: Cambridge University Press, 1975), 2.
30. R. C. Bendi, "The spirituality of the Syriac speaking Christians", in *Christian Spirituality: Origin to the Twelfth Century*, ed. Bernard McGrinn & John Meyendorff, (New York: Crossroad, 1988), 157.
31. Bishop Thomas Dabre, "Towards and Indian Theology", 30

32. Placid OIC, "An Indian approach to the celebration of the mysteries" in *Theologizing in the Malankara Catholic Church*, 178-192
33. Ibid., 182.
34. John Berchmans OIC, "Liturgy of St. James, Celebration of Salvation History as God's Self Disclosure and Human's Response to it", in *Liturgy of St. James: its Impact on Theologizing in India*", ed. John Berchmans OIC and James Puthuparampil OIC (Pune: BVP Publications, 2009), 75-111.
35. Jacob Parappally, MSFS, "The Trinitarian Worship in the Liturgy of St. James and its Relevance for the Church in India," in *Liturgy of St. James*, 292; see also, James Puthuparampil OIC, "From Liturgy to Life: A Study Based on the Eucharistic Liturgy of St. James" in *From Streams to Source*, 339-341.
36. V. Lossky, *Mystical theology of the Eastern Church* (London: James Clarke & Co. Ltd., 1973), 9.
37. Joseph Kallarangatt, "Dimensions of Perspectives," 97.
38. *Instrumentum Laboris* (of Asian Synod), *L'Osservatore Romano*, 25 (February, 1998), 47.
39. R. Murray, "The characteristics of East Syriac Christianity," in *East Byzantine-Syria and Armenia in the Formative Period*, ed. N. C. Garroien et al. (Washington: Dumbarton Oaks Pub Service, 1982), 5-6.
40. K. Tong, "A Study of Thematic Differences Between Eastern and Western Religious Thought", JES 10 (1973): 341.
41. Msgr. Seely J. Beggiani, *Early Syriac Theology* (Boston: University Press of America, 1983), 1-9
42. Pope John Paul II, *Orientale Lumen* (Trivandrum: Carmel International Publications, 2005), 6
43. Tomas Spidlik, *The Spirituality of the Christian East* (Michigan: Kalamazoo, 1986), 327-349.
44. Evagrius, *De Oratione*, 60: PG 79:1180 B
45. Pope John Paul II, *Redemptoris Missio* (7 December 1990), 91; AAS 83 (1991), 338
46. George Thomas OIC, "Role of Monasticism in the Development of Theology in the Oriental Churches." in *Theologizing in the Malankara Catholic Church*, 301
47. Vat. II, UR, 15
48. *Orientale Lumen*, 9
49. Ibid.
50. Archiemandrite Boniface, *Eastern Monasticism and the Future of the Church* (Stamford: Baselios Press, 1993), 83.
51. Arthur Voobus, *History of Asceticism in the Syrian Orient*, Vol. I (Louvain: CSCO, 1958), 10-30.
52. Abhishiktananda, *The Further Shore* (Delhi: ISPCK, 1975), 1.
53. S. Dutt, *Early Buddhist Monasticism* (Bombay: Munshiram Manoharlal Publishers, 1960), ix.

54. George Thomas OIC, "Role of Monasticism, 311.
55. Jacob Parappally, "The Trinitarian Worship in the Liturgy of St. James and its Relevance for the Church in India", in *Liturgy of St. James*, 290-291
56. Tomas Spidlik, *Spirituality of the Christian East (Kalamazoo, Michigan: Cistercian Publication, 1986,* 125-50.
57. Mathai Kadavil, OIC,"Towards an Ecotheology from the Oriental Christian perspective", in *Theologizing in the Malankara Catholic Church*, 251-265; Mathew Jayanth, SJ, "Ecotheology from the Perspective of the Subsistence Needs of the Poor in India", in *Theologizing in the Malankara Catholic Church*, 284-300; Job Kozhanthadam, SJ, "Science and Ecotheology" in *Theologizing in the Malankara Catholic Church*, 266-283.
58. Jacob Parappally, MSFS, "Towards and Indian Christology" in *Theologizing in the Malankara Catholic Church*, 143-153.
59. Antony Kakkanatt, "The image of Christ in the liturgy of the Malankara Church: An Introduction to Malankara Christology," in *Theologizing in the Malankara Catholic Church*, 154-175.

Chapter 9

Reading the Bible in the Indian/ Asian Context

Rekha M. Chennattu, RA

The Paper begins with preliminary observations on biblical hermeneutics in general, followed by an assessment of the Indian biblical hermeneutics in particular. The article proposes *rootedness in and fidelity to* the biblical text as well as *sensitivity to and relevance for* the Asian contexts and world-views as hermeneutical keys for an Asian reading of the Bible.[1]

1. Preliminary Observations

As Lucien Legrand observes in his review of the book, *Waters of Fire*, "Christian theology itself is the outcome of an encounter between the message, culled in the thought patterns of the Semitic world, and the thinking of Greece, of Rome, of successive ages, and now of the age of modern science, sociology, psychology and already of the computer era."[2] Going back to the New Testament times, let us take the example of Saint Paul who was trained to interpret the Torah and belonged to the group that was responsible for the ongoing interpretation of the

Torah and its faithful transmission (1Cor 15:3). Paul was convinced that "the word of God is not chained/imprisoned" (*ho logos tou theou ou dedetai* [2 Tim 2:9]) by time and space or by any culture, language or people, and can be experienced and interpreted in a variety of ways. This is what Paul was doing after his encounter with the Lord on the road to Damascus – reinterpreting the Torah in the light of the Christ event (Gal 3; Rom 4) and interpreting the Christ event in the light of the Torah as well as the new pastoral concerns of the growing Church in the Gentile world (Gal 3; 1Cor 15; see also Acts 17). Paul was, therefore, a key figure in extending membership of the Church to non-Jews, in defining Christian identity through his law-free gospel and in developing an inculturated Christian theology.[3]

Similarly, the four evangelists interpreted the Christ-event differently. Although we have only one historical Jesus, we have four gospels giving us four different faces of Jesus. Each evangelist interpreted the story of Jesus in response to the needs of their respective communities. For example, by presenting Jesus as the *logos*, the fourth evangelist uses a concept that is familiar to the Jewish, Samaritan and Greek Christians, and reinterprets the meaning and significance of the Christ-event for the Johannine community.[4] The mystery of the Incarnation transcends the boundaries of Hellenistic philosophical thought and Jewish religious traditions and becomes a cross-cultural and inter-religious expression of the Divine. Therefore, Saint Paul and the four evangelists seem to be good biblical models for reading the Bible in the Asian context. On the one hand, they remained faithful to the experience of the Christ-event and, on the other, they made it meaningful to the new members who embraced the WORD by being sensitive to their cultures and religious traditions. I think we are called to do the same thing.

There is a growing awareness among biblical scholars today that the biblical texts are not unbiased, that biblical interpretations are not neutral, and exegetes are not without their presuppositions. We no longer regard the historical critical method as an objective, neutral and scientific approach to the Bible which can provide correct and meaningful interpretation of the text. This is so, because in biblical interpretation we are dealing with words/expressions – the articulations of human experiences which are conditioned by history, cultures and traditions. So one cannot talk about an Asian Chemistry, but can talk about an Asian exegesis.[5]

Asia is blessed with a great diversity of religions, languages and cultures. Almost all great religions originated in Asia and lived side by side peacefully for many years. Among other things, most of the Asian countries also suffer from massive poverty and gender discrimination. In an Asian Biblical Hermeneutics, one reads the Bible with an Asian pre-understanding, shaped by Asian realities and spiritualities as well as Asian exegetical traditions. In other words, an Asian reading should either use Asian methods of interpretation or be guided by the concerns of Asian cultures or provoked by questions emerging from the contemporary socio-political realities of Asian society.

2. Indian Readings of the Bible

It seems now appropriate to focus on one of the Asian contexts, namely, the Indian traditions. The quest for an Indian biblical exegesis is not a recent phenomenon. Many attempts have been made to revive the ancient Indian hermeneutics of "story telling" and to work out a method for an Indian biblical hermeneutics. Indian traditional methods were mostly synchronic. As Lucien Legrand puts it, "India has rich traditions of exegesis which have never fallen a victim to the lures of diachronic interpretation."[6] The Indian tradition seems to be closer to the Semitic tradition on this point. For example, the Aramaic versions of the Old Testament (*Targums* or *Targumim*) are not literal translations of the Hebrew bible, but colourful retellings of the old biblical stories for a new life context in the history of Israel. Similarly, for ages Indian *gurus* (religious teachers) have been using hermeneutics as a means of retelling the sacred stories for new generations.[7]

Some fifteen years ago, the late George Soares-Prabhu (an Indian biblical scholar) identified four ways (a list that is indicative or illustrative rather than exhaustive) of reading the Bible from an Indian perspective which are very significant for our discussion. Soares-Prabhu wrote:[8] An Indian reading of the Bible might mean any one of the following:

1. Reading the biblical text using traditional Indian methods of interpretation (like *dhvani*).
2. Reading the Bible in the light of specifically Indian concerns (like poverty or caste).
3. Reading the Bible with an Indian mind, that is, with the sensibilities of the great or little traditions of India (like the *vedantic* reading of John or a tribal reading of the Exodus).
4. Reading a biblical text along with a parallel text from an Indian Scripture – not to compare their respective religious world-views, but to gain new insights into the biblical text from its similarity to or difference from its inter-text.

I shall briefly deal with the three methods which are more common: 1) The use of the Indian traditional methods; 2) The *dhvani* interpretation; 3) Readings based on Indian realities and concerns.[9]

2.1. The Use of the Indian Traditional Methods

This reading goes back to the Vedic or Upanishadic experience of God and tries to understand the biblical symbols and narratives from the framework of the Indian religious mind. In this process, biblical symbols are placed on a par with Indian ones or replaced by Indian symbols from the Sanskrit literary tradition. Examples include the works of Krishna Mohan Banerjee, who found similarities between Vedic texts and biblical narratives and claimed Indian Christians as the spiritual heirs of Aryan Hindus[10]; Swami Abhishiktananda, who presented the Gospel of John as a Christian Upanishad[11]; T. M. Manikkam, who studied both the literary evolution of the Dharmasastras[12] and the Pentateuch and compared the teachings of Manu with the laws of Moses from philosophical, social and religious perspectives[13]; Bede Griffiths, who interpreted the Christian doctrine of the Trinity in the light of the *advaitic* (non-dualistic) experience of *Saccidananda*[14]; Vandana Mataji, who studied the Johannine symbol of *logos* in the light of the Upanishadic concept of *aum* and the symbol of water in the light of Hindu scriptures and traditions[15]; and Corona Mary, who used the Tamil Saiva-Siddhanta tradition to interpret biblical texts.[16] Such readings require an in-depth knowledge of both Hindu and Christian Scriptures to do justice to both traditions.

2.2. The Dhvani Method of Interpretation

The *dhvani* theory goes back to the 9th century linguistic studies in India and was first proposed by Anandavardhana of Kashmir in his work, *Dhvanyaloka*.[17] Anandavardhana argues that beyond the primary meaning (*abhidha*) and the secondary meaning (*laksana*) of a word, there is something real and beautiful which he calls "*dhvani*", the suggested or evoked meaning. Anandavardhana further explains the *dhvani* theory through similes and metaphors; he compares *dhvani* with the charm in a young woman. This charm is not identified with any individual part of the body or with the ornaments she wears, but it stands out. Similarly, the suggested meaning or *dhvani* shines above the individual words and their meaning. The suggested or evoked meaning creates an ambience of pleasant surprise among the readers or hearers.[18] In the words of A. Amaladass, "*dhvani* is something like an echo or resonance creating newer and newer echoes (*anuranana*). The popular etymology of the word *dhyanyate* brings out this aspect, 'that by which the real meaning (of the poem) resounds."[19] Unlike the primary and secondary meanings, *dhvani* thus provides new meanings to new readers. A. Amaladass further explains the role of *dhvani* with the traditional, stock example of *Gangayam ghosah* (literally "the village on the Ganga" [Ganges river]) which suggests or evokes an ambience of serenity, peace and holiness associated with the sacred river.[20] George Soares-Prabhu regards *dhvani* as a metaphor because *dhvani,* like a metaphor, "does not communicate a lesson, but evokes a limit experience – an experience of the transcendent which is so utterly beyond conceptualization."[21] The Indian *dhvani* reading comes very close to the semiotic analysis of the West.[22] The *dhvani* method pays special attention to the evocative process at work through various factors like structure, style, diction, intonation or gestures.

2.3. Readings Based on Indian Realities and Concerns

The contextualized readings display a special sensitivity to the Indian social realities like mass poverty, social discrimination and political corruption. Among these readings, two perspectives stand out: (1) Social and political perspectives (e.g., *dalit* readings from the point of view of the socially marginalized outcastes or *dalits* [literally, oppressed] and tribal readings from the point of view of the Indian tribal communities); (2) Feminist readings from the point of view of the experience of women in India who are victims of a double discrimination in society.

2.3.1. Social and Political Readings

The biblical stories were looked at from social and political perspectives. Following the principle of equality and justice, biblical texts have been interpreted from the perspective of the poor, the oppressed and the marginalized. The late George Soares-Prabhu, Samuel Rayan and the late Sebastian Kappen were pioneers in this field in India.[23] Indian social readings emphasized both personal conversion and structural change to bring about a just society that makes God's reign visible here on earth. A *dalit* reading is an Indian offshoot of the social reading as it interpreted the Bible in the light of the experience of the *dalits* (one of the most discriminated against groups which are said to be outcastes, i.e., considered lower than the lowest caste).[24] It developed a spirituality of confrontation against the enslaving social structures that perpetuate unjust and unequal relationships in society. Biblical texts are also interpreted from a tribal perspective. In an interpretation of Exodus 1–15, for example, Peter Haokip tried to show parallels between the exodus story of Israel and that of the tribal people of North East India.[25]

2.3.2. Indian Feminist Readings

Although many attempts have been made to develop an Indian feminist theology[26], we have not done much in articulating a biblical hermeneutics from an Indian woman's perspective. Pauline Chakkalakal is one of the pioneers who contributed to this area by reading the biblical texts with special sensitivity to the patriarchal bias in the Bible.[27]

What is the unique and distinct way in which Indian women respond to the present situation of cultural alienation, religious deprivation and male domination? The following observation seems timely and relevant. The conventions such as "being submissive" or "to cultivate a capacity to endure suffering and humiliation" still reflect in many ways what Indian women were taught (and still believe) as the most natural, normal and noble way of behaving in society. What seems appropriate in handling these issues is the strategy of constructive dialogues in view of challenging and changing the gender stereotypes in the Church and society being sensitive to the deepest aspirations of Indian women. Theological illiteracy is indeed one of the reasons for the subordination of women in the Church. Adequate biblical and theological formation will empower women to play their rightful role in the Church.

Jesus' vision of God's reign (Luke 4:16-21), Paul's dreams of an egalitarian society (Gal 3:28) and the significant roles played by biblical women have been a source of inspiration for Indian women. Courageous biblical women (e.g., the midwives in the story of the Exodus, the mother of Moses, Miriam, Deborah, Judith, Ruth, Esther, etc. in the OT, Mary, the mother of Jesus, Mary and Martha, Mary Magdalene, as well as the four women mentioned in the genealogy of Jesus in the Gospel of Matthew) not only reflect the socio-cultural reality of the biblical world but also foreshadow the ideals, aspirations and struggles of contemporary Indian women.[28] Sandra M. Schneiders discusses a three-fold mission of the Feminist biblical hermeneutics which is very relevant: it has the mission of liberating all oppressed in general and the Church from a gender biased world-view which alienates women from decision-making bodies as well as the text from its own participation in the discrimination against women.[29] An integrated approach that focuses on liberating God experience leading to the empowerment of women (at the personal level) and social transformation will be the hallmark of Indian feminist readings of the biblical narratives.

3. Towards an Asian Biblical Hermeneutics

We begin with a discussion of the Hindu world-view, which will hopefully help identify the hermeneutical key for an interpretation of the Bible in Asia today.

3.1. Asian/Hindu World-view

The focus here is the impact of Asian/Hindu (major or *brahmanic* tradition) understandings of God's word and Asian/Hindu world-view on the Christian appropriation of God's word and reading of the Bible. Lipner makes a helpful distinction between Hinduism and "Hinduness" – while Hinduism stands for "a family of religious traditions", Hinduness refers to the distinctive characteristics of the family of Hinduism, viz., "a particular orientation in the world, a specific way of being, a distinctive *mentalité*."[30]

The Hindu mind generally believes that God upholds the values that sustain and preserve the universe and is at work in human history. In the words of Vensus A. George, "the concept of the *avatara* of Lord Visnu in Vaisnavism and the concept of *Sakti* of the Lord Siva in Saivism point to the immanent aspect of the supreme God as active in the world respectively."[31] It seems that the fundamental unity pervading the Hindu traditions consists in a world-view that propagates the sacredness of the universe. Some Hindu schools like Sri Vaisnavism or Visishtadvaita (of Ramanuja and others of this school) regard the whole universe as the body of God. Vensus A. George refers to this unity as a "spiritual perspective with which the whole universe is viewed and understood" in Hinduism.[32]

The Asian religious tradition in general seems to consider that, more than the accumulation of information and speculation on dogmas of faith, the purpose of the study of the Scriptures is enlightenment or liberation (*moksa*). In the words of Sister Vandana, "reflection and commentaries on the Scriptures – *bhashya* – are the normal mode used in India for a growth in the spiritual life, for that is the goal of all theologizing – coming closer to God till we are one with him."[33] The knowledge sought after in the Scriptures, especially in the Upanishads, "is not that of ritual techniques or even of ritual-based homologies, but a graspable, revelatory and experiential knowledge of the self as one with the ultimate reality. In the early Upanishads this experience is formulated as the realization of ultimate connection', the oneness of *Atman-brahman*, a connection knowable only in the context of communication from *Guru* to disciple."[34] The exegetes are called to experience the divine presence and then to clarify the vision of the divine word (*vak*) which had been experienced by the ancient authors.[35] In Hindu exegesis, reason and revelation are regarded as complementary. Reason alone is empty and powerless when it comes to revealing and possessing the knowledge of the divine, but reason is necessary to remove doubts and obstructions.

The Hindu *mentalité* (to use an expression from Lipner) encourages open-ended inclusion and healthy relativism. It usually prefers a "*both-and*" to an "*either-or*" approach to reality and doctrines. Hindu traditions maintain an overall integrity and interrelatedness.[36] Asia's relativistic and inclusive world-view is expressed in the logical axiom of *sive-sive* "be it this way, be it that" or in other words "this as well as that," which coordinates rather than dissects. Julius Lipner shows that the analogy of a magnificent banyan tree explains well the polycentrism as well as the organic oneness of the diverse religious traditions grouped together under the umbrella of Hinduism.[37] The Hindu mind is characterized by an integrated diversity that upholds both unity and pluralism.

3.2. Hermeneutical Keys for an Indian/Asian Reading

As one of the Asian traditions suggests, the purpose or goal of interpreting God's Word is not mere knowledge but rather enlightenment or transformation because our interpretation strives to lead "the reader to a depth-meaning which is experienceable but not expressible."[38] To achieve this, when the exegetes deal with the Gospels, the interpreter needs to take into consideration *the world behind the text* (Christian communities responsible for the Gospels), *the world of the text* (the plot in the Gospels) and *the world in front of the text* (the contemporary Asian context).[39] The interpretation needs to be rooted in the biblical traditions as well as be relevant to the Asian contexts. *Rootedness in and fidelity to* the biblical text (the *centripetal* aspect of Asian reading) as well as *sensitivity to and relevance for* the Asian contexts and world-views (the *centrifugal* aspect of Asian reading) should function as hermeneutical keys for an Asian reading of the Bible.

3.2.1. Rootedness and Fidelity

In order to make an Asian interpretation of the text a Christian reading (which is different from a Hindu or Buddhist reading, for example), the interpretation should be faithful to the religious experience that is being communicated to the reader. The reader meaning (what is understood by the reader) should be in continuity with the author meaning (what is meant by the author). This process demands rootedness in the biblical tradition and fidelity to the text under consideration. Mastery of the biblical languages such as Hebrew, Greek, Syrian and Latin is crucial for an informed reading of biblical texts. Considering the richness and diversity of biblical texts, exegetes need to use a variety of complementary methods. Integration of various diachronic as well as synchronic methods becomes imperative.

An Asian reading should use different scientific methods to ensure fidelity to the text. Textual criticism helps one to deal with issues concerning the variant readings of the passage under consideration. Grammatical criticism responds to the questions pertaining to the biblical languages in general and the syntax of the sentences in particular. Literary criticism deals with style, character, compositional technique and the rhetorical patterns of the given text. The literary context or the location of the passage and its function within the larger literary units are important for the interpreter to be in continuity with the author meaning. Rhetorical analysis explores how biblical texts employ literary devices to persuade their readers. The Bible contains a rich diversity of literary genres and forms such as hymns, parables, allegories, prophetic speeches, pronouncement stories, miracle stories, diatribes, type scenes and metaphors, to mention a few. Questions concerning the literary forms and genres constitute the field of form criticism. Redaction criticism seeks to understand the changes the text might have undergone in the editorial process and focuses on the final form of the text under consideration.[40] Moreover, biblical exegetes need to revive the ancient Asian hermeneutics of "story telling" by exploring narrative criticism and reader-response criticisms.[41] The exegetes need to learn to ask right questions and learn to answer them in a coherent and meaningful way.

3.2.2. Sensitivity and Relevance

In order to make an Asian reading more meaningful and relevant for our times, the interpretation should be shaped by Asian social realities we well as the Asian world-view and spiritual quest. Asian biblical hermeneutics should, therefore, take care of the relevance of the interpretation for the Asian readers.[42] An integration of a variety of readings such as tribal, dalit, feminist, political, cultural and social perspectives will bring out the richness of the biblical texts for Asia.[43] A dialogue between the biblical world and Asian socio-political realities and religious traditions becomes imperative in the process. It challenges the interpreter to be deeply rooted in and sensitive to the Asian realities and worldviews in order to make the interpretation relevant and meaningful.

Asian sensitivity demands an inclusive approach which upholds the dignity and right of women and a social sensitivity that takes care of the poor and less privileged sections of society as well as the sustainability of the universe. The interaction with the Word of God brings about both personal conversion (*metanoia*) and social commitment to build up a more just and humane society. As George Soares-Prabhu puts it, "'Liberation' for the Asian psyche is not only liberation from poverty, but equally the liberation which leads to that 'poverty' which is freedom from illusion, attachment and greed."[44] It implies an integration of biblical exegesis, theology and spirituality. The primary purpose of biblical hermeneutics for Asians should be an encounter with God which results in personal *metanoia,* brings about social transformation and protects the cosmos for future generations. This personal experience of God, in the process of exegesis, empowers the interpreters to share in the life of God leading them to become instruments of God's reconciling or redemptive work (2Cor 5:18-21).

Conclusion

The real challenge is to get all the three horizons – the biblical traditions, ancient Asian traditions and the contemporary secular contexts – to interact with one another and enter into a process of dialogical engagement. [45] An Asian reading of the Bible is therefore characterized by both *centripetal* (maintaining rootedness and continuity) and *centrifugal* (encouraging sensitivity and diversity) aspects of hermeneutics. On the one hand, the interpreter needs both the historical and the literary critical methods in order to be rooted in the biblical text and to be faithful to the religious experience transmitted to us by the early Christian community. On the other hand, the interpreter needs to be familiar with ancient Asian traditions and be sensitive to the realities of the contemporary Asian society in order to make his/her interpretation relevant to the modern readers of Asia.

Endnotes

1. This article is a revised version of the Keynote address given at the International Conference on "Doing and Teaching Biblical Studies in East Asian Contexts" organized by Loyola School of Theology (LST) and the Catholic Biblical Association of the Philippines (CBAP) at Ateneo de Manila University Campus, July 15-17, 2010. It was first published in *Reaping a Harvest from the Asian Soil: Twenty Five Years of the OTC/FABC,* ed., Vimal Tirimanna (Bangalore: ATC, 2011), the Felicitation Volume on the occasion of the 25th year of service of the Office of Theological Concerns (OTC) in collaboration with the Federation of the Asian Bishops Conference.
2. Lucien Legrand, "Book Reviews," *Indian Theological Studies* XIX, No. 2 (1982): 172.
3. Rekha M. Chennattu, "Challenges of St. Paul to the Mission of the Church in Asia-Pacific," *East Asian Pastoral Review* (2009): 46-58.
4. Rekha M. Chennattu, "The Word Became Flesh (John 1:1-18): A Cross-cultural/religious Expression of the Divine," in *Cross-cultural Encounter: Experience and Expression of the Divine,* ed., Mohan Doss and Andreas Vonach (Innsbruck: Innsbruck University Press, 2009), 43-51.
5. George Soares-Prabhu, "Interpreting the Bible in India Today," *The Way Supplement* 72 (1991): 70-71.
6. Lucien Legrand, "New Horizons in Biblical Exegesis," *Indian Theological Studies* 21 (1984): 205.
7. The works of the great missionaries like Robert de Nobili (1577-1656) and Constant Joseph Beschi (1680-1746) show that they have followed the Indian

tradition of "story telling" and "retelling of old stories" for a new audience living in a different context. Following the example of two of the Hindu Sanskrit epics, the *Ramayana* and the *Mahabharata*, Beschi wrote an Indian Christian epic, a poetical work on the life and teachings of Jesus Christ, called *Thembavani* (*The Unfading Garland*) in which St. Joseph is portrayed as the hero.

8. George Soares-Prabhu, "Editorial," *Jeevadhara* xxv, No. 146 (1995): 104.
9. For reading a biblical text along with a parallel text from an Indian Scripture, I suggest the article of Soares-Prabhu on "Two Mission Commands" which interprets Matthew 28:16-20 (the mission command in Matthew) in the light of a Buddhist text. See *Biblical Interpretation* 2 (1994): 264-82).
10. Krishna Mohan Banerjee, *The Relation between Christianity and Hinduism* (Madras: Christian Literature Society, 1892). As Kaj Baago puts it, Banerjee "tries to prove two propositions: (i) that the Christian doctrine about salvation finds a remarkable counterpart in the Vedic principles of primitive Hinduism in relation to the destruction of sin and redemption of the sinner by the sacrifice of Prajapathi, the Lord and Saviour of Creation. (ii) That this Prajapathi is Jesus Christ." See, *Library of Indian Christian Theology: A Bibliography* (Madras: Christian Literature Society, 1969), 9.
11. Swami, Abhishiktananda, *Hindu-Christian Meeting Point: Within the Cave of the Heart* (Bombay/Bangalore: IIC/CISRS, 1969). See also *Saccidananda: A Christian Approach to Advaitic Experience* (Delhi: ISPCK, 1974).
12. *Dharmasastra* is the name for a traditional (ancient) Hindu text or book that contains laws or codes (corresponding to the Catholic Canon Law). There are several such *Dharmasastra* books; the most important are the codes of Manu and Yajnyavalkya.
13. T. M. Manikkam, *Dharma According to Manu and Moses* (Bangalore: Dharmaram, 1977). Manikkam also presents the thematical scheme of the laws of *Dharma* in *Manusmrti* and that of *Sedaqa* in Pentateuch; see pages 328-40.
14. See Bede Griffiths, *Return to the Centre* (London: Fount paperbacks, 1978); *The Marriage of East and West* (London: Fount paperbacks, 1983). *Saccidananda* is one of the later definitions or descriptions of Brahman (or the Supreme Being) in the *Upanishads*: *Saccidanandam Brahma*. So Brahman is Being, Consciousness, Bliss. These characteristics or qualities are identical with Brahman, who is one Person. However, Brahmabandhab Upadhyay, in his hymn *Vande Sac-cit-anandam* appeared in the monthly journal *Sophia* in October 1898, established a correspondence between *Saccidananda* and Christian Trinity (which is three Persons): *Sat* refers to the First Person (Father), who is Being, since the First Person is the "Creator"; *Cit* refers to the Second Person, the Logos, the Word, the Son; *Ananda* refers to the Third Person, the Holy Spirit. Cited in George Gispert-Sauch, "The Sanskrit Hymns of Brahmabandhav Upadhyay," *Religion and Society* 19:4 (1972): 60-77, especially, 65-77. For a scholarly explanation of

the hymn, see also Julius Lipner and George Gispert-Sauch, eds., *The Writings of Brahmabandhab Upadhyay* , Vol. 1 (Bangalore: The United theological College, 1991) 125-45; Julius J. Lipner, *Brahmabandhab Upadhyay: The Life and Thought of a Revolutionary* (Delhi: Oxford University Press, 1999) 199-204.

15. Vandana Mataji, "The 'Johannine-Upanishadic' Experience: An Indian meditation on John's Prologue," *Indian Theological Studies* 16 (1979): 153-68; *Waters of Fire* (Madras: Christian Literature Society, 1981).
16. See Corona Mary, "Divinization through Grace: Understanding a Johannine Theme in the Light of Saiva-Siddhanta," *Jeevadhara* 25 (1995): 161-72.
17. Anandavardhana, *Dhvanyaloka,* trans. K. Krishnamurthy (Delhi: Motilal Banarsidass, 1974).
18. Anandavardhana, *Dhvanyaloka,* 6.18-19; cited by A. Amaladass, "'Dhvani' Theory in Sanskrit Poetics," *Biblebhashyam* 5, No. 4 (1979): 262-75. See also his book, *Philosophical Implication of Dhvani: Experincing the Symbol Language in the Indian Aesthetics* (Vienna: Gerald & Co., 1984), 79-80.
19. A. Amaladass, "'Dhvani' Theory in Sanskrit Poetics," 262. See also Francis X. D'Sa, "*Dhvani* as a Method of Interpretation," *Biblebhashyam* 5, No. 4 (1979): 276-94.
20. Amaladass, "'Dhvani' Theory in Sanskrit Poetics," 263.
21. George Soares-Prabhu, "And There was a Great Calm: A Dhvani Reading of the Stilling of the Storm (Mark 4:35-41)," *Biblebhashyam* 5, No. 4 (1979): 301.
22. For a discussion of semiotic analysis and *dhvani*, see Joseph Pathrapankal, "The Way to the Kingdom of God: A Semiotic Reading of a Markan Pericope (Mark 10:2-16)," *Jeevadhara* 25 (1995): 120-22. Among scholars who tried to interpret the Bible using the *dhvani* method include George Soares-Prabhu, Matthew Vellanickal, Anand Amaladoss and R. J. Raja. See George Soares-Prabhu, "And There was a Great Calm: A Dhvani Reading of the Stilling of the Storm (Mark 4:35-41)," 295-308; Matthew Vellanickal, "Drink from the Source of the Living Water," *Biblebhashyam* 5, No. 4 (1979): 309-18; Anand Amaladoss, "Dhvani Method of interpretation and Biblical Hermeneutics," *Indian theological Studies* 31 (1994): 199-217; R. J. Raja, "Seeking God, Sought by God: A Dhvani-Reading of the Episode of Zacchaeus (Lk 19:10)," *Jeevadhara* 25 (1995): 139-48.
23. George Soares-Prabhu, "'Good News to the Poor'; The Social Implications of the Message of Jesus," *Biblebhashyam* 4 (1978): 193-212; "Jesus and Social Justice," in *Jesus for Our Times: Towards a Spirituality of Social Action* (Manila: FABC Office of Human Development, 1986) 34-52; "Class in the Bible: The Biblical Poor a Social Class?" in *Voices from the Margin: Interpreting the Bible in the Third World* (Maryknoll, New York: Orbis Books, 1991), 147-71; Samuel Rayan, "Jesus and the Poor in the Fourth Gospel," *Biblebhashyam* 4 (1978): 213-28; "Jesus and the Struggles of the Masses in India," *Third Millennium* 11

(1999): 18-31. Sebastian Kappen, *Jesus and Freedom* (Maryknoll: New York: Orbis, 1977); *Jesus and Society: Selected Writings of Sebastian Kappen, SJ,* (Delhi: ISPCK, 2002). See also L. Legrand, "'There is neither Slave nor Free, neither Male nor Female': St Paul and Social Emancipation," *Indian Theological Studies* 18 (1980): 135-63. See also Simon Samuel, "The *Kairos* of the *Galilaioi*: An Indian Liberationist Reading of John 1-7," *Jeevadhara* 25 (1995): 149-60. More than a decade ago, I did a political reading of the good shepherd metaphor in John's Gospel when India celebrated the 50th anniversary of her Independence from British rule. See Rekha M. Chennattu, "The Good Shepherd (Jn 10): A Political Perspective," *Jnanadeepa: Pune Journal of Religious Studies* 1:1 (1998): 93-105.

24. See for example, A Maria Arul Raja, "The Authority of Jesus: A Dalit Reading of Mark 11:27-33," *Jeevadhara* 25 (1995): 123-38. For *dalit* theology in general, see, for example, Peter Arockiadoss, *Equal and Free,* ed., Michael Amaladoss (Dindigul: Vaigarai Publications, 2010).
25. Peter Haokip, "A Tribal Reading of Exodus 1-15," Jeevadhara XL, No. 236 (2010): 89-108. For tribal theologies, see also the *Journal of Tribal Studies*; James Massey and Shimreingam Shimray, ed., *Dalit-Tribal Theological Interface: Current Trends in Subaltern Theologies* (Jorhat: TSC/WSC and Delhi: CDS, 2007).
26. For example, see Pearl Drego, "The Place and Role of Women in Church and Society in the Light of Vatican II," in *Quest for an Indian Church: An Exploration of the Possibilities Opened up by Vatican II,* ed., Kurien Kunnumpuram and Lorenzo Fernando (Anand: Gujarat Sahitya Prakash, 1993), 181-212; Shalini Mulackal, "Political Economy of Participation: Women in the Life and Mission of the Church," in *Ecclesia of Women in Asia: Gathering the Voices of the Silenced,* ed., E. Monteiro and A. Gutzler (Delhi: ISPCK, 2005),184-94. See also R. S. Shrivastava, "Women Empowerment: Some Critical Issues," in *Modernity, Feminism and Women Empowerment,* ed. A. Avasthi and A. K. Srivastava (Jaipur and New Delhi: Rawat Publications, 2001), 171-81; Mary C. Grey, *A Cry for Dignity: Religion, Violence and the Struggle of Dalit Women in India* (London: Equinox Publishing, 2010).
27. See Pauline Chakkalakal, *Discipleship: A Space for Women's Leadership* (Mumbai: Pauline Publications, 2004). Rekha Chennattu, "Women in the Mission of the Church: An Interpretation of John 4," *Vidyajyoti: Journal of Theological Reflection* 65 (2001): 760-73; Trans, "Les femmes dans la mission de l'Église: interpretation de *Jean* 4." *Bulletin de Litterature Ecclesiastique* CVIII, No. 3 (2007): 381-96; "Asian Feminist Christology," in *Asian Faces of Christ: OTC Theological Colloquium,* ed., Vimal Tirimanna (Bangalore: Asian Trading Corporation, 2005), 183-202. See also the whole issue of the journal, "Jesus and Women," *Jeevdhara* XL, No. 237 (2010): 175-252.
28. See Rekha Chennattu, Rekha Chennattu, "Biblical Women as Agents of Justice and Peace," in *Word of God: Source of Justice and Peace,* ed., A Peter

Abir (Tindivanam: CBF, 2008), 124-58; Evelyn Monteiro, "Re-imaging Woman and Reshaping Her Destiny: An Indian Feminist Reading of the Bent Body," in *Body and Sexuality: Theological-Pastoral Perspectives of Women in Asia, eds.,* Agnes M. Brazal and Andrea Lizares Si (Manila: Ateneo de Manila University Press, 2007), 139-50.

29. Sandra M. Schneiders, *Written That You May Believe: Encountering Jesus in the Fourth Gospel* (New York: The Crossroad Publishing Company, 1999), 126-34; idem., "Feminist Ideology Criticism and Biblical Hermeneutics," *Biblical Theology Bulletin* 19 (1989): 3-10.
30. Lipner, "Ancient Banyan: An Inquiry into the Meaning of 'Hinduness'," *Religious Studies* (1996): 112.
31. Vensus A. George, *Paths to the Divine: Ancient and Indian.* Indian Philosophical Studies XII (Washington, D. C.: The Council for Research in Values and Philosophy, 2008), 294.
32. Ibid., 295.
33. Vandana, *Waters of Fire* (Madras: Christian Literature Society, 1981), xvii.
34. Alf Hiltebeitel, "Hinduism," in *World Religions: Selections from the Sixteen-Volume Macmillan Encyclopedia of Religion* (New York: Macmillan Publishing Company, 1987), 488.
35. Harold Coward, *Sacred Word and Sacred Text: Scripture in World Religions* (Maryknoll, New York: Orbis Books, 1988), 122-28.
36. Tinu Ruparell, "Hinduism," in *Encountering Religion,* ed., Ian S. Markham and Tinu Ruparell. 2nd ed. (Oxford: Blackwell Publishing, 2005), 167.
37. Julius Lipner, "On Hinduism and Hinduisms: The Way of the Banyan," in *The Hindu World,* ed., Sushil Mitta; and Gene Thursby (New York and London: Routledge, 2004), 9-34, esp. 24-25. See also Rekha M. Chennattu, "*Verbum Dei* nel Contesto dell'Induismo," Paper presented at the Settimana Conclusiva dell' Anno Centenario del Pontifical Biblical Institute on May 5, 2010, Rome, Italy.
38. D' Sa, "*Dhvani* as a Method of Interpretation," 279.
39. See Sandra M. Schneiders, *The Revelatory Text: Interpreting the New Testament as Sacred Scripture.* 2nd. ed. (Collegeville, MN: Liturgical Press, 1999). See also Rekha M. Chennattu, "The *Svadharma* of Jesus: An Indian Reading of John 5:1-18," in *Seeking New Horizons: Festschrift in Honour of M. Amaladoss, SJ,* ed., Leonard Fernando (Delhi: Vidyajyoti Education and Welfare Society & Indian Society for Promotion of Christian Knowledge, 2002), 317-35.
40. See Peter S. Williamson, *Catholic Principles for Interpreting Scripture: A Study of the Pontifical Biblical Commission's The Interpretation of the Bible in the Church* (Subsidia Biblica 22; Roma: Editrice Pontificio Istituto Biblico, 2008). For these criticisms in detail, see Wilhelm Egger, *How to Read the New Testament: An Introduction to the Linguistic and Historical-Critical Methodology,* ed., Hendrikus Boers (Peabody: Hendrickson Publishers, 1996). See also

Metodologia dell' Antico Testamento, ed., Horacio Simian-Yofre (Bologna: Edizioni Dehoniane Bologna, 1995).

41. Jean Louis Ska, *"Our Fathers Have Told Us": Introduction to the Analysis of Hebrew Narratives* (Subsidia Biblica 13; Roma: Editrice Pontificio Istituto Biblico, 1990); Mark Allen Powell, *What is Narrative Criticism? A New approach to the Bible* (London: SPCK, 1993).
42. See Soares-Prabhu, "Interpreting the Bible in India Today," 77-79; R. S. Sugirtharajah, ed., *Interpreting the Bible in the Third World* (Maryknoll, New York: Orbis books, 2006).
43. See, for example, R. S. Sugirtharajah, *Asian Biblical Hermeneutics and Postcolonialism: Contesting the Interpretations* (Sheffield: Sheffield Academic Press, 1999).
44. George Soares-Prabhu, "Inculturation – Liberation – Dialogue: Challenges to Christian Theology in Asia Today," in *Biblical Themes for a Contextual Theology Today: Collected Writings of George M. Soares-Prabhu, SJ*, Vol. 1, ed., Isaac Padinjarekuttu (Pune: Jnanadeepa Vidyapeeth, 1999), 56. See also Samuel Rayan, "Asia and Justice," in *Liberation in Asia: Theological Perspectives,* ed., S. Arokiasamy and G. Gispert-Sauch (Anand: Gujarat Sahitya Prakash, 1987), 3-16; Kurien Kunnumpuram, *Towards a New Humanity* (Mumbai: St Paul's, 2005), 131-57.
45. See, for example, the editorial and articles in *Towards an Indian Biblical Hermeneutics,* ed., Rekha M. Chennattu, *Jeevadhara* XL, No. 237 (2010): 87-168.

Chapter 10

Methods and Models of Education
Reflections on Re-Visioning the Teaching and Learning Process

Mathew Jayanth, SJ

Introduction

Methods of teaching and learning constitute a complex field of research that involves theories of learning, models of education, pedagogy or methods of teaching, methods of evaluation, understanding the student profile, awareness of the prerequisites for learning as well as other areas such as syllabus, curriculum design, and resources. However, very little time and energy is spent in our theological and philosophical institutions on the question of methods of teaching and learning. In practice, professors in the faculties of philosophy and theology engage in the teaching and learning activity without any conscious knowledge of the theories of education that are implicitly present in their very activity. Bringing some of these theories into our conscious awareness could help us improve our teaching and learning process.

Understanding 'Method'

The term 'method' is ambiguous. When applied to the process of teaching and learning, it can be understood in two ways. First, it could mean the concrete ways adopted or steps taken in the teaching and learning activity. For instance, a teacher may employ the lecture method, the methods of lecture cum discussion, small group discussions with presentations, seminars, power point presentations, field studies, debates, panel discussions, participant observations and exposure program in his/her teaching and learning process. These are teaching methods in the sense that they are concrete steps taken or tools employed in order to achieve and realize the goal of education.

Second, 'method' could also be understood more abstractly as the assumptions, presuppositions, visions and goals of the total process of teaching and learning. In this sense, it stands for the theoretical structure or the conceptual framework of the teaching and learning activity. This structure or framework provides the rationale for the pedagogy used for the educational purpose. In reality, pedagogy evolves from the conceptual framework with which an educator operates and, hence, an analysis of one's pedagogy will unveil the theories of education on the basis of which the teacher is functioning. That is to say, method as understood as the structure or theoretical framework is seldom present in the conscious awareness of the teacher unless he/she is formally introduced to the theories of teaching and learning.

The primary focus of this paper is on method understood in its second meaning. The reasons for giving priority to the second understanding of method are the following: First, there is much chaos created in our discussion on improving the teaching methods on account of confusion caused by the mix-up of the two different understandings of method. Second, we often talk about pedagogy focusing exclusively on the first meaning of method and give little attention to the models of education or the theories of teaching and learning. As a consequence, we fail to make any headway in improving our pedagogy. Third, we are unaware that a specific pedagogy is built on a particular theory of education. It implies that one's conception of pedagogy differs from others depending on the underlying theories of education one has. It is important, then, that a certain level of consensus on the theories of teaching and learning is ensured before we can meaningfully talk about pedagogy. Finally, there is an immediate and urgent need to introduce new pedagogies into our teaching and learning process. For this, it is necessary to begin with some of the theories of education, because new pedagogies presuppose new theories of education. In other words, any significant change in the pedagogy is predicated upon our conceptual framework for teaching and learning.

From this perspective, the primary goal envisaged in this paper is to introduce ourselves to some of the models and accompanying theories of education with a view to initiating creative thinking in the field of pedagogy or methods of teaching. The assumption behind this is that familiarity with the models and theories of education as well as some of the theories of learning may prove to be of immense help for us to revision our pedagogy, our syllabus and curricula, and the process of assessment and evaluation. Accordingly, I shall discuss the four basic models of education and the various models that derive from them. While discussing these models, I offer a brief critical assessment of the teaching and learning processes that go on in our philosophical and theological institutions and suggest some of the crucial elements that need to be incorporated into our educational process. In conclusion, I shall highlight some of the insights that can be utilized for improving the methods of teaching and learning.

I. Models of Education Based on the Teaching and Learning Activity[1]

The educational model based on the teaching and learning activity in the classroom classifies the process of teaching and learning on the basis of the levels of the teacher input and the student input. Accordingly, this model generates four different sub-models. A grid could help understand the sub-models that emerge[2]. Here the teacher input is placed on a horizontal axis which marks a continuum from low teacher input to high teacher input. Similarly the student input is placed on a vertical axis representing a continuum from low student input to high student input. This generates four quadrants representing four sub-models of education.

1. MODELS OF EDUCATION
Based on the Teaching and Learning activity

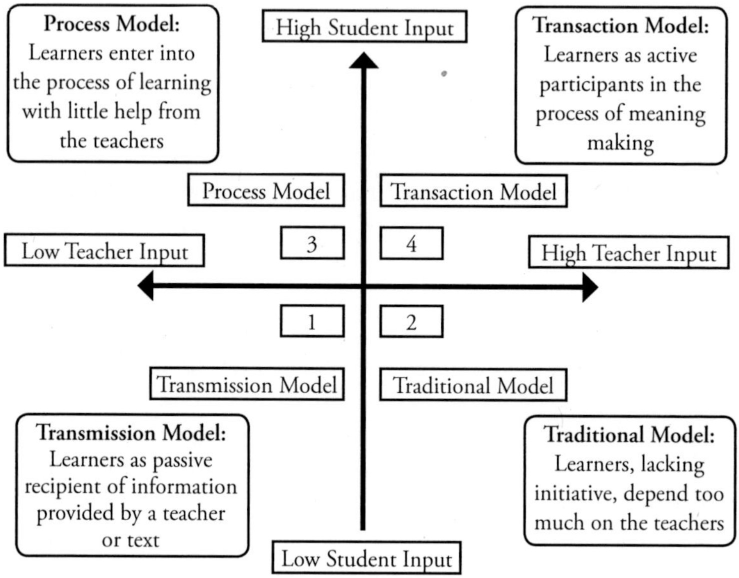

Quadrant I: Low Teacher Input and Low Student Input. The quadrant one (1) is characterized by minimum classroom activity from the side of both the teacher and the student. This is called the Transmission Model. In this model, students remain as passive recipients of information that the teacher imparts. The educational process depends heavily on lectures and class notes, prepared notes and reading material, and very limited and restricted student responses. As a consequence, a minimum is taught, a minimum is learned. The teacher is happy because there is hardly any demand on the teacher; the student is happy because not much effort is needed to learn the minimum that is taught. The student evaluation places emphasis on the student's ability to memorize what is taught. Since there is not much to memorize, it is possible for all students to perform well and score high marks in the examination. In the teacher evaluation, it is very likely that the teacher would be rated high since students easily understand the minimum that is taught, and especially so if he/she has a good sense of humor and has good communication skills. In an atmosphere that encourages high criticism of teachers that could endanger their teaching career, teachers may be tempted to adopt this model as a survival mechanism.

Quadrant II: High Teacher Input and Low Student Input. The second quadrant is marked by high teacher input and low student input. It is called the Traditional Model. Like the previous model, this model is also marked by passive learning and the educational process follows a similar pattern. However, there is one major difference, namely, that the teacher in this model is more active than in the previous case. This model can also be called the "banking model" because the teacher's primary function is seen as 'depositing' his/her knowledge into the students and the student's role is to take in what is deposited. The teaching method may include prepared notes, dictated notes, extensive use of blackboards, and/or power point presentations. Here the demand on the teacher is high. However, the student's capacity to think is stifled. Since the teacher does the thinking, the student is discouraged from thinking. This will contribute to the frustration of the intelligent students who place a premium on thinking. Students could perform excellently well solely by memorizing the content of the elaborate notes painstakingly prepared by the teacher. In the teacher evaluation students who have a penchant for gathering information (a majority of our students prefer this to independent thinking!) may rate the teacher high.

An Observation: In most of our philosophical and theological institutions we still operate according to models represented by Quadrants I & II. The teacher is concerned with giving more and more information to students. The role of the student is to "know' the information given and to reproduce it from memory. The focus of evaluation is to determine the amount of information the student has gathered in the process of attending a course. If the teacher and the student are operating with these models, it would be nearly impossible to bring about any substantial change in the teaching and learning process. No further explanation is needed to ascertain what our institutions stagnate!

Quadrant III: Low Teacher Input and High Student Input. The third quadrant, which is called the Process Model, is characterized by low teacher input and high student input. Within this model students enter into the process of learning on their own without much assistance from the teacher. This model may be appropriate for highly motivated self-starters as it gives them ample opportunity to study and do research independently. However, the average student will be in the lurch as they are deprived of their primary source of learning. Even the intelligent students would experience the deprivation since they lack the much needed feedback from the teacher as well as the opportunity to benefit from the teacher's knowledge, experience and guidance. As a consequence, they may not make as much progress as they could have made with the help of the teacher.

We find, in our institutions of philosophy and theology, students who fall into the category of self-starters who are normally highly intelligent and capable. They might find the normal classroom activity inadequate and frustrating. If our teaching and learning activity is not going to rise to the level represented by the Fourth quadrant, then, it is important to identify the self-starters in the group and to offer them the needed assistance by way of feedback and guidance to do independent study and research. This is particularly important in large classroom situations.

Quadrant IV: High Teacher Input and High Student Input. The specific marker of the fourth quadrant, called the Transaction Model, is the high input both from the teacher and the student. In this model both the teacher and students are actively involved in the teaching and learning process. Both are fully engaged in and committed to the principle of participatory learning in which students as well as the teacher are beneficiaries since both teach and both learn. Accordingly, the responsibility for learning and making decisions is shared by the teacher and students in their differing capacities.

The Fourth quadrant represents the ideal scenario of teaching and learning from the perspective of the model we are discussing. Here the process of teaching and learning operates on the basis of a contract between the teacher and students. The function of the teacher is to facilitate the learning of students and students take responsibility for their learning. This responsibility is vested solely in the students and it is not to be transferred to the teacher. If such transference occurs, it will pave the way for high teacher criticism which must be perceived as a camouflage for the students to debunk their own responsibility for learning. Encouraging such a tendency and making it a pattern of students' academic life in our institutions may be counterproductive in the long run as it encourages among teachers a corresponding tendency to seek cheap popularity by awarding high marks in examinations and to avoid criticism by means of adopting the model of teaching as represented by the first quadrant. This is becoming more and more a curse on our philosophical and theological education.

In addition, the model represented by the fourth quadrant is difficult to achieve precisely because the teachers in the institutions of philosophy and theology are disadvantaged on three accounts: first, they inherit the methods of teaching and learning as represented by quadrants I and II that are prevalent especially in the Indian educational system and they find it difficult to transcend the inherited models. Second, they have no formal learning in the theories and principles of education as required of ordinary primary and secondary school teachers. And third, the students they are dealing with are trained according to the models of the first and second quadrants. Therefore, teachers face a constituency that refuses to change over to any other model because they are unwilling to face the demands of the change. In addition, inadequate emphasis on accountability, lack of motivation and incentives make the situation worse. In my opinion, if we could adequately respond to the first two disadvantages, the handling of the third disadvantage would be easier.

II. Models of Education Based on the Outcome of the Teaching and Learning Process[3]

The first model based on the teaching and learning activity in the classroom is foundational and is applicable to the remaining three models of education because the teacher and the student inputs are basic to every type of educational process. It would suffice, however, to keep it in mind while discussing the other models. The models of education based on the outcome of the teaching and learning process consists of two subsidiary models, namely, the facrtory or industrial model and the womb model. The focus in both models is on the intended outcome or the end product of the educational process.

1. The Factory or Industrial Model: This model is particularly promoted by the corporate world that needs professionals to run the various departments of the corporation. In our institutions this model gets valorized when the church itself is seen as a big corporation in need of professionals. When this happens the philosophical and theological formation moves in the direction of a factory model. Accordingly, the institutions of philosophical and theological learning become factories or industries and the process of education assumes the nature of a mechanical, industrial process. Just as a car is fabricated in a factory, a church professional is fabricated in our institutions. Just as the process of producing a car begins at the beginning of a conveyor belt and comes out as a finished product at the end of the conveyor belt so also a church professional begins to be formed in the minor seminary or pre-novitiate and comes out as a finished product at the end of the conveyor belt of years long formation. From this perspective, the student is looked at as a factor of production to be assembled and put to work. A student who does not think and who does not ask critical questions would be considered as material of the best quality. The purpose or goal of the educational process becomes no more than the mass production of 'factors of production' to be used for the manufacture of wealth/ goods (services). The teachers are like industrial robots that produce well-trained products with competence, especially with the excellent qualities of submissiveness and total inability for critical thinking. Their competency is judged on the basis of their ability to produce professionals as required by the managers to run the corporation. For this purpose, the content (what is to be taught) and method (how it should be taught) are dictated to them and seldom are they given the necessary freedom for curriculum design.

According to this model, the purpose of reform and renewal of the educational process would be to make the institution more machine-like; production more mechanical; and products more 'efficient'. In order to achieve this goal, emphasis is often given to greater standardization and stricter regimentation. The ultimate consequence of such standardization and regimentation would be the total dehumanization of education itself.

This model in its starkest form may not be present in our philosophical and theological institutions. However, the restriction of the freedom of research and expression imposed on the teachers and, to a limited degree, on the students, and the constant supervision of the content and process of education with the help of 'invisible hands' point to the direction of a factory model of education. Moreover, the quality of the end products judged with the measure of personal conviction, initiative, creativity and commitment, and seeing the conspicuous lack of these qualities, one may be justified in thinking that the product is coming out of a conveyor belt. Further, the evaluation system focusing more on awarding marks for information reproduced than on personal transformation in terms of developing strong convictions, perspectives and commitments also may testify to a machine-like production process in our institutions.

2. The Womb Model: The womb model of education has great relevance for the life of the church. Here the church is understood as a community that needs nurturers rather than a corporation requiring professionals. Accordingly, school and education are viewed as a place the process of birth takes place – birthing a new generation of priests and religious who will carry forward the culture of the community. Here students are seen as human beings to be nurtured rather than machines to be fabricated. They are nurtured and set to thinking so that they may become agents of ecclesial and social regeneration. In conformity with this view of the student, the purpose of education is envisaged as individual cultivation of human maturity in order to give birth to thoughtful human beings who will embody and model the church's values for succeeding generations. Here the role of the teacher becomes delicate and challenging. They are seen as nurturers of human persons and midwives of a new generation of thoughtful priests and religious. This model of education also envisages the need for reform and renewal. However, the purpose will not be to make the educational process more mechanical and products more efficient. It will rather be to create space for personal growth; to promote individual initiative and freedom and to facilitate the generation of agents of ecclesial and social transformation.

The womb model of education, as mentioned earlier, has great significance for the church in India, especially because the church itself is considered as the Mother of the faithful. If the church is mother, then her primary function is to nurture and promote life. Priests and religious are people who are specially called to participate in the nurturing function of the church and, therefore, the institutions of philosophy and theology have the responsibility to create nurturers who are capable of giving witness by embodying the true nature of the church. This can be achieved only if teachers themselves become nurturers with the required competency to assist the birth process of a new generation of priests and religious. This does not rule out the need for professionals since the church is also an institution. The real problem emerges when the professional aspect overrides the nurturing dimension of the educational process. In fact, this is happening in our institutions under the impact of globalization where efficiency and professionalism is valued at the expense of everything else. The church values professionalism and efficiency, but it ought to value the nurturing dimension more and create in her professionals the ability to become nurturers. Accordingly, the process of reform and renewal of our institutions of philosophy and theology need to aim at transforming them into places of rebirth and regeneration, the teachers into nurturers and midwives of a new generation of priests and religious and students into embodiments and carriers of the values of the church for future generations.

III. Models Based on Orientations to Learning[4]

While the focus of the first models was on the teaching and learning activity in the classroom and that of the second on the outcome of the educational process, the emphasis of the third models fall on the learning theories and particularly on orientations to learning. Here learning is viewed not as a product in terms of acquiring knowledge, skills, methods and the ability to apply them to various circumstances of life. If we look at learning as a product – the outcome of a process – then learning becomes external to the learner. Rather, in the third models learning is seen as a process of change and transformation and, hence, learning as internal to the learner. It is different from the models represented by quadrants One and Two in the first models and from the factory model where learning is perceived as something the teacher does to the student. When looked at learning as a process, it is something that happens to the student as a consequence of the participatory teaching and learning process as represented by the fourth quadrant in the first model, and the nurturing of the persons as seen in the womb model of education. That is to say, there is something personal about the educational models based on orientations to learning.

There are four orientations to learning, namely, the behaviorist orientation, the cognitive orientation, the humanist orientation, and the social/situational orientation. Each of these orientations enshrines specific views of learning, the purpose of learning, the role of the teacher as well as the manifestation of this orientation in adult learning. These orientations to learning show various aspects of learning involved in the process of education which need to be taken into account.

1. Behaviorist Orientation to Learning[5]

View of the learning process:

The behaviorist orientation to learning views education as a process leading toward a change in behavior. The change is perceived predominantly as a function of the environment. More than the learner himself or herself, it is the elements in the environment that are considered to be decisive for what one learns. Therefore, the behaviorist orientation to learning gives great importance to the environment of learning in the process of learning that leads to the formation of habits indicating changes in behavior. However, the behaviorist orientation in its emphasis on the environment tends to overlook other factors in the learning process which the other orientations highlight.

Purpose in education:

Consonant with the view of learning as a process, the purpose of learning is conceived as producing behavioral changes in the desired direction. Knowledge and theory have no relevance in themselves. They are significant insofar as they help bring about changes in behavior.

Educator's role:

Accordingly, the role of the teacher is to arrange the environment to elicit the desired response. The learning environment needs to be such that it makes learners active rather than passive. For the behaviorist orientation to learning presupposes that activity is important for learning to take place. Moreover, constant practice is also a necessary element for effective learning. Together with repeated practice, there is also the aspect of positive reinforcement by way of rewards that plays a significant role in the learning process. Finally, to better facilitate learning, the objectives of learning need to be made clear to the learners. In these ways the teacher creates and arranges the environment for learning and facilitates behavioral changes.

Manifestations in adult learning:

Since in the behaviorist orientation to learning the emphasis is on the outcome of the learning process in terms of behavioral changes, the learner manifests one's learning in effecting behavioral objectives, especially the desired changes in behavior. Second, competency-based education focusing on developing capabilities to do things rather than merely having theoretical knowledge and skill development are other manifestations of behaviorist orientation in adult learning.

We shall now briefly look at the significance of the behaviorist orientation to learning for the philosophical and theological education. Effecting change and transformation of behavioral patterns in the direction of an authentic Christian life is a central concern of our philosophical and theological formation. However, living in a society that is steadily becoming more and more consumerist, it is undeniable that people tend to adopt consumerist values and patterns of life. Consumerism exercises a strong influence both on teachers and students in our institutions. This is the environment of our education and it leads our students to adopt behavioral patterns contrary to what is desired and intended by our educational process. The primary question for us educators at this juncture is: what should be the nature and characteristics of the environment in our institutions and how can we transform it so that our teaching and learning will effect change in our students in the desired direction of Christian values and patterns of life? This question highlights the vital need to pay greater attention to the behaviorist orientation to learning in our educational process.

2. Cognitivist Orientation to Learning[6]

View of the learning process:

The focus of the cognitivist orientation to learning is on the individual's internal mental processes including insight, information processing, memory, and perception. That is to say, it is concerned with cognition itself, namely, the act or process of learning. Learning takes place through inferences, expectations and making connections. From a cognitivist perspective, rather than acquiring behavioral habits as in the case of behaviorist orientation to learning, learners acquire the ability to make plans and strategies through the learning process.

Purpose in education:

From the perspective of cognitivist orientation, the purpose of education is to develop capacities and skills to learn better. Behavior, tasks and skills need plans and strategies to put them into effect in actual practice. It is the primary function of education to provide the ability to plan and develop strategies to execute tasks which come from the knowledge acquired through the process of learning.

Educator's role:

The primary role of the teacher envisaged in the cognitive orientation is to structure the content of the learning activity. This role of the teacher takes into account some of the key principles of the cognitivist orientation to learning. They include the need for the teacher to organize the instructions well because well organized material can be easily learned and remembered. The cognitivist orientation requires the teacher to clearly structure the instruction taking into account that the subject matter itself has inherent logical relationships among key ideas and concepts that link the parts together and it is the responsibility of the teacher to explicate these relationships. The teacher also needs to be aware of the knowledge level of the learners so that new learning can be incorporated into things that are already known by students. This presupposes that there are differences in individual learners. Finally, the teacher needs to give cognitive feedbacks, that is, providing information about the results of learning. This will reinforce the learning process. In this way, the teacher plays a constitutive role in the cognitive orientation to learning.

Manifestations in adult learning:

In adult learning, the cognitive orientation to learning is manifested in the cognitive development of the learner which includes development in the internal mental processes such as insight, information processing, memory, and perception. The growth in intelligence is manifested in the ability of the student to make inferences and to establish connections among key ideas. In the practical realm the student will show competence in making plans and strategies for achieving the desired goal.

The cognitive orientation to learning has great significance for our philosophical and theological education. What we witness at present in our institutions is an increasing disdain for intellectual excellence. It is evident in the overemphasis given to extracurricular activities in our institutions, often at the expense of the academic side. Sports and games, musical and cultural performances, various competitions, celebrations, program and shows, and pastoral and social activities easily substitute serious academic activities. The teaching and learning itself is approached as a burden helplessly borne and as a necessary evil to be patiently endured. The tragedy is that even the educators seem to encourage and promote this view by lowering the standards, relaxing the demands, and rewarding mediocrity, thereby enabling students to perform well in the examinations even without any serious application to study.

While this is happening in our institutions, the secular world throws up challenges and questions from varied fields starting from the religious, socio-cultural, economic and political, environmental spheres and reaching up to the most challenging fields of science and technology. Often the questions coming from secular fields have a direct bearing on our faith. And yet the priests and religious who come out of our institutions find themselves inept in facing these questions and responding to these challenges. Helplessly settling for simplistic answers learned in earlier catechism classes becomes the only pastoral option for many as a result of the neglect of intellectual and academic excellence.

In the emerging situation, it is incumbent upon our philosophical and theological institutions to ensure that the cognitivist orientation to learning is given adequate importance. They should do this knowing that the pastoral ministry is not narrowly limited to what our students understand and that it involves much wider and complex areas than preaching, teaching catechism, conducting choirs and administering sacraments. Pastoral ministry in the modern world calls for adequate intellectual preparation as emphasized in the cognitivist orientation to learning.

3. Humanist Orientation to Learning[7]

View of the learning process:

In the humanist orientation to learning, the stress is neither on the change of behavior nor on the mental processes that go on in the learner, but on the potential for human growth. Rather, the process of learning is seen as a form of self-actualization of the whole person which is considered as the highest good desired in the learning process. Learning is approached as a personal act to fulfill one's potential. In the humanist orientation the learning process engages the whole person with his or her experiences. As a consequence, the humanist approach to learning combines the logical and the intuitive, the intellect and feelings. The critique of the humanist orientation to learning is that it tends to be narrowly individualistic and self-centered.

Purpose in education:

In conformity with the humanistic vision of the learning process, the purpose of learning is perceived as becoming a self-actualized person. Self-actualization is understood as the capacity to make full use of and give full expression to one's talents, capabilities and potentialities. Self-actualization also entails becoming autonomous persons not in the sense of having no social responsibility but capable of fulfilling the social obligations without losing one's own integrity or personal independence. The social existence of the self-actualized person need not necessarily limit one's horizon as not to see other possibilities of self-actualization. If necessary, he/she may be also prepared to transcend the socially prescribed ways of acting in order to reach one's full potential as a human person.

Educator's role:

The teacher's role is limited solely to facilitating the development of the whole person. It implies that the teacher should ensure the personal involvement of the whole person. That is to say, the feeling and cognitive aspects of the person needs to enter into the learning process. The teacher may provide external impetus or stimulus; however, he/she should realize that learning is self initiated and that understanding and comprehension come from within the learner. Similarly, the teacher should be conscious of the fact that learning could exert influence on the behavior, attitudes and personality of the learner and make a difference. However, it is the learner's responsibility for this to happen. Furthermore, it is important to know that in this approach the learner is also the evaluator. The teacher could assist the learner to see whether the learning process meets the needs of the learner and provide the necessary help to achieve what the learner wants. And, finally, the teacher should realize that the essence of learning is making meaning for one's life and, therefore, the teacher should make sure that meaning is built into the whole experience of learning.

Manifestations in adult learning:

The primary manifestation of the humanistic orientation to learning is in the sphere of self-directed learning. The adult learner knows what he/she wants and takes the initiative to get fully involved in the learning process and ensures that he/she achieves the goal one sets for oneself. It is in the self-directed learning that one manifests one's journey toward self actualization.

The humanist orientation to learning could shed light on certain ambiguous areas of our philosophical and theological education. Often questions are raised about the appropriateness of philosophy and theology professors being considered as formators. It is argued that the job of professors is to teach and the formation should be delegated to a different agency called 'the formators'. The humanist orientation to learning shows that personal growth and actualization of the self are strong components of education. Teaching and formation constitute two inseparable sides of the whole teaching and learning process. The responsibility to facilitate the personal development of students through their teaching is vested on the teachers. This makes it clear that teaching cannot be confined to transmission of information but also includes the inculcation of the formative value of the subjects taught. For this, the teachers themselves would have to personally experience and live those values inherent in the subjects. In other words, witnessing by life is integral to the teaching and learning process. Teachers, by giving witness to a Christian way of self-actualized life by their pattern of life, facilitate the self-actualization of students. The humanist orientation to learning needs to take this direction in our institutions of philosophy and theology.

4. Social and situational orientation to learning[8]

View of the learning process:

From the perspective of the social/situational orientation to learning, the process of learning is situated in the context of social relationships, in situations of co-participation. Learning takes place through interactions/observations in social contexts. Here the focus is not on cognitive processes and conceptual structures but on social engagements that provide the context for learning. Learning is seen as a process of social participation and, hence, participation in communities of practice is essential for learning to take place. People often begin learning at the periphery of a community and gradually move to the centre of a community of practice. The increasing participation in the communities of practice is seen as authentic learning and it involves the whole person acting in the community and the world. The social/situational orientation emphasizes the situated nature of learning. Learning is always contextualized.

Purpose in education:

In the context of a relational view of persons and learning, the purpose of education is understood as full participation in communities of practice and utilization of resources. Since the social orientation to learning does not envisage learning as acquisition of knowledge and information by individuals, but as a process of participation in the socio-cultural practice of the community, the purpose of education is to enable persons to become full participants in the community and through the community to engage in the world.

Educator's role:

As both the vision and purpose of education underscore the centrality of participation in a community of practice, the teacher's role in the learning process is to work to establish communities of practice in which conversation and participation can occur. The teacher needs to explore all possible avenues with people in communities to ensure that all are accorded full participation. The teacher should be especially sensitive to the power relations existing in communities that might prevent some from becoming full participants in the socio-cultural practices of the community.

Manifestations in adult learning:

The social/situational orientation to learning is manifested in the degree of social participation of the people. High levels of participation and engagement would indicate the depth of one's learning. Moreover, since learning is not the private possession of individuals but an integral part of various conversations in a community, adults give expression to their learning by becoming partners in conversation at various levels.

While discussing the significance of the cognitive orientation to learning the tendency to overly engage in extracurricular activities was exposed and critiqued as an excuse to evade the demands of academic excellence. The social orientation to learning, on the other hand, reveals the significance of social and pastoral involvement for the teaching and learning of philosophy and theology. Students often complain about the irrelevance of what is taught in our institutions. The major reason for this complaint is the lack of orientation of our teaching and learning to the ecclesial and social life. Our philosophical theological education has become decontextualized in the sense that it is unrelated to and irresponsive to the questions arising from our life situations. The teachers are excellent thinkers, no doubt, but their isolation from and lack of lived experience of the life-context of the people make their teaching insular and irrelevant. Students who often have much greater exposure and experience of the living conditions of the people bemoan the inability of teachers to link their teaching with the pressing issues arising from society.

Contrary to the current isolation of both teachers and students from the context of a living community, the social orientation to learning emphasizes the need for our teaching and learning activity to be concretely situated in the life of a community and learning to emerge from involvement and engagement in the life of the people. This specific orientation reminds us that authentic learning has to evolve from the interaction between the learning activity proper and participation in a community of practice. Learning is not something done but it is something that happens in the interface of participation in social/ecclesial life and formal learning.

To conclude, teaching and learning is not to be guided by a single orientation. It involves multiple orientations and all are important. These orientations constitute the different components of the total educational process. The weakness of our institutions is that most of our teaching focuses on the cognitivist orientation and, as a result, it becomes, as we shall discuss in the following model, reductionist. This explains the fragmentation of our education. The challenge before us is to incorporate all orientations into our teaching and learning process.

IV. Models Based on the Dimensions of Education[9]

Educational process is a very complex reality as it entails different dimensions of thinking and varied levels of awareness. If in the earlier times the approach to education was characterized by a simplistic concept, the complex nature of education is being acknowledged and accepted in the contemporary times. Based on the emphasis given to the dimensions of education, it is possible to classify education as conventional or unidimesnional and holistic or multidimensional education.

(a) Conventional Education (Unidimensional)

All of us are familiar with the conventional, unidimensional education since it was probably the only type of eduaction that we have been introduced to and the only model we employ in our current educational activity. Hence, without going into details, we shall briefly delineate the main characteristics of this type of education.

In conventional education, the focus is exclusively on the cognitive dimension of the learning process. As a result, all learning is seen as a cognitive process involving the mind and all the mental processes such as reasoning, logical ordering of ideas, making inferences, memorizing, remembering and everything associated with mental activity. Accordingly, the academic task is considered exclusively as the development of the intellectual capabilities of students. Nothing else is given importance. The student is like a robot that must assimilate information unilaterally provided by the teacher. The unidimensional education is, thus, similar to the models represented by the first and second quadrants in the models based on the teaching and learning activity that we discussed in the beginning. It is also similar to the Factory model of education.

The cognitive vision of learning is one-dimensional and, hence, reductionist. Education is reduced to a single dimension, namely, the cognitive, and, accordingly, places emphasis on memorizing, and intellectual, rational, linguistic, linear and materialistic training. As we shall see, the unidimensional cognitive vision leaves out other important and fundamental dimensions of education that are taken seriously in the holistic approach to teaching and learning.

(b) Holistic Education (Multidimensional)

Unlike the conventional model, the holistic model of education attempts to take into account the entire field of thinking, learning and expression of the whole person. This model views teaching and learning as a pluri-dimensional and multilevel task related to the total awareness, experience and expression of the student. It considers education as an integral process involving various dimensions of thinking and different spheres of awareness. In other words, the holistic vision of education focuses on the total body-person with his/her personal, intellectual, psychological, moral, aesthetic, social, ecological and transcendental dimensions and awareness.

The holistic model identifies, in particular, six dimensions of the teaching and learning process. They are: Cognitive Dimension, Social Dimension, Emotional Dimension, Corporal or Physical Dimension, Aesthetic Dimension and Spiritual Dimension.

1. **The Cognitive Dimension** focuses on the thought process and the capacity to reason logically. This dimension takes seriously the intellectual nature of human persons. As intelligent and rational beings, human persons thirst for truth. Seeking and finding the truth about the natural world, about humans and their societies, as well as about God are integral to human existence. Every educational process, therefore, requires to give importance to the cognitive dimension of education.
2. **The Social Dimension** emphasizes the social nature of human existence. Human beings are social beings who can become humans only in the context of a society. Precisely because humans are social, all learning happens in a social context of shared meaning. Accordingly, social interaction and social participation, as the social orientation to learning has pointed out, have a significant role in the learning process. The social dimension of education, thus, emphasizes the interrelated

nature of human existence and its importance for the teaching and learning process.

3. **The Emotional Dimension** gives due importance to the fact that human persons are psychological beings. Feelings and emotions play a significant role in making us who we are. The Stoic concept of human persons as rational who would be best if untouched by emotions is seen as a distortion of what it means to be real humans. The multidimensional education understands that all learning is accompanied by an emotional state which can greatly affect the learning outcome and, hence, it recognizes the role of emotions in the educational process.
4. **The Corporal or Physical Dimension** is an important factor in teaching and learning that has been sidelined for too long. Human persons are essentially body persons and the embodiment is the substratum for all other dimensions of human existence including the teaching learning process. The holistic education acknowledges this truth about human persons and recognizes that all learning occurs in a physical body. Therefore, the mind-body harmony is an important element in the quality of learning. What we learn, we learn in our bodies and there can never be any learning outside the body. In a way, the physical dimension is central to the learning process.
5. **The Aesthetic Dimension** is another aspect of human existence that has also been ignored in the educational process. Along with truth and love, beauty is a key aspect of human existence. Holistic education realizes this truth and considers the aesthetic dimension as an important element is the educational process. By emphasizing the dimension of beauty, it directs our attention to the interiority of the learner and underscores the need for giving expression to the interior life of a person as a significant dimension of the educational process. It sees artistic expression of inner life as a key to a happy life. This makes it mandatory that the teaching and learning process gives due importance to the aesthetic dimension in education.
6. **The Spiritual Dimension** is the third and crucial aspect that has also been overlooked in the teaching and learning process. The reason for ignoring the place of spirituality in education is

that, first, it wrongly gets associated with sentimentalism and superstition. Then it is judged to be unscientific and unfit for consideration in the educational process. And finally it is delegated to the sphere of emotionalism emerging from a pre-scientific mindset. However, the spiritual dimension of a person is a much deeper concept that views human persons as transcendent beings who seek to go beyond the limitations imposed by embodiment as well as the space and time categories. Spirituality is, thus, seen as a person's capacity to open oneself to the totality of reality that confronts us at every moment of our existence. Holistic education considers the spiritual dimension to be the total and direct experience of universal love that establishes a sense of compassion, fraternity and peace toward all beings. The spiritual dimension of education broadens one's sphere of existence so as to include the cosmic and transcendental levels.

The emphasis given to the six dimensions of thinking and learning testifies that the holistic approach to education focuses on the total person who is, at once, embodied and sensual, intelligent and capable of emotions and feelings, aesthetic and social, moral and spiritual. The complex nature of human persons makes the educational process itself complex. Each of the dimensions of the human person is involved in the teaching and learning process. Overlooking any of the dimensions would make education somewhat truncated. Therefore, it is essential that all genuine educational process should take the total person into account. Education becomes genuinely holistic when each of the six dimensions of thinking is given due importance.

Besides the six dimensions of thinking, the holistic model also identifies five levels of awareness and experience that are seen as integral to the teaching and learning process. They are: Personal Level, Community Level, Social Level, Planetary or Environmental Level and Kosmic[10] or Spiritual Level of awareness and experience. The last level should not be seen as one along with the other four levels. It must be viewed as inclusive of all the individual, community, social, and environmental levels. The holistic education visualizes the Spiritual level as a presupposition for all other levels for the reason that a deep level of awareness and experience is fundamental to all genuine education.

1. **The personal or individual level** of awareness and experience looks at the person as an independent unit. Here the focus is on the self-awareness of the person. One acquires the awareness of the self through personal or individual experiences. It is this awareness emerging from personal experiences that constitutes one's identity. This identity allows one to expand one's awareness and experience to wider levels. It is important that the process of teaching and learning should shape this identity by deepening one's self-awareness through personal experience. This will facilitate the movement of a person to wider levels of awareness.
2. **The community level** of awareness and experience is wider than the first in the sense that here the person is concretely situated in the context of a community where face to face relationships exist. The community provides the locus for the self-awareness and experience to take place. From this perspective it can be said that learning is primarily communal and teaching and learning is basically community education. A person's relatedness to the community in terms of interactions and exchange contributes to the expansion of one's awareness as a person and as a member of a community.
3. **The social level** of awareness and experience, predicated upon social education, entails a much wider awareness. The person at this level becomes aware of the cultural heritage of the society of which he/she is a part. Transcending the personal and communitarian levels, the social level of awareness enables a person to critique and expose the cultural and ideological distortions operating in a society. The function of social education is to make a person responsible for the well-being of society. The holistic education focusing on the social level of awareness and experience should equip the person to become a consciously active member of a society.
4. **The planetary or environmental level** of awareness and experience that has been sidelined for the greater part of the history of education has received importance and relevance with

the realization of the impact of ecological degradation on the survival of humans and other life-forms. The holistic model of teaching and learning emphasizes the role of environmental education for the further expansion of one's awareness and experience to a higher level. At this level one's awareness encompasses the planet and one perceives oneself as a knot in the planetary web of relationships. The consciousness of being a part of the entire planetary life process enables a person to be a responsible and active member of the earth community.

5. **The Kosmic or spiritual level** of awareness and experience is seen as the heart of holistic education because it encompasses all other levels of awareness and provides an integral vision of education. Therefore, this level of awareness that has so far been excluded from education has assumed centrality in holistic education. For this level of awareness is seen as the sphere of love and wisdom that allows us to perceive ourselves as spiritual beings. The awareness of our essential nature as spiritual beings takes a person to the vantage point from where he/she could experience universal love, compassion for all living beings, solidarity, fraternity, peace and harmony. This awareness and experience is considered to be the ultimate goal of the educational process.

The five levels of awareness highlight the dynamic process involved in education. It is marked by a movement from self-awareness toward the spiritual awareness through community, social and planetary levels of awareness. This expansion of awareness is not chronological but synthetic in the sense that at every level all the other levels are present in a greater or lesser degree. At the same time, each of the higher levels encompasses the lower levels. Thus, the community level includes the personal; the social level includes the personal and community levels; and the planetary level includes the personal, community and social levels. The spiritual level of awareness not only encompasses the personal, community, social and planetary levels of awareness, but it also facilitates the integration of the cognitive, emotional, physical, social, aesthetic and spiritual dimensions of the teaching and learning process. Therefore, the spiritual level of awareness marks the culmination of the educational process. The challenge of holistic education for the philosophical and theological formation is to approach each of the levels of awareness and each dimensions of thinking from the spiritual level of awareness that alone can give coherence to any authentic education.

Conclusion

Our discussion so far has convincingly shown that teaching-learing is a complex porcess that involves theories of education, pedagogy, prerequisites for learning, understanding the student profile and methods of assessment and evaluation. Added to them are other elements such as the syllabus, schedule and resources. In this paper we have focused mainly on theories or models of education. We have discussed four models of education based on the teaching and learning activity, the expected outcome, the orientations to learning and the dimensions of teaching and learning. The main purpose of the discussion was to sharpen our perception of what is entailed in genuine education and the processes involved.

We have realized that authentic learning presupposes participatory learning as exemplified in the fourth quadrant of the first model. The teacher's participation must be characterized by the quality of nurturing as shown in the womb model of education. Moreover, the teaching and learning process needs to incorporate the various orientations to learning as discussed in the third model. And, finally, and most importantly, the educational process must take into account the various dimensions of thinking and the different levels of awareness as shown in the holistic model of education.

These insights, if incorporated into our philosophical and theological education, can enrich our teachig and learning activity in our institutions. For this, there is a need to transcend the factory model and the unidimensional model of education that have, perhaps, become the only models we employ in our teaching of philosophy and theology. Familiarity with other models and the possible contributions that they can make to education can help us go beyond the unconsciously inherited models on which depends our current practice.

It also presupposes that we redesign our syllabus and rearrange our schedule in such a way that they facilitate the introduction of new models of education into our institutions. Only with this kind of reform and renewal can we think of introducing new pedagogies. For, improvement in the teaching and learning process is predicated upon the models of education that we adopt. The attempt to introduce new pedagogies without altering the models of educaton would inevitably end up as an exercise in futility. Hence, the primary challenge before us is to seek appropriate models of education and suitable pedagogies will follow in its trail. At the same time, it must be clearly borne in mind that it is not possible to bring about such reforms overnight. Hence, the process should be viewed as a long term project or goal which needs to begin now.

Endnotes

1. For this section I am indebted to Doug Noon, "Models of Education: Overview". Accessed 5 November 2010. Available from http://borderland.northernattitude.org/2005/12/13/models-of-education-overview/
2. The graphic is adapted from Lucy Calkins as presented in Doug Noon "Models of Education". I have elaborated it to serve the purpose of this article.
3. The reflections in this section are based on Robert Freeman, "Competing Models for Public Education: Which Model is Best?" Accessed 7 November 2010. Available from http://www.commondreams.org/views05/0226-25.htm
4. The inspiration for this section comes from Smith, M. K. (1999) 'Learning theory. Accessed 13 November 2010. Available from *the encyclopedia of informal education*, www.infed.org/biblio/b-learn.htm, Last update: September 03, 2009
5. Discussions in this section are based on Smith, M. K. (1999) 'The behaviourist orientation to learning'. Accessed 2 January 2011. Available from *the encyclopedia of informal education*, www.infed.org/biblio/learning-behavourist.htm, Last update: September 03, 2009.
6. The ideas developed in this section are based on Smith, M. K. (1999) 'The cognitive orientation to learning'. Accessed 2 January, 2011. Available from *the encyclopedia of informal education*, www.infed.org/biblio/learning-cognitive, Last update: September 03, 2009
7. This section is developed with the help of Smith, M. K. (1999) 'The humanistic to learning'. Accessed 2 January 2011. Available from *the encyclopedia of informal education*, www.infed.org/biblio/learning-humanistic.htm, Last update: September 03, 2009

8. The basic ideas for this section are borrowed from Smith, M. K. (1999) 'The social/situational orientation to learning'. Accessed 2 January 2011. Available from *the encyclopedia of informal education*, www.infed.org/biblio/learning-social.htm, Last update: September 03, 2009.
9. The discussion on holistic education is based on Ramon Gallegos Nava (2000) Power Point Presentation at the 8th International Conference on Holistic Education. Guadalajara, Mexico, November 2000. Accessed 16 December, 2010. Available from http://www.ramongallegos.com/englishversions.htm#ancla2
10. Ramon Gallegos Nava uses the neologisms 'Kosmos' and 'Kosmic" to differentiate it from the planetary level and to indicate the larger spiritual sense in which he is using the term.